Praise for Knocked Up

"*Knocked Up* is what woul⋯⋯⋯⋯⋯⋯⋯⋯⋯⋯lly impregnated by Mark Darc⋯⋯⋯⋯⋯⋯⋯⋯Eckler has covered the basics of y⋯⋯⋯⋯⋯⋯quirky and outlandish way."

—New York *Daily News*

"Painfully funny . . . Readers are treated to Eckler's biting wit. . . . It's fun to watch [Eckler] change from the woman who dreaded seeing mothers with infants . . . to being a mother herself."

—*Los Angeles Times*

"[Eckler's] frankness, quirky style and light touch are a winning combination."

—*Kirkus Reviews*

"Hit[s] the mark among twenty- and thirtysomething mothers."

—*Library Journal*

"*Knocked Up* is the best cure for morning sickness! *Knocked Up* is the answer to postpartum blues! *Knocked Up* can cure preeclampsia! Yes, *Knocked Up* can solve gestational diabetes! *Knocked Up* even works on stretch marks! Like Prozac, and safe to take while nursing—this is a hilarious book!"

—Molly Jong-Fast, author of
The Sex Doctors in the Basement and *Normal Girl*

"*Knocked Up* is a delightful story about getting knocked up, popping the baby out, and everything that happens in between. Rebecca Eckler's hilarious and candid account of what seem to be the longest nine months of her life will go down as smoothly as a well-mixed cosmopolitan."

—Amulya Malladi, author of
Serving Crazy with Curry

Rebecca Eckler

● ● ● ● ● ● ● ● ● ● ● ● ● ● ● ● ● ● ●

Ⓥ VILLARD *New York*

Wiped!

Life with a Pint-Size Dictator

For Susan, Glenda, and Rowan Joely

Preface

● ●

Here's the thing: you could say I didn't exactly enjoy being pregnant.

I woke up, knocked up, just over a year ago. It had been the first, and only, time the Fiancé had . . . you know . . . in me.

We had been at our engagement party, not even thinking about the possibility of one day becoming parents. Life, it turns out, doesn't happen when you're busy making other plans. Life, apparently, is what happens when there's an open bar. That's what happened to us anyway.

After way too many cosmopolitans, me stupidly (but passionately) calling out, "Just cum in me!" and the idiot Fiancé actually listening (in his defense, he was drunk too), our engagement party turned out to be our "conception party." Four home pregnancy tests—or was it five?—and one blood test later, the Fear that I was pregnant was a reality.

I was knocked up, not married, and not even living in the same city as the Fiancé. But I convinced myself, and the Fiancé, that having a baby was not going to change our lives. Not. One. Little. Bit.

Yes, I had to change cities, leave my friends and family, and, for the first time, actually live under the same roof as the Fiancé. But I could handle all that. Surely life with a baby would be easier than being pregnant!

I was not good at being pregnant. By the end of my third trimester, I had gained forty-seven pounds (almost half my body weight), walked like a penguin, had wrist fat, couldn't see my cheekbones, and was wearing red slippers in public and asking the Fiancé, "Is my ass fat?" three times a day. (Okay, three times an hour.)

But I had survived being unexpectedly expecting. I remember being pretty damn positive that once this thing came out, I would get my old life back. I would party with friends again. I would get back to the career I loved, writing at the newspaper. And I would lose the baby weight as quickly as Heidi Klum lost hers, and maybe even faster.

But, somehow, it didn't happen.

I went from being knocked up straight to being, well, knocked down. I'm a friggin' idiot for thinking my life would ever be the same. It's not entirely my fault for being so naïve.

How was I to know that pregnancy would be a ninety-minute massage compared with life now?

No one warned me I'd be so wiped. No one warned me about a lot of things. Why didn't anyone warn me?

Ten Mommy Moments People "Forget" to Mention

1. You will feel like a walking, talking zombie.
2. You will obsess about the baby weight gain, which is not coming off.
3. After the flurry of congratulations, you will realize it's not "all about me anymore." It's all about the baby.
4. The father of your baby will annoy you.
5. Your in-laws will annoy you.
6. From the moment you bring baby home, all conversations will be only about baby.
7. Newborns are cute, but they are boring too.
8. You will find yourself aimlessly walking the streets almost daily.
9. You will say your baby is sick, even though she is fine, when you want to cancel plans.
10. If you have a boy, he will be mistaken for a girl. If you have a girl, she will be mistaken for a boy.

The Fourth Trimester (0 to 3 Months)

What's My Name?
Seriously, What's My Name?

Present day . . . or is it night?
Sometime, somewhere, some year

● ●

"OH SHIT!"

The pain hits, without warning, as if someone has just thrown a brick at my face. I fall to the floor. "Shit!" I cry out again, blinking back tears.

"What? What is it? What happened?" the Fiancé asks in a loud whisper, after racing in to find me rocking back and forth, groaning, on the floor, in a ball.

"Shit! Shit! Shit!" I shriek. I'm seeing stars and fighting the urge to pee, which is always what happens when I hurt myself. What the *hell* just happened to me? What the *hell* did I just do? Where the *hell* am I? Who the *hell* am I? Shit!

"Shhh!" the Fiancé demands. He doesn't sound as compassionate as he should, especially upon finding me, supposedly *the love of his life*, writhing in pain on the floor. "You have to be quiet! What happened?" he asks, hovering over me.

Is it just me, or does he sound incredibly annoyed? As if I *wanted* this to happen! What *had* happened?

I lift my head and see the red digits on the alarm clock. It's 3:37 A.M. "Turn on the light! Just turn on the light!" I say, not even attempting to keep my voice down. Now I'm the one who sounds irritated.

He flicks on the switch. Right. I'm in our bedroom. Right. I haven't been to sleep yet. Right. I haven't slept a full eight hours in weeks. I touch my nose and feel wetness. I look at my hands. They're covered in blood.

"I think I just broke my nose!" I cry, letting the tears fall.

"What the hell happened?" he asks, looking at the blood pouring out of me like my nose is a tap. My entire face is pounding. I have a sudden migraine. I'm sweating. Even my teeth hurt. I think I might very well be one second away from throwing up.

I'm now in full-fledged sob mode. I manage to stutter, "I, uh, walked, uh, right into the, uh, wall! I, uh, think my nose, is, uh, broken!"

"Oh God! Oh God! How did that happen? Okay, I'm going to get you some ice and a towel. But please, try to be quiet! You have to be quiet!" He still sounds annoyed. His tone infuriates me. I didn't mean for this to happen! I fight the impulse to tell him to go screw himself. *He's* not the one who's bleeding! *He's* not the one who just broke his nose! *He's* not the one who just walked smack into a wall! He has *no idea* how much pain I'm in.

I know he's right though. I have to calm down. I have to be quiet. I pick myself up off the floor and wobble back into our king-size bed, trembling and sobbing like a baby. Of course I know now that babies don't exactly sob. No, "sob" is definitely not the right word. Babies scream bloody murder, for hours, and for no reason. Whoever came up with the phrase "sobbing like a baby" apparently never had a baby, and certainly never lived with a newborn, like we do, in a two-bedroom condominium.

4:00 A.M.

I'm lying in bed with a bag of frozen peas on my face and two pieces of tissue stuck up my nose. I wonder where the Fiancé found the bag of frozen peas, since I don't recall us ever eating frozen peas. Then I remember that I feel like I'm dying. I kind of wish I were dead. Why we have frozen peas in our freezer is the least of my worries.

"At least she's finally asleep," the Fiancé grumbles, climbing back into bed beside me. "I thought she'd never shut up. I can't believe I have to get up and go to work in two hours!"

I've always pitied the Fiancé, not only because he's a corporate lawyer but also because he has to wake up at such ungodly hours to do whatever it is he does all day being a corporate lawyer. I should say something sympathetic to him right now like "I know, sweetie, I know. I feel for you." But I'm too tired, and in too much pain, to feel sympathy for anyone other than myself. I'm the one so exhausted I just walked directly into a friggin' wall!

The Fiancé did, to his credit, halfheartedly suggest we go to the emergency room. I declined. "I'm too tired. I'm just so tired," I said. Plus, the baby was finally asleep. After four hours of nonstop crying, the baby was asleep. Not even to find out if I had a broken nose, not even if I was having a heart attack, not even if Johnny Depp called and asked me to come over to his place, would I dare go anywhere if it meant possibly waking the baby.

It was my fault I may have just given myself the nose job I've always thought I might like to have. I had been trying to get the baby to fall asleep for what seemed like six months. I couldn't take it anymore. I had called out to the Fiancé, who was in bed, "Can you come in here? Please?"

I knew he hadn't fallen asleep yet either. There was no way. A fire alarm was a more soothing sound than this baby's wails.

"I can't take it anymore. I just can't! I might hurt her if you don't take over now!" I had told him. It was the first time I had actually thought about dumping the baby into her crib, putting a pillow over my face to drown out her cries, and giving up. I had tried everything to get her to fall asleep. I'd run tap water. I'd put her in her car seat. I'd rocked her. I'd sung to her. I'd put her in the swing. I'd walked around with her. I'd changed her. I'd fed her. I'd burped her. I'd put her in her bassinet. I'd done everything I could think of.

But every time I thought, "This is it. She's finally down! God doesn't hate me after all!" and attempted to tiptoe out of her room, she'd start wailing all over again. I honestly felt that if the Fiancé didn't take over, I might injure the baby. At least I knew enough to know that I had had enough. I didn't really want to harm the baby. I just wanted her to shut up, shut up, shut up!

When the Fiancé came into the baby's room, I handed her over and headed back to our bedroom. That's when I walked straight into the wall. Fuck.

"It's so rewarding, isn't it?" the Fiancé asks as I rearrange the bag of peas on my pounding face. I'm too tired to even attempt a smile. In fact, I don't think it's funny at all. How is it all those parents had told me when I was pregnant that having a baby would be "so rewarding"? Liars, all of them. Did their babies not make them want to run away from home and check in to the

Four Seasons for a week? Or was it just this baby? Or was it just me? At what point would having a baby become "so rewarding"?

8:20 A.M.
I'm awake. I think.

For the past few weeks, I've constantly felt half-asleep, or is it half-awake? I haven't been optimistic lately, so I choose half-asleep. I cannot tell you what day of the week it is, although I do know it is a weekday. I know this because the Fiancé is not beside me, which means he's left for work. Pre-baby—was it only five weeks ago?—the Fiancé would have kissed me good-bye on my forehead before leaving and told me he loved me. That was when he liked me though. He's been in a less-than-cheerful mood since I came home from the hospital . . . with the baby. He's been downright grumpy. I hear the clatter of dishes in the kitchen.

Nanny Mimi must be cleaning up our dishes from dinner last night. What did the Fiancé and I even eat for dinner last night? Did we eat? I have no idea. I hear no sounds from the baby's room, which means she's gloriously still asleep. I manage to force myself out of bed and head directly to the place I've gone first thing every morning since the baby came home.

No, I don't go check on the baby, which is probably what I should want to do. I head immediately to our washroom, where I look in the large mirror over the sink and lift my shirt while sucking in my gut. Phew. My stomach is going down. There is a God!

My favorite part of waking up each morning is looking at my stomach to check on its progress. Because I had a C-section, I'm not supposed to work out for six weeks. I now think not being able to work out for six weeks is a definite argument against having a planned C-section.

Sure, a planned C-section meant it only took twenty minutes for my baby to come into this world. Yes, I felt as elated as any mother who went through natural birth when I saw my daughter for the first time. Sure, I knew exactly when she was arriving, so I could prepare the baby's room and make sure my mother was in town for the big day. Sure, I actually chose to have the baby cut out of me because the only other way the baby could come out of me made me hyperventilate at the very thought.

But my best mother friend, Ronnie, who has given birth to three children, said she was back on the treadmill a week after each birth. I'm regretting not having had natural birth, only because I'd like to get on a treadmill and walk the fat right off of my ass. Every time I moan, "I just want to work out already!" the Fiancé tells me that not working out for six weeks, in the big picture, is not a big deal. *He* hasn't gained forty-seven pounds in nine months! How can *he* possibly understand what it feels like to look at your body and not recognize it?

Don't get me wrong—I'm not some fanatic workout freak. I hate working out. But even more than I hate working out, I hate how when I lie down my ass feels like its own entity. My ass fat spreads out beside me, taking up half the bed.

When I was pregnant, one of my mother friends told me that my ass would "never be the same again" after having a baby. I laughed then. As if!

But I'm not laughing now. I hate how I still look six months pregnant, even when I wear a baggy sweatshirt. Except now the skin around my stomach isn't tight like it was while I was pregnant. My stomach is simply a blob of mushy, droopy flesh, like a three-day-old helium balloon.

I've seen photographs of me holding the baby, taken during the first couple of weeks after she was born. They're not pretty. I mean, I'm not pretty. I've debated cutting myself out of the photos because the sight of my bloated stomach is not something I want to be reminded of. Ever. I also hate that I've lived in sweatpants and extra-large T-shirts for almost an entire year now.

And I really hate it when people tell me, "Well, it took nine months to put the weight on, so it will take nine months to come off." I just want to tell them to shut up.

Ronnie had a horrible thing happen to her once. She was picking up child number one at school and another parent asked her when she was due. The problem was, Ronnie wasn't pregnant. She had given birth three weeks earlier. You always hear these stories, and you'd like to believe they're just myths. They're not. It happens.

At least that hasn't happened to me. Yet. Of course, I've barely left the house since giving birth, and when I do leave, I make sure the baby is with me, so people know that I just gave birth and that's why I'm fat.

There's no way it's going to take me nine months to get all this weight off. My glee in looking at my slowly deflating stomach immediately vanishes when I see my face, something I've tried to avoid doing for the past few weeks.

Even after getting out of the shower, washing my face, or brushing my teeth, I make sure to avert my eyes from mirrors. I've learned that no good comes from looking at my reflection. The dark bags under my eyes depress the hell out of me and make me look how I feel—haggard. Haggard at age thirty-one.

This morning I catch a glimpse. (Okay, I always catch a glimpse. It's so hard not to look in mirrors!) I see two black eyes. Fuck! The wall. Right. I had walked into a wall only five hours ago. My nose, aside from being swollen, doesn't look crooked. I'm sure it's not broken. But it could have been! How is it possible that I haven't had a drink in months, yet I still look worse than I ever did hungover, after a long night of partying!

Who am I? How did I get here? What has happened to my life? This is not my life.

8:30 A.M.

I suppose I should go say good morning to Nanny Mimi and check on the baby. My heart pounds. I'm still not used to these two new humans in my condo. Every morning I wake up feeling like it's final-exam day, something I just have to face, get through, and that there's a good chance I could fail miserably. The baby makes me nervous. The nanny makes me nervous. I'm always nervous.

I remember first coming home from the hospital to see Nanny Mimi waiting for us in our condo, her arms wide open to hold the baby for the first time. I remember thinking how cute it was that this nanny was wearing overalls and had her hair in two ponytails. I remember thinking how skinny Nanny Mimi was too, and that kind of made me hate her immediately.

It was always our plan that we would have a nanny, mostly because neither the Fiancé nor I had any clue what to do with a baby, and we still wanted to have lives. Even my own mother, who raised four kids without any help, suggested I get a nanny. It hadn't disturbed me that everyone seemed so worried about me finding help once I gave birth.

The fact was, I was worried too. I knew I needed help. I'm not beyond asking for help. For the first couple of weeks, having Nanny Mimi in our two-bedroom condo was exactly like having a stranger in our two-bedroom condo. Mostly I tried to hide, which, as you can imagine, is kind of hard to do in a two-bedroom condo.

When Nanny Mimi was in the kitchen, I'd go into the living room. If she was in the living room, I'd head to my bedroom.

Granted, I am recovering from the C-section—a major operation, as I keep reminding the Fiancé when I am too lazy to fetch myself a Diet Coke—but mostly I have no idea how to interact with this woman, who is my—gaa!—employee. I am her boss!

I have never been a boss. I've only had bosses. I don't know how to be a boss. I only know the thoughts I've had about some of my bosses, and they aren't exactly kind thoughts. I certainly don't want Nanny Mimi thinking bitchy things about me and complaining about me to her friends, like I complain about my bosses to my friends.

Making conversation with Nanny Mimi is like being on the longest, most uncomfortable blind date in the world. Except this blind date begins every morning and lasts eight hours, five days a week.

"Hi, how are you?" I always ask when she arrives.

"Fine. How are you?" she says politely.

"Fine."

Uncomfortable silence.

"So, did she sleep last night?" Nanny Mimi asks.

"Not really."

"Oh. Well, she's a baby," Nanny Mimi says.

"Yeah, that's true," I respond. "She is. She's a baby."

Uncomfortable silence.

"Well, I'm going to go check on her and do some of her laundry," Nanny Mimi says.

"Okay, then. Thanks!"

I have been on blind dates in which the conversation is less stilted and forced. Am I supposed to tell Nanny Mimi what to do? What is there to tell her, really, except to feed my baby, change her diaper when she's wet, and keep her alive? She's a nanny! She knows that stuff.

I have other worries. Should I brush my teeth and hair before Nanny Mimi sees me? Does she think I'm fat? My friend Vivian, who had given birth six weeks before I did, had a nurse live with her and her husband for the first three weeks. One day last week I had been whispering on the phone to Vivian, who asked me why I was acting all strange.

"Um, the nanny is right in the next room," I whispered.

"I know. It's weird, isn't it?" Vivian said. "We would hide up-stairs whenever the nurse was around."

I'm sure I hadn't been saying anything even remotely inter-esting to Vivian, but I still felt like I was talking to a boy for the first time, with my parents hovering around eavesdropping, whenever Nanny Mimi was within hearing distance of any of my conversations with friends.

I knew nothing about Nanny Mimi, except that she came highly recommended, had worked with newborns for eight years, and was taking care of the most important person in my entire life.

The Fiancé and I had met Nanny Mimi when I was six months pregnant, at a coffee shop. That had been our first un-comfortable meeting with many uncomfortable silences. We had prepared, well, nothing to ask her, except whether she had worked with babies before, if she would be available October 17, the day the baby was coming home, and what her salary expec-tations were.

Nanny Mimi is thirty-eight and very attractive, which posed more pressing concerns. Not only was she older than me (how can I boss around someone who is older than me?), she obviously knew way more than I did about babies, because I knew almost nothing about babies. What if I suggested something that she didn't agree with?

I had also worried that the Fiancé would pull a Jude Law on me. I'd heard stories about men ditching their wives for nannies. They couldn't all be myths, could they? How would I ever explain to my friends and family that the Fiancé had thrown me over for the nanny? But I had (mostly) gotten over that worry. I mean, if the Fiancé did ditch me for the nanny, he would have much more explaining to do than I would.

I didn't know if Nanny Mimi had a boyfriend, enjoyed reality television, thought Leonardo DiCaprio was hot, loved cookie-dough cheesecake, and was obsessed with handbags. You know, the things everyone should know about another person to see if you really could get along and be friends. Was she even supposed to be my friend?

Nanny Mimi also made me feel guilty about everything. I felt guilty for wanting to hold my baby when Nanny Mimi was around, because that's what she gets paid to do. I felt guilty turning on the television, because I didn't want her to see me in the middle of the afternoon watching bad talk shows. I felt guilty every time I asked Nanny Mimi a question, like "Has the baby eaten?"

If the baby pooed while I was holding her, there was no way I could feel comfortable passing her over, even though changing her diaper is what she was supposed to do. Or could I? I felt guilty that we had no food in our fridge for Nanny Mimi. I felt guilty that she made our bed every day, even though we never asked her to and it wasn't in her job description. (But, I admit, I also enjoyed it. Though I'd thought about telling her, "You don't have to make our bed!" I hadn't. It is so much nicer getting into bed when someone else makes it for you—kind of like living in a hotel.)

I also felt guilty hiding out in my room, with the door shut, to take a nap. I didn't want her to think I was being rude or lazy and didn't care about the baby. Basically, I had no idea how I was supposed to act around her. I had no idea if there was even a new politically correct term for "nanny." Do I introduce her to my friends as "the nanny"? Do I say, "This is my nanny"? Do I say, "This is the baby's nanny"? Or do I introduce her by her name? Argh. I knew nothing about the etiquette of having a nanny.

I also worried about whether Nanny Mimi felt as awkward around me as I did around her. I definitely didn't want Nanny Mimi to think I was a bad boss, though I wasn't sure how she could perceive me as a bad boss considering I hadn't asked her to do anything yet. Unless not asking her to do anything made me a bad boss. Argh. Argh. Argh.

In any case, I know I have to put on a bra before saying good morning to Nanny Mimi. I definitely am not at the point where I feel comfortable walking around braless in front of her, which, frankly, considering it's my home, I would like to do. But, like at a first sleepover with a guy, I keep my bra on around her at all times. I enter our walk-in closet in our bedroom and find the most comfortable granny bra and put it on under my T-shirt. I'm still wearing the bras I bought and wore when I was pregnant. I'm happy my boobs are still larger than they were pre-baby, even though I'm not breastfeeding. That's right. I'm bottlefeeding the baby.

Breastfeeding was another discussion the Fiancé and I had had while I was pregnant—in about two minutes. Actually it was I who decided I wasn't going to breastfeed, because I knew, from other mommy friends, what happens when you breastfeed. I knew if I breastfed, no one else could feed the baby in the middle of the night and I couldn't leave the house for long periods of time because the baby would need my boobs. Also, the thought of a pump freaked me out. While it doesn't bother me when other women pull up their tops in restaurants, I couldn't picture myself being one of those women. I didn't really want the Fiancé's friends to see my boobs. I didn't really want my father to see my boobs.

Of course, I did take into consideration the argument that you lose the baby weight more quickly when you breastfeed. How could I not? But, I figured, the argument was a wash. I mean, I could lose weight by breastfeeding, or I could leave the baby with someone else, because she wouldn't be tied to my boob, and go to the gym.

Before heading out of the bedroom, I look at all my pre-pregnancy clothes hanging in the closet and think, "I miss you, clothes. I miss you. You have no idea how much I miss you."

8:40 A.M.

"Hi, Mimi," I say, trying to sound cheerful but sounding flat.

"Hi, how are you?" she says, actually sounding cheerful. She is always cheerful, and that kind of weirds me out. How is it she can sound so cheerful knowing she's going to have to be with the baby all day long, a baby who just sleeps, screams, eats, and needs diaper changes? The thought of taking care of my own baby for an entire day freaks me out, and I'm her mother!

"Great! It was a good night. She fell asleep around four," I say.

"Well, she has her days and nights mixed up still. She's a baby."

"Yes, she is. She's a baby," I say.

Uncomfortable silence.

"Excuse me," I say shyly, while I grab a spoon out of the drawer to eat a bowl of cereal. I'm even afraid to ask Nanny Mimi to move out of the way so I can get my own spoon out of my own drawer in my own kitchen!

Nanny Mimi is at the stove, boiling a pot of bottles. Our stove has never been used so much as it has been since the baby arrived. Before the baby came home, I think we made soup on the stovetop once. And we used to use it to light our cigarettes.

Now Nanny Mimi, the Fiancé, and I are constantly boiling bottles in water to sterilize them. Also, we are constantly making formula, buying formula, and running out of formula. Maybe it is easier to breastfeed. It's certainly cheaper if you breastfeed, and you'll never find yourself running to a twenty-four-hour grocery store, like we had to do the other night, when we ran out of formula.

It's become a joke when I make the formula, taking out the measuring cup, measuring the exact amount, and mixing the white powder with boiled water, before pouring the mixture into the bottles. "Look!" I'll say to the Fiancé. "I'm cooking!" He'll roll his eyes.

Well, it is kind of like cooking, I don't care what he thinks.

Just then—thank God—I'm rescued from making any more small talk because from the baby monitor in the kitchen we hear the baby stirring in her room. Not that we actually need a baby monitor. Our condo is that small. The baby could sneeze at one end of the condo and we'd hear her from the farthest end.

Nanny Mimi races out of the kitchen to go fetch the baby. I finish my cereal and call the Fiancé, who picks up immediately.

"Hi, it's me," I say.

"Hi."

"You never said good-bye this morning," I moan.

"You were sleeping. I didn't want to wake you."

"Oh. How are you feeling?" I ask.

"Like shit."

"Me too. I have two black eyes from walking into the wall. I'm still not sure how that happened."

"I'm going to get fired if I don't get any work done. I'm making major mistakes on multibillion-dollar deals here," the Fiancé responds, as if we are in a competition to see whose problems are worse.

"My eyes hurt they're so tired," I tell him. "And I have two black eyes!"

"I don't even remember getting to work today," he continues. "So how is the Devil Child?"

"Hey, thanks for asking about me, dude," I think. "She's just getting up now," I tell him. It kind of annoys me that he calls the baby "the Devil Child." I mean, sure, she is a Devil Child and I sometimes call her the Devil Child, but I'm her mother. I can call her whatever I want.

"Okay, so I guess I'll call you later?" says the Fiancé. He sounds exhausted, as if the very effort of forming a sentence feels like running a marathon.

"Okay, bye," I say.

Obviously, the Fiancé isn't in any mood to give me sympathy. But that's okay. I'm not in the mood to give him any either. We're in this baby thing together, aren't we? Except why do I feel like I'm in it more?

9 A.M.

I need compassion. I'm a walking zombie. And I almost broke my nose. Honestly, I'm so tired that if you asked me my name, I would have to think about how to answer. Who would give me the sympathy I need after walking into a wall and surviving another night with the baby? Of course! My mother. I feel like a child who has a child, a woman in a generation of women who have babies but still need their mommies. My mother would give me the sympathy I so deserve. She's my mother after all. She loves me. She's been a new mother herself, having had four babies. She would know how I feel. Plus, giving me sympathy is her job.

"Hi, it's me," I say when my mother picks up.

"Hi! Hi! Hi!" she says excitedly, like she hasn't heard from me in months, and not just since yesterday. Ever since I became a mother, I've called my mother daily. Pre-baby, I could go days, weeks even, without calling my mother. This is only one of very many things that have changed in my life.

My mother does sound thrilled to hear from me, unlike some people, and that cheers me up.

"So how's the baby?" is her first question.

Oh. Wait. I get it. I realize instantly that my mother is not, in fact, so thrilled to hear from me. She's only excited to hear about the baby. I'm no longer cheered up. "Oh, she's fine. I think I broke my nose," I tell her.

"So what's the baby doing now?" my mother asks.

Hello? What? Did my own mother not hear what I just said? The part about me—her only daughter—almost breaking her nose? "Did you hear what I said? I walked into a wall last night because I was so tired. She was up practically the entire night. I have two black eyes. There was blood everywhere. I almost went to the emergency room." I hear my voice rising.

I was a drama queen in my pre-baby days. That hasn't changed. Why doesn't anyone seem to care about me?

"Ooh, poor, poor baby," my mother coos. Okay, maybe she finally heard me. "So is she sleeping now?"

Again, that "poor, poor baby" wasn't for me. It was meant for the baby.

"God, I miss her," my mother continues. "Maybe she had a tummy ache? Maybe she was hungry? Maybe her diaper was wet?"

Maybe she's just a bad, bad baby, I say to my mother. Okay, I don't really say that. I don't say anything. I just sit there, silently, holding the phone to my ear, letting my mother carry on about her first grandchild. What's the point of saying anything? It's not like I've done anything remotely interesting in the past twenty-four hours anyway. Clearly, I no longer matter. I had done what

I was supposed to do in life, which is provide her with a grand-child. No matter how well I had done in school, no matter what my career accomplishments were, my mother had never been so proud of me as when I gave birth. And really, studying for exams was way harder than getting knocked up. What had been the point of getting A's in school? What had been the point of going to university? What had been the point of working so hard at my career if it all gets forgotten when you give birth?

Whatever. Clearly, I'm nothing more than a baby machine now.

10 A.M.

Along with two black eyes, a mother who no longer cares about my well-being, a fiancé too tired to say more than three words to me, and a new nanny who I have no clue how to talk to, I also have a Diaper Genie.

I don't know what's more painful: my almost broken nose, making small talk with the nanny, feeling like no one cares about me, or this thing that looks like a garbage can that is sup-posed to make my life easier but is, in fact, making it hell.

The Diaper Genie is one of those baby items that every other mother I knew had told me I needed to have.

Well, it's been six weeks and we have yet to use this must-have baby item because we can't figure out how it works. We managed to put in the Baggies, but whenever we turn the top, the Diaper Genie won't do what it's supposed to do, which is magically show up with a new Baggie, making the old Baggie filled with a dirty diaper disappear into the ether.

This is not a Diaper Genie. This is a Diaper Bitch.

It has become sort of an obsession though. Every day I fiddle with the Diaper Genie, but I always become as frustrated as someone watching a three-year-old trying to tie his shoelace.

How has the biggest worry in my life come to be wondering where the new Baggie is?

We've been using plastic grocery bags to put the dirty diapers in. And until I can figure out how this thing works, we will continue to do so.

I'm feeling blue. I kick the Diaper Genie, which makes me feel a little better. So I kick it again.

10:30 A.M.

Pre-baby, I'd probably still be sound asleep now. Pre-baby, I would have spent last night with friends at a bar. Pre-baby, I'd be at work in an hour or so, writing fun columns for the newspaper I work for, about fashion, style, trends, and new bar and store openings. Pre-baby, I would be talking to friends on the phone throughout the day about their dates and sex lives. Pre-baby, the Fiancé would have missed me during the day and would have already called me three times by now to tell me so. Pre-baby, I'd worry about whether I was too bloated to wear my new designer jeans that I had spent half a month's rent on.

Post-baby, I change from sweatpants to sweatpants and worry about a nonexistent plastic Baggies to put the baby's dirty diaper in.

11 A.M.

I decide to call Ronnie, my best mother friend. She has three kids, so I know she'll be glad to listen to me moan about living with a newborn. She's been there, done that. Maybe she even knows how to work a stupid Diaper Genie.

"Hey, it's me!" I say.

"Hey, how are you?"

"Great! So—"

"Listen, I can't talk right now. Kyle has a cold, and Brad has a playdate, and I have to make lunch for them. Poppy also needs to be fed."

"Okay, call me later," I say.

"Kyle! Stop that right now! Okay, I'm going to count to three! What did you just say to me?"

"Are you talking to me?" I ask.

"No, I got to go. I'll call you later."

Clearly, Ronnie is busy being a mother. A decade ago, Ronnie and I would talk on the phone for hours. We'd go to bars late at night and pull all-nighters studying for exams. Now she's married with three children and scheduling playdates and making lunches and counting to three.

I can't imagine having three children at my age or any age. I don't even know how I'm going to deal with the one I have now. I don't really even understand the concept of a playdate. I should ask Ronnie what exactly a playdate is.

11:05 A.M.

I decide to call Heather, one of my closest friends, who also writes for a newspaper. She's single and fabulous and will have a ton to tell me about what I'm missing in the outside world, a world that I used to embrace with a passion. I want to know what's happening in her life, who she's fucking, and, I'll admit, I want to brag about my newborn and how cute she is. Sure, Heather may be out fucking guys and going on dates and not walking into walls, but I have a baby.

"Hey, it's me!" I say when she picks up, saying her name. Wow, she sounds so professional. I can't remember the last time I answered a phone saying my name. I can't remember the last time the phone rang for me.

"Hey, how are you?" she asks.

"Great! So what's—"

"Listen, I can't talk right now. I have a deadline and then a meeting. Can I call you later? Actually, can I call you tomorrow? Because I have to rush and meet someone for lunch. And then I have an interview to do after that. God, I have so much to do. I got to go. I got to go! My editor is giving me the evil eye."

"Sure," I say, trying not to let disappointment (or is it envy?) drip from my tongue. Why do people pick up the phone when they're too busy to talk? Maybe she just doesn't want to talk to me? I didn't even get a chance to tell her how cute the baby is. I didn't even get the chance to pretend that life was A-okay. And why didn't Heather even ask how the baby was? I mean, isn't that kind of rude?

I know my mother asked me how the baby was, and that annoyed me. But it annoys me too when people don't ask how the baby is. I'm a sleep-deprived new mother who can't work a stupid Diaper Genie. I'm allowed to be annoyed about whatever I want, whenever I want.

11:10 A.M.

I call my friend Sara, who had a baby two weeks ago, right after I did. She must be like me, yearning for adult conversation. I had tried Vivian, who had a baby six weeks before me, but she wasn't home. Sara is practically in the same stage I'm at, and it would be fun to moan about our lives. We always have liked to complain.

"Hi, you've reached Sara, David, and Ella," goes her voice-mail message.

I can't believe it. This is a woman I used to go drinking with, and now she's changed her home voice-mail message to include her three-week-old baby? I'm so shocked that I hang up without leaving a message. Is there something wrong with me for not changing my voice-mail message? The thought of changing our outgoing message to include the baby didn't even occur to me. Um, I don't know much about babies, but I know newborns can't speak.

God, it's amazing that the people you least expect to embrace parenthood are the ones who surprise you the most. Who would have thought Sara, who loved to complain about being pregnant with me, would embrace new parenthood with such a vengeance and want the world to know—via outgoing voice-mail message —that she was a proud mother?

I leave messages for three other friends on their work machines. I don't know what to do with myself. I feel guilty going back to bed so soon after getting out of bed. I don't think I can fall asleep anyway. I'm past the point of tired, entering the over-tired phase, when you're too tired to sleep. Nanny Mimi is in the baby's room, watching her sleep and organizing her sleepers, folding and refolding, like she works at Baby Gap. The Fiancé is at work, all my friends have jobs, and my mommy friends have their children to look after and, apparently, their voice-mail messages to change. All I have is thirty-eight pounds to lose, two black eyes, and a woman in my house who I don't know how to talk to. Make that a woman in my house whose very presence is a constant reminder that she is skinny and I am not.

I need to turn off my brain, because over the past few days, it's really started to sink in that life did not stop, as I thought it would, when I had the baby.

The newspaper I write (wrote) for still appears on my doorstep every morning, much to my shock and dismay. How can they possibly manage without me? How can they possibly put out a good newspaper, when I'm not writing for them? When did I go from feeling special, like I had everything—a fiancé, a great job, a fun life—to feeling nonexistent, with nothing to do? Am I really so replaceable?

Is this what being a mother is really like? Sara couldn't wait to go on maternity leave. Though she's never said this, I think one of the reasons she got pregnant was so she could go on maternity leave. I, however, have always loved my job. Sure, when I had bad days, I'd moan, "I should just get pregnant and go on maternity leave."

But now that I am on maternity leave, I'm not spending my days shopping for clothes (still too fat), meeting friends for lunch (they're all working), and seeing matinees (by myself?), which is what I thought people did on maternity leave. Or at least it's what I imagined I would be doing.

When I first came home from the hospital, I felt like a beauty pageant queen, the center of attention. There were bouquets upon bouquets of flowers, which had arrived after the news spread of our baby's birth. I felt like I had done something truly special. I have never received so many gift baskets and flowers in my life, even if I counted up all my birthdays and Valentine's Days. People had never been so happy for me. They had left messages asking all about the baby, yes, but they asked about me too. Everyone wanted me to call back with all the news—the baby's name (Rowan Joely), her weight (7 pounds, 3 ounces).

But over the last couple of weeks, the flowers stopped coming, and so did the phone calls. The Fiancé went back to work, and the newspaper continued to show up on my doorstep, as if nothing had changed. I am on maternity leave, supposed to be bonding with my newborn, and basically, I hate my new life.

1 P.M.
"Hi!" I say, calling the Fiancé at his office.
"Hi."
"So, when are you coming home?" I ask, trying to sound like

I don't really care. The thing is, I do care. I really want to know when he's coming home.

"Beck, it's one o'clock."

"I know. So when are you coming home?"

"I'll be home when I get home," he snaps.

"So, like around five?"

"Beck!"

"Fine! Bye!" I say, hanging up.

This conversation—rather, me asking the Fiancé, "When are you coming home?"—has become a daily ritual. Along with asking, "Am I getting skinnier?" I can't help but call the Fiancé a half dozen times a day, asking when he'll be home. I'm bored.

It's not even that I miss him. It's just that I want someone around, someone I can complain to, someone who understands that this is hard. Why am I feeling this way when there's actually a new person in my life who is supposed to bring me nothing but joy? Do other new mothers call their husbands at work, at 10 A.M., asking when they're going to be home? Or is it just me? At least today I waited until after lunch to ask. Last week I asked when he thought he'd be coming home . . . before he even left the house.

1:30 P.M.

I'm lying in bed, wishing I still had some Tylenol with codeine left over from when I had my C-section. God, those pills were good. I'm too tired to read. I'm too tired to watch television. I close my eyes, playing over in my head the moment the doctor held up the baby for me to see for the first time. I cried, for the first time in my life, tears of joy. She was *so* cute and slimy and red. She was *so* beautiful. She was *so* perfect. My stomach knots with happiness and tears of joy appear behind my closed lids as I replay the moment. The first time I saw the baby is a thought I replay in my head every time I close my eyes, like replaying the first time some guy you love kissed you. Seeing the baby for the first time was the happiest moment of my life. I actually ache thinking about how much I love her. I fall asleep, smiling. Life isn't that bad. No, life couldn't be better.

5:15 P.M.

Someone kissing my head wakes me up.

It's the Fiancé. I have somehow been asleep all afternoon.

"My parents invited us over for dinner," he says, sitting on the bed.

"Okay," I say.

"We don't have to go if you don't want."

The Fiancé knows me well and knows how I've felt lately about going to his parents'.

"No, we can go," I say, not adding, "What else are we going to do?" which is what I'm thinking.

It's not that I don't love my in-laws. I do. They are the most generous, kind in-laws a girl could ever hope for. It's just that sometimes they annoy the crap out of me.

When you have a baby, no one warns you about how painful sleep deprivation is, and no one warns you how annoying relatives become. Was I just so tired all the time now that everybody annoyed me? Or was it everyone else who had changed? Sure, people told me I absolutely needed a Diaper Genie, but no one bothered to warn me that my in-laws were going to drive me bonkers after I had a baby.

"Hey, you have to look at this," the Fiancé says, lifting his pant legs.

"What?"

"I'm wearing one black sock and one blue sock, that's how tired I was this morning. I can't even dress properly anymore."

Pre-baby, the Fiancé dressed well. Now, not only does he constantly look kind of rumpled, like all his clothes have been run over by a truck, but he's wearing mismatching socks.

I don't dare huff, "Well, at least you still get to get dressed because you're a productive member of society, unlike me, and get to go to work."

The baby, of course, is sleeping. Of course she is sleeping now, at dinnertime, because that means she won't sleep later, when we want to sleep, you know, at the normal hour humans are supposed to go to bed. I get out of bed and go in to look at her. I love the smell of her room. It always smells like baby powder, even though we don't actually use any baby powder on her. Do all babies smell as good as mine? God, she is beautiful when she sleeps.

I notice a pad of lined paper on the baby's changing table. Nanny Mimi, upon my recommendation—my only recommendation to her—has begun to keep a log of when the baby pees, poos, and feeds. It's like the most boring schedule you've ever seen. Today, Nanny Mimi has written:

9:00 A.M.: pees.
9:15: feeds.
10:30: pees.
Noon: feeds.
1:45: poos and pees.
2:00: feeds.
2:30: pees.
4:00: feeds and poos.

I had thought I would eventually see rhyme and reason to the schedule and that that would be helpful. Like, every day at 2 P.M. the baby poos, and I'd make sure I was "busy" taking a shower.

But the only thing I've learned about babies from this schedule is there really is no rhyme or reason to when they eat or poo, at least from what I can see. I stopped taking notes about her bowel movements and eating schedule two weeks ago. What was the point? It changed daily. I think that Nanny Mimi, however, feels important taking the notes, so I haven't bothered to tell her she can stop if she wants to.

6:30 P.M.

We're at the Fiancé's parents' condo, which, depending on your sensibility, is either in a great location or the most unfortunate location ever, next to living at an airport. The Fiancé's parents' condo is in the tower right next to ours. It's in a great location for us because we don't have to go outside to visit them, which means the baby can just be in her sleeper and we don't have to worry about bundling her up, and the in-laws are readily available if we need them to look after the baby, or if they just want to, as they say, "pop by." If we're at their place and she needs a change of clothes, we can just run back to our condo and be back at theirs in two minutes. We can take the indoor hallways from our condo to theirs in a minute and a half, in fact.

The proximity of their condo to ours is unfortunate because it's located in the next tower and we can get there in a minute and a half, and they can easily "pop by." Which they do. Often. They never "popped by" our condo before the baby. This is new.

The baby is asleep in the portable bassinet when we walk into the in-laws' condo.

"I saw this really interesting show on Dr. Phil," the mother-in-law says as we sit down at the kitchen table.

I'm convinced that no good sentence has ever begun with "I saw this really interesting show on Dr. Phil." It didn't when I was single and childless, and it sure doesn't now. "It was about how to get your baby to sleep through the night," she continues. Ever since I gave birth, most of the mother-in-law's sentences begin with "I read this really interesting article" or "I saw this really interesting show" or "My friend's granddaughter." And all the shows and articles and conversations she tells us about are about babies.

I know the mother-in-law means well, but I'm not interested in what experts have to say about getting your child to sleep. If I were, I would have read books. Every mother has told me it takes about three months before they sleep through the night. I don't need experts. I don't need books. Plus, what do people think? That new mothers don't pay attention to this stuff? If there were a foolproof way to make sure your baby slept through the night at six weeks, don't you think I would have done it by now? I try not to roll my eyes. I don't say anything like "Oh, tell me about what Dr. Phil has to say, please, please, please!" because I know she's going to anyway.

It's been hard on the Fiancé to mediate between his parents and me ever since the baby came into our lives. He's an only child and a bit of a mama's boy, as most male only children are. And he's caught in the middle when his parents tell him to do something with *our* baby and I tell him to do something else. He doesn't want to hurt their feelings, and he definitely doesn't want to hurt mine, especially since I'm still pretty hormonal and if he uses even a slightly harsh tone with me, I'll cry. In fact, if the Fiancé even looks at me strangely these days, I cry.

The other day there was almost a blowup between the in-laws and me, and the Fiancé, of course, was stuck in the middle. The in-laws offered to pick up a jumbo box of diapers and wipes for us, which was a very thoughtful and considerate thing to do. "That would be great," I told the Fiancé over the phone, when he called to tell me his parents would do this for us. Like Nanny

Mimi, the in-laws aren't exactly comfortable with me either, which is why they call the Fiancé at work to ask him questions and then he calls me to pass them along.

"Tell them we need Pampers diapers and Huggies wipes," I told the Fiancé. I'm not sure how I knew I wanted Pampers diapers and Huggies wipes, but I know that's what I wanted. I think Ronnie, who has three children and thus is an expert in the variety of diapers and wipes on the market, told me. I didn't need to read any parenting books, because Ronnie was a walking, talking parenting book. Whenever I had a question, I'd call her.

"Okay," the Fiancé said.

Two minutes later he called me back. "My mother told me she heard that Huggies were better diapers than Pampers," he said.

I immediately felt all my muscles tighten and my jaw clench. I was immediately annoyed. All I wanted was Pampers, and it had turned into an *issue*.

"What, did she hear it on Dr. Phil or something? Did she read an article about it?" I asked, the sarcasm dripping off my tongue like thick chocolate sauce (mmm . . . chocolate).

"No, I think her friend's granddaughter uses them," he answered, ignoring my tone.

"Whatever. So, what did you tell your mother?" I asked, trying to hold in my anger.

"I told her you were the mother and that if you said Pampers diapers were better, we're getting Pampers," he said. "We almost got into a fight. I was very short with her."

"Well, thank you for siding with me," I said.

"You know, they're just trying to help," he said.

"Then why don't they just do what we say?" I asked. "Why do they always have their own opinions? Why couldn't they just go and get Pampers?"

"Because they think they know best."

"Well, they don't."

"I never said they did."

"So, when are you coming home?" I asked, trying to change the subject.

"Good-bye, Beck!"

I knew he wanted to get off the phone with me so he could call his mother to apologize for being short with her. If there's one thing the Fiancé hates just as much as pissing me off, it's feeling guilty about hurting his mother's feelings. This is annoying but is also what makes him a good father. When my single friends wonder if their partners would make good fathers, I always say, "Look at how he treats his mother." If men treat their mothers well, you can be pretty sure they're going to treat their children well. At least that's my theory.

7:30 P.M.

After dinner, the mother-in-law puts a box of chocolate-covered coffee beans on the table.

I take one. If I nibble on it like I'm a mouse, this one chocolate-covered coffee bean could possibly last me ten minutes. Was it only months ago I was polishing off entire large bags of Cheesies, and eating two Big Macs a day without thinking twice about it, because it felt so good to give in to every craving? After all, it was the baby in me who was craving the Cheesies and Big Macs. Or that's what I had told myself.

"You're being so good," the mother-in-law says. "I would never have that kind of willpower." It's true, I am being good. Since the baby came out of me, I've cut out most carbohydrates and I try to eat only two meals a day; my treat is one chocolate-covered coffee bean a day. Still, the weight is not coming off. I've never had to diet before. I have a newfound respect for any-

one who has tried to lose weight, because it's really fucking difficult.

I don't think I really have that much willpower. I thought the
cravings for french fries and chocolates would go away once the
baby came. They haven't. I still crave chocolate. I still crave po-
tato chips. In fact, I could easily go for a Big Mac and super-size
fries right now. The only thing stopping me is that I'm wearing a
pair of the Fiancé's trackpants. The only thing worse than wearing a pair of the Fiancé's trackpants would be to be seen eating a
Big Mac and super-size fries while wearing the Fiancé's trackpants.

November 10
2 P.M.

I decide to take a shower. I think I fall asleep in the shower. Is it
possible to fall asleep standing up? Well, elephants do it. When
I get out, I know something is just not right. I know I've missed
some process of showering. Did I forget to soap myself? No. Aha!
I forgot to shampoo my hair. That's it! I remember putting conditioner in, but I don't remember rinsing out any suds. Right.
This is what they must mean by "mommy brain." I remember
feeling this way when I was pregnant, too, forgetting to do basic
things, like putting shampoo in my hair. From pregnancy brain
to mommy brain—will it ever end? Will I get my brain cells
back? That reminds me. I must get the Fiancé to take a roll of
film in for developing.

The Fiancé and I now spend a lot of time taking pictures. We
have throwaway cameras all over the condo, along with two digital cameras. Though we have taken literally hundreds of digital
photographs of the baby, we have yet to e-mail them to anyone.
This is because the Fiancé can't figure out how to do it, and nei-

ther can I. (Hey, we're the only two idiots who can't figure out how to work a Diaper Genie too. And it took three hours for him to put the stroller together.) Because we have taken so many pictures, it would take hours to pick out the good ones (otherwise known as the ones I don't look fat in). So we also take photographs of everything the baby does with the throwaway cameras as well. Mostly these are pictures of her sleeping, because that's mostly all she does.

But we also take pictures of the baby naked. Or we put a cell phone next to her ear and think it's adorable and snap away. We put stuffed animals by her and think it's the funniest thing we've ever seen. We take rolls upon rolls of pictures of the baby, who does nothing but eat, sleep, pee, and poo. I then ask the Fiancé to take them in and get triples. We have piles of photographs of the baby on countertops, on bookshelves, on end tables. We have yet to put any of them in the many photo albums we received as presents. I put that on my "must do" list, along with figuring out how to use the Diaper Genie, getting skinny again, being more patient with the in-laws, remembering to use shampoo next time I take a shower, and maybe shaving my legs.

7 P.M.

I realize that tomorrow will mark six weeks since I had the C-section. I can start working out! Tomorrow I can also have sex. It will be six weeks since the baby came into our lives. It only *feels* like six years since she came into our lives. It also feels like six years since I've gotten laid.

8 P.M.

"I can't have sex," I tell the Fiancé. Technically I can. I just don't wanna.

"I know," he says.

"I can't have sex for another three weeks or so. I really want to, but I can't. Doctor's orders," I tell him, acting like I'm sad about the whole thing.

I'm not though. Well, I'd like to have sex. I just don't want to be seen naked and have sex. How could I possibly want to be naked when I feel so not sexy? Who would even want to have sex with me? And how can I have sex when I'm so tired? I suppose I could just lie there.

I had to say something about us not having sex. It's been almost two months since we've been intimate. I feel like the Fiancé and I are losing that close feeling couples have, that you can only get back after a passionate night (or ten minutes) in bed. I needed to say something. It's like the Fiancé has become my roommate. This thought saddens me. But not enough to want to get naked and have sex.

I know that guys like to have sex. Heck, I even like(d) to have sex. I only feel slightly guilty lying to him about the doctor's orders. Am I the only woman to add on an extra few weeks to when the doctor said was an okay time to get back at it? There is no way I could climb on top of him looking like this. I could hurt him. And there is no way I want him to grab my big ass.

"It's okay," he says. "I'm too tired anyway."

Um, hello?

The Fiancé is too tired? It's okay for *me* to be too tired, but *he's* not supposed to be too tired! You know your relationship is in trouble when your male partner is telling you he's too tired to have sex with you, which is the female equivalent of "I have a headache," usually a lie.

Is it because I'm still fat? Is it because having sex is what got us where we are today—with a baby? Is it because he sees me as I see myself, as a gross blob of unsexy flesh? Is he worried I could hurt him?

I've never met a guy who was "too tired" to have sex. Even though I don't want to have sex either, my feelings are hurt.

I head to the washroom to get ready for bed. Every time I open the washroom cupboard to get toothpaste or mouthwash, I swear the box of condoms we keep there is mocking me. I can't stop myself from opening the box. I take out the condoms and count them. Phew. They're all there. I know the Fiancé would never cheat on me. One of my friends who had a baby told me that she and her husband used to have sex almost every night. Until they had a baby. And now they have sex, like, once a month. I'm just being paranoid. It must be the post-baby hormones. I'm also being paranoid about the fact that none of my friends have called me back, right? And I'm being paranoid worrying that the in-laws are going to drive me mental for the rest of my life, right? It has got to be the hormones. Please, dear God, let it be the hormones.

November 11
10 A.M.

I get my period. It shocks me, like I'm thirteen all over again and it's the first time. At least I have a good reason now not to have sex. At least for a couple of days.

I think I remember someone telling me I shouldn't use tampons the first period after having a baby. Whatever. I'm already not feeling sexy, and a maxi pad isn't going to make me feel any sexier, that's for sure. I find a tampon and look at it like I've never seen one before. I kind of miss them, which, I know, is weird.

I guess I can start having babies again. The thought mortifies me.

"I got my period," I say to the Fiancé, calling him at his office.

It's the biggest news, the only news, of my day. I want to share it with someone.

"Congratulations," he says.

"So, when are you coming home?"

"Good-bye!"

I wonder how much longer I have before he decides to never pick up his phone when he sees that it's me calling. Or maybe he'll start getting his assistant to tell me that he's in a meeting. All day. Forever.

10:30 A.M.

I take a shower and get into another pair of trackpants. I'm pathetic. I did get out of my sweatpants once, two weeks ago, when I was trying to look like I had my shit together. In the city I now live in, with my family—I can't believe I have a "family"!—the government sends a nurse to your home a few weeks after you give birth. They say this is to see how the parents are holding up, but who are they kidding? I know it's really to see how the baby's holding up, living with us. Today is the day of our visit.

I think, "What would a capable mother, one who knows what she's doing, one who loves being a mother, one who has her shit together, wear for the visiting nurse?" My options are minimal at best. I had made the mistake of trying on a pair of pre-pregnancy jeans, which was probably the worst decision I'd ever made in my life. I couldn't get them up past my knees. Had I really been that skinny once? I cried for twenty minutes after that.

So I put on a pair of stretchy workout pants, which are slightly more fashionable than sweatpants. In other words, not very. The Fiancé, who came home from work for this appointment, or test, or whatever it was, is wearing a suit. "He's so lucky to look so professional," I think bitterly.

I give our condo the once-over, making sure that it looks like competent parents live here, ones who are raising a baby in a healthy, safe environment. Is it clean enough? Will the nurse care that absolutely nothing has been babyproofed? Should I hide all my *Us Weeklys* and put out some parenting magazines? Will the nurse care that this condo still looks like a designer bachelor pad, aside from the baby's room, which is straight out of the Pottery Barn showroom?

I have dressed the baby in a brand-new onesie and sleeper. I am completely nervous. What if the nurse can tell that I am an absolute mess, that I have no idea what I'm doing, that I have no business being responsible for a newborn?

"Fuck," I say to the Fiancé when I hear the doorbell. "She's here." It's judgment time.

"Don't worry," the Fiancé tells me. "We'll be fine."

"Hello. I'm Meredith," says the woman at the door.

"Hi," we say in unison, and the Fiancé introduced us.

"Would you like a cup of coffee or some juice?" I ask, thinking, "Please don't want coffee or juice." I am pretty positive we don't have either. I do have a lot of formula though.

"No, no. I'm fine. Let's go see the baby," she says, getting down to business.

"Please don't take my baby away," I think. "Please don't take my baby away. If you don't take my baby away, I will promise to be nicer to the Fiancé, stop moaning about the in-laws, and give a lot of money to charity."

"Why don't you undress her so I can measure her?" says the woman, taking a measuring tape from her bag.

I nervously pick up the baby, which is weird, because I have never been nervous picking her up before. Holding the baby is one of the things I had been most paranoid about before I gave birth. But immediately, when the doctor had handed her to me,

she just fit in my arms perfectly. It also wasn't nearly as hard as I
had imagined to change her diapers. I almost kidded myself that
I was a natural at this mommy thing when she first came out of
me. And I was, for the first ten minutes, before she starting crying and I had no idea why.

The baby started to fuss when I undressed her with Meredith
watching. "Oh, God, don't cry now," I think. "Please don't cry
now. Don't make me look like I don't know what I'm doing.
Don't act unhappy now, of all times. You're making me look
bad!"

"So, is she breast- or bottlefed?" Meredith asks.

Crap. This is another question I hate. At least she's a professional and has more of a right to ask this question than some
people. Perfect strangers, when they see me with the baby, have
asked me this. Though I'm completely comfortable with my decision to formula-feed, I'd learned the whole "Are you bottle- or
breastfeeding?" discussion was one I never wanted to get into.
You can never tell what people's reactions will be.

"She's bottlefed," I say firmly, with a "Don't fuck with my decision" undertone. I am lucky. Meredith doesn't seem to care.
Well, not entirely.

"Was that your choice, or was there a medical reason?"

"Um, it was my choice," I answer, again with the "Don't fuck
with my decision" undertone.

My friend Vivian calls certain people breastfeeding Nazis.
"I got two calls after I came home from nurses who kept trying
to convince me to breastfeed," she had told me. "I dreaded
picking up my phone." I couldn't believe that people actually
did that. Breastfeeding Nazis were worse than telemarketers.
I wasn't breastfed, and I, mostly, turned out okay. The Fiancé
wasn't breastfed, and he is a corporate lawyer, with four de-

grees. He really turned out okay. Plus, my friend Ronnie, who breastfed all three of her children, was constantly complaining about her sagging boobs. "They're ruined for life," she's always moaning, and she wonders how she can save money to get a boob job. She also wants a tummy tuck, but that's another issue.

Not that the possibility of sagging breasts was the reason I had decided not to breastfeed. Well, that wasn't the sole reason. What can I say? I like my breasts.

The checkup goes fine. I guess we pass, because Meredith packs up her things and says she is heading off, but not before asking us if we have any questions for her. Once again, the Fiancé and I have nothing prepared to ask. Meredith looks at us expectantly. I feel bad. I make a mental note to think up questions to ask these professionals, who always want to know if we have any questions. I kind of think it makes us look bad, you know, the fact that we never have anything to ask about our baby (although it would be nice if someone we knew could tell us how the Diaper Bitch works).

We should have a million questions, shouldn't we? We really should. Shouldn't we?

November 14
9 A.M.

I wake up to hear laughter in the kitchen. I wonder who could be here at this hour, aside from Nanny Mimi and the baby, who definitely doesn't laugh. As I head down the hallway toward the kitchen, I recognize the voice. It's the mother-in-law.

As soon as I walk into the kitchen, she starts explaining that she just stopped by to drop off some new undershirts that she had bought for the baby. Maybe she's aware that I don't exactly love these surprise drop-ins because she's telling me why she's here and I haven't even asked.

This is the fourth time she just "had to stop by to drop something off for the baby" in the last week.

I say a grumpy hello, grab my cell phone, and head back into my bedroom. I'm still not a morning person, and I don't like speaking to anyone before a cup of coffee. I don't like it either that the mother-in-law seems to get along better with the nanny than I do. I'm her boss! Nanny Mimi should want to suck up to me, not my mother-in-law!

"Why doesn't your mother just say she wants to see the baby?" I ask the Fiancé when he picks up the phone. "That would be okay, you know. She doesn't have to make up an excuse and buy something for her every time she wants to see the baby. It bothers me that she does that."

"They're just trying to be helpful," he says. If I hear one more time that "they're just trying to be helpful . . ."

"Do you know what it's like for me to not even feel comfortable in my own house? I don't want to wake up to have them here. I don't want to see people when I just wake up," I moan. "Can't they just call first? How hard is it to pick up a phone?"

"Well, what do you want me to do?"

"They're your parents! You tell them they have to call first."

"Okay, I'll say something, but it's going to start a fight," he huffs.

"I don't think it's too much to ask for a phone call before they come over."

I'm torn. It's true, they do mean well, and they're always happily buying things for the baby. They do make our lives easier. I don't know why I'm being so unreasonable. I just feel like being unreasonable, that's all. I feel like starting a fight with the Fiancé. I feel like being a royal bitch.

4 P.M.

Do all mothers dread weekends? Weekends used to be fun for me. Weekends used to mean sleeping until noon, going to a spin class, going out to brunch, taking a nap, and going out for dinner or drinks. Now it just means I'm going to have to take care of the baby all by myself for forty-eight hours. The Fiancé, don't get me wrong, is super-supportive and helpful and will be with me for the next forty-eight hours. But for some reason I believe I can feed the baby and hold her and calm her down better than he can. Every time he picks her up, and she doesn't stop screaming immediately, I take her from him. Every time he tries to feed her, I'm convinced he's not doing it right. Every time he goes to burp her, I'm convinced he's going to drop her. But maybe I'm supposed to feel like I know better. I'm her mother after all. Isn't it true that mothers know best?

"So, when are you going to be home?" I ask when I call the Fiancé.

"Beck . . ."

"What? I'm just asking when you're going to be home. I'm allowed to ask you a question, aren't I?"

"Soon. I'll be home soon."

"Okay, good. See you soon."

It was only the fifth time today I've asked him that question. I think I'm progressing.

8 P.M.

We had decided to meet friends for dinner at a Chinese restaurant. We now only seem to go out to eat ethnic foods, which I like, don't get me wrong. But mostly the reason we go to these types of restaurants is because they're always full of customers, which means they're always loud. If the baby acts up, we feel less guilty about it. Plus, all the action in these noisy restaurants tires her out, so she sleeps. Luckily, the baby sleeps through the entire dinner, which is a blessing. I barely eat anything and stay away from all the fried foods. I think I'm getting used to feeling like I'm always starving. I know that all doctors would tell me that the way I'm dieting is unhealthy. But I don't care. I just want to lose the damn weight already.

"Stop!" I yell at the Fiancé as we're driving home.

"What?" he says.

"You just went through a red light!"

"I did?"

"Yes!"

"Oh God, I'm so tired," he moans.

"Be careful! God, we have a baby here!" I say.

I'm starting to understand those BABY ON BOARD bumper stickers. Not that I'm ever going to get one. Please. I'm not that type of person.

8:02 P.M.

"Stop!"

"Shit!"

"You did it again!" I cry.

"I didn't even see that stop sign!"

"We're going to die," I moan. "We're going to die!"

"I really shouldn't be driving."

"That's for sure."

I laugh, though. And so does the Fiancé. It's the first time we have laughed together in a while, even if it's because we could have gotten into a car accident. Maybe I *am* the type of person who would drive around with a BABY ON BOARD bumper sticker. You know, they're not a bad idea. Not at all. I know now that what the signs really mean is "Sleep-deprived parent behind the wheel. Watch out!"

8:15 P.M.

We're at home. It's a miracle. I wonder how many traffic accidents are a result of sleep-deprived parents of newborns driving. I open the back door and take the baby, in her car seat, out of the car. I feel like kissing the concrete floor of the underground parking garage. But I don't want to make the Fiancé feel worse than he already does about almost killing us, so I just silently thank God we're alive.

"Are you going to take her out of the car seat?" he asks.

"No."

"Good."

I can't believe the baby has been sleeping so long.

"I just hope she doesn't get used to sleeping in the car seat," the Fiancé says.

It's true. The baby spends more time sleeping in the car seat than anywhere else. She just seems to like it better than her comfortable crib, which cost a small fortune, and her bassinet, which is so soft that if I were smaller, I'd sleep in it.

"Do you really care where she sleeps as long as she sleeps?" I ask.

"No."

"Thought so."

9:30 P.M.

We're both in bed.

"I can't tell you how happy I am to be in bed," the Fiancé says.

"Me too." The baby woke up for a feeding and we changed her diaper and her sleeper. We played around with her a bit and then she started getting cranky. We put her in the swing and she fell asleep. She spends a lot of time sleeping in the swing, too, come to think of it. I'm okay with that, as long as she sleeps.

"Maybe she'll sleep through the night," the Fiancé says.

"Don't say that! Why the fuck did you have to say that?"

"What? What did I say?"

"You said, 'Maybe she'll sleep through the night.' You've just jinxed it."

I've learned never to think, let alone say, "Maybe this will be the night she sleeps through," because as soon as I do say it, or even think it, she starts screaming bloody murder.

Waaa!!!

"Fuck," he says.

"I'll go get her," I say, like I'm doing him the biggest favor in the world. "I told you not to say that! I told you!"

Don't you just love being the one who gets to say "I told you so"?

November 15

11 A.M.

Having a newborn is like going on the longest walk in the world. Sometimes I feel like the Fiancé and I are homeless when we go out for walks with the baby, which is what we do every Saturday afternoon now.

We don't have a destination when we leave the house. We just need to get out. We need to do something. One can stay in a two-bedroom condo with a newborn for only so long.

"You know," the Fiancé says, "before we had her, we never went on walks. Can you ever remember us going on walks?"

"Not unless it was from the car to the restaurant or from the car to the movie theater," I answer.

"I'm now convinced that the only people who go on long walks are new parents," he says.

He's completely right. The Fiancé and I had never walked so much in our lives as we have in the past couple of months. We walk and walk and walk, pushing the stroller, with no place to go. Not only because it's something to do, but the fresh air knocks the baby out. In fact, I've learned that if we walk directly into the sun, it will force the baby to shut her eyes, and then she'll fall asleep. There should be a book called *Tricks to Get Your Child to Sleep*. I'd probably pick up that book.

"So, you want to go to the drugstore?" I ask the Fiancé.

"Why? Do you need something?"

"No. But why not?"

"I guess we could."

"Okay, let's go then."

This is another thing. I now make up destinations. I may already have two tubes of toothpaste at home, but I'll walk with the baby to the drugstore convincing myself that we need more toothpaste, or we will one day. I mean, a person always needs toothpaste. These days I'm always too tired to read, but I'll spend hours browsing in the bookstore and buying novels that I would love to read when—and if—I get my brain back. I may not want a coffee, but I'll go to Starbucks just to kill an hour, with the baby beside me in her stroller.

In fact, where I once noticed cute guys in drugstores and bookstores and coffee shops, now all I seem to notice are all the parents of newborns, who clearly are also out killing time, drinking coffee they don't really want, and buying books they'll never read. At least the in-laws offered to babysit tonight, so the Fiancé and I can have a nice, quiet dinner together, which is something to look forward to. We haven't been alone, just the two of us, in a long time.

When we get back to our condo, after getting a tube of toothpaste, a couple of magazines, and a coffee, I feed the baby and give her a bath.

I like the baby today. She's been good. She's been an angel. I put her in her swing. And then she's not good. She starts crying.

Every time she starts crying, I look at the Fiancé to see if he'll get up and get her. Sometimes he does. Sometimes he looks at me as if to say, "Your turn."

"You know," he says, "she's like a dictator. Every time she starts screaming, we come running. She's a pint-size dictator. And that's what I'm going to call her from now on."

"My Pint-Size Dictator," I repeat. "Yes, it really does have a nice ring to it, doesn't it?"

Later that night

We're home from dinner by 8:30 P.M.

"Well, you guys didn't go out for very long," the mother-in-law said when we went to their place to pick up the baby.

We had gone out for sushi. Our meal lasted forty minutes.

It's just that I missed my baby horribly.

When Ronnie gave birth to her first child, she didn't go out and leave the baby with a sitter, or even her parents, for six months. When she had her second child, she went out without him after two months. After her third child, she was going out after a week.

I'd never had a problem leaving the baby. I mean, I only had a problem in the sense that right after I left her, I wanted to be back with her again. Why is it that after I spend the entire day with the baby, I can't wait to leave her, but then, ten minutes after I leave her, I want to see her again? Why is it that when I hold her I want to put her down, but when someone else picks her up, I want to grab her from whoever is holding her so I can hold her again? Why is it that I can't wait for her to fall asleep, and then, when she finally does, I find myself wanting her to wake up again?

It's kind of like whatever section of the newspaper the Fiancé is reading, I want to read that section immediately.

Not only had I missed the baby horribly over dinner, I am also hating the fact that the Fiancé and I seem to have become worse than just roommates. We don't have anything in common anymore but the baby, or so it seems, because that's all we talk about.

"Isn't she cute when she wakes up?" I said to him over dinner.

"Yes, she's very cute."

"Doesn't she have the most beautiful eyes?" I asked.

"Yes. Isn't it amazing how she'll sleep all day and then be up all night?"

"Yes."

"I just love her so much, don't you?"

"Yes."

I don't remember what we used to talk about pre-baby. We haven't seen a movie in months, so we can't talk about movies. I can't complain about work, which previously took up most of our conversations, because I haven't been working. He never talked about his work with me before, because I don't quite understand what it is he does. I can't even tell him what books I've been reading, because I don't remember how to read. My party friends don't call anymore, so I have no gossip to pass on to him.

We do talk about one other thing: my big butt. But that topic can only last five minutes before he tells me that "it took nine months to put on the weight and it will take nine months to get off," and that just puts me in a foul mood.

There's no kidding ourselves. We have turned into, um, parents. I don't think either one of us wanted to prolong our night out. He knew my mind was on getting back to see the baby. He knew I couldn't wait any longer.

The baby was lying quietly when I raced to see her, sleeping in her car seat on the in-laws' kitchen table.

"She was perfect. Just perfect!" the mother-in-law said. Why is it every time we drop her off at their place, the baby is perfect? Why is it she only screams bloody murder when the Fiancé and I are with her, and not anyone else? I think the in-laws were lying.

The mother-in-law has also told me that when her son was a baby, she had "trained" him to never poo from nine to five, during the hours she was at home alone with him. I don't believe that, and I don't believe that the baby is always "perfect" when she's with them.

"Don't you dare wake her!" the mother-in-law told me when she saw me hovering over the baby. Which immediately made me want to wake her. She was my baby—*mine*—and if I wanted to wake her, I would damn well wake her. Who was she to tell me what I could and couldn't do?

The fiancé sided with his parents on that one.

"Beck, if she's sleeping, that means she's tired. She needs to sleep. Don't wake her."

"Well, she wakes me up when I'm sleeping, so why can't I wake her up when she's sleeping?" Okay, I knew I was being ridiculous.

"What are you, a child?" the Fiancé asked.

I continued staring at the baby, and the second she made a movement, I picked her up. The in-laws and the Fiancé stared at me like I'd done something horribly wrong, like I'd murdered someone.

"What? She was getting up anyway! I didn't wake her!" I protested. (Unless me blowing air on her face woke her . . .)

The Fiancé shook his head. The mother-in-law shook her head. So did the father-in-law. I didn't care what any of them thought. She was my baby and I could hold her whenever I wanted to.

November 17

8:15 A.M.

I'm holding my baby, who looks like she's been in a cat fight. Her face is covered with scratches.

"What happened?" Nanny Mimi asks.

"I don't know. She woke up like this!"

There's nothing in her crib, where she slept last night for the first time, that could possibly have scratched her. Except her.

I actually have a couple of scratches on my face, too, thanks to the Pint-Size Dictator. She's a dangerous little thing, or she has been since her nails have grown. I've tried putting those sock mittens on her hands, but they never stay on very long.

"Someone needs their nails clipped," Nanny Mimi says.

I find baby nail clippers, which we have, who knows why or how we got them. I hand them over to Mimi. "You do it. I can't," I say. I'm scared shitless to clip her nails. Her hands, and her nails, are so tiny. What if I accidentally cut off some skin? I never want to hurt the baby. Never.

"We have to wait until she's asleep, and then I'll do it," says Nanny Mimi. Why didn't I think of that? Ahh, the baby's first manicure. I have to remember this moment. I don't want to take my baby out in public looking like this, all scratched up. What if people think I did this to her?

November 18

10 A.M.

It's Tuesday morning and I'm excited to get started on my day. Today will be the first day I've exercised in, what, nine months? I had meant to keep up with my workouts during my pregnancy, but I gave up after month four. I was enjoying giving in to my every craving way too much. I had done the math. I would have had to do eighteen hours of spin classes just to work off what I ate in one meal, so what was the point?

"Hey, Mimi," I say, "I'm just heading downstairs to work out for a bit." Nanny Mimi is feeding the baby, and I kiss her on her forehead. The baby, I mean, not Nanny Mimi. She smells yummy. The baby, that is, not Nanny Mimi.

"Okay, bye!"

The one nice thing about living in a condo (aside from the fact we have a garbage chute in our laundry room, which goes directly to a bin in the basement, which means the dirty diapers get out of our place fast. It actually also means we don't really even need the stupid Diaper Genie. Anyway . . .) is that we have a small gym on the main floor, which means I'll have no excuse not to work out, once I get back into the routine. I'm going to walk on the treadmill for at least one hour and then go on the elliptical trainer for twenty minutes. I can already feel my ass getting smaller.

It's funny, but when I was sixteen I used to be embarrassed about my body. Then when I was twenty-eight, I missed that sixteen-year-old body of mine. And now that I've had a baby, well, let's just say I want any body but the one I have now.

10:15 A.M.

"You're back already?" Nanny Mimi asks.

"Yes," I say quietly.

"Oh," she says. She hasn't moved since I left . . . five minutes ago.

Uncomfortable silence.

I could barely walk on speed 2.1 on the treadmill. Before the baby, I was running at 5.3. I suppose this is what eight months of lying on your ass and eating jumbo bags of Cheesies in bed does to a person.

So I do what anyone else would do upon saying they were going to work out, only to return five minutes later.

I lie.

"I actually felt a little pain, so I thought it was better to stop."

"That's probably best," she says.

Uncomfortable silence.

I head to the bedroom and call the Fiancé to moan.

"Well, you just had a major operation. It'll take time to get back into the swing of things," he says.

Why does it seem like it's been years since I had the C-section? When the Fiancé said, "It'll take time to get back into the swing of things," was he talking about me working out, or our lives?

Even though I walked on the treadmill slower than a ninety-nine-year-old with a cane who's just had hip-replacement surgery, for a whole four minutes, I'm exhausted. But before I can despair about the sad state of my body, Heather calls me back. Finally.

"So, how's being a mother?" she asks.

"It's great. She's so cute," I lie. Not about the baby being cute, which she most definitely is, but about being a mother being great. It's definitely different. But I'm not sure "great" is the right word to describe it.

"So, have you lost all the baby weight yet?" she asks.

"No. But I just worked out," I tell her.

"So, are you ready to have another yet?"

Gaa!

"Another what?" I ask. Maybe Heather was asking me about coffee.

"Another baby!"

"Um, no. I've barely gotten used to this one," I say. "I'm not even sure if my stitches have healed yet!"

This baby has only been in my life for, what, almost two months? The funny thing is, Heather is not the first person to have asked me this question. Ronnie had asked when I was going to start trying for a second.

"No way," I had told Ronnie. "There's no way. I think that's it for me. I'm done."

"Wait. You'll see," she had said. "You just wait." As if!

"So, are you planning to ever get married?" Heather asks. Why is she asking me all these questions?

"I don't know. Maybe when I lose the baby weight," I say, only half joking.

I realize that getting married is no longer a priority in my life. The Fiancé and I pretty much stopped all wedding talk when I got knocked up at our engagement party. Plus, the Fiancé and I are living like an old married couple already. We don't have sex. I call him a billion times a day, asking when he's going to come home. I realize that not even my parents have been asking me when we're going to get married. It's all about the baby now.

Anyway, most people, I'm convinced, get married only to have a baby. And I have a baby. Why do I have to get married now?

Midnight

The Fiancé is lecturing me like I'm five.

"If you wake her up, you'll have to deal with her," he tells me.

The baby has been asleep for hours and hours, and I miss her.

I can't believe how much I miss her, even though she's right in the next room. I just want to hold her. The problem is, once I start holding her, I want to put her down after ten minutes, and once I pick her up, she doesn't want me to put her down.

"Fine. I'm not going to wake her. But she's been asleep for so long now. I just want to hold her," I tell him. "Can't you understand that?"

"If you wake her, you deal with her," he says again, like I'm in a china store with the "You break it, you buy it" rule.

I walk next door into the baby's room. She looks so peaceful and cute I just want to hold her close to me and smell her. I'm not going to though. But she's just so cute. It's amazing that it seems I spend all my time when she's awake trying to get her to go to sleep. Maybe if I just gently rub my finger across her cheek. There. Her skin is so smooth. She doesn't move. Maybe I can gently pick her up without waking her. I slowly put my arm under her head. She doesn't stir. Perfect. I pick up her entire body and inhale her beautiful scent, getting the baby fix I was jonesing for. No other baby in the world smells as good as—

WAAAAA!!

Fuck. Fuck. Fuck.

"I told you!" the Fiancé yells out. "I told you not to touch her, and now look at what you've done."

"I told you I'd deal with it and I will!" I scream back.

"Fine!" he screams.

"Fine!" I scream.

"Fine!" he screams again.

"Fine!" I scream back at him.

It only takes three hours to settle her down. I've learned my lesson. Boy, have I learned my lesson. Never wake a sleeping baby, even when you ache for her. It's not worth it. Especially when someone tells you "I told you so."

The Fiancé and I are heading for a divorce, I'm sure. It seems we bicker a lot, and he refuses to talk to me right now. Not that I'm talking to him either.

November 19
10:15 A.M.

Today I learned that having a child with a unisex name poses hurdles. We're at the pediatrician's for a checkup. I walk up to the counter to announce our arrival. The nurse pulls out the baby's file, and I see the male symbol next to her name.

"Actually," I tell the woman, "she's a girl. Rowan's a girl."

"Oh, I never heard of that name for a girl. Interesting," says the nurse.

Interesting? What does that mean? Interesting in a good way or interesting in a bad way? I convince myself that she would have noticed that the baby is a girl if she had seen the pink blanket and her pink sleeper and her pink hat. But she was behind a counter.

The nurse leads us to an examining room and tells us to undress the baby.

"Totally?" I ask.

"Yes, even her diaper."

Shit. The Fiancé and I look at each other. We didn't bring the diaper bag. Instead, I had just thrown a bottle into my purse. I figured we wouldn't be here very long. I undress her, trying to untape the diaper carefully to reuse it.

"I'll be right back," I tell the Fiancé, handing over the baby.

"Where are you going?" he asks, alarmed that I'm leaving him alone with the naked baby on his lap.

"I'll be right back! I have to do something."

"What?"

"I'll be right back!"

Okay, I could lie and say that I was searching for diapers. The truth is I had noticed a scale in a room next to us. I hop on it to see what I weigh, since we don't have a scale at home. The Fiancé won't let me have a scale at home. Which is for the best. I'd be weighing myself every two minutes. So is it any wonder that when I see a scale I want to jump on it?

I can't believe this. I'm still thirty-some-odd pounds heavier than my pre-baby weight.

Mortified, I go back to the examining room, where I pray the baby hasn't peed on the Fiancé, because he'd be in a pissy mood.

"I just weighed myself," I tell the Fiancé.

"I can't believe you just did that. God, what's wrong with you? We're here for her, not you!"

"I've been walking on the treadmill and everything, and nothing is happening!"

"Beck, it took nine months to put on, so it—"

Thank God the doctor walks in so I don't have to hear the rest of that sentence. The doctor is a very affable man who checks out the baby and tells us she's at the fiftieth percentile of height and weight.

"Do you have any questions for me?" he asks.

The Fiancé and I look at each other. Fuck. I forgot to take diapers, and I forgot to come prepared with questions.

When I was pregnant, Ronnie had warned me that obstetricians were impossible to get a hold of and I should come to each appointment with a list of questions. I guess this was the same idea. The problem was, again, I really didn't have any questions. Again, I feel like a bad mother for not having questions. I should be worried about something, shouldn't I? But the fact is, she eats okay, she goes to the washroom okay. She was okay. There doesn't seem to be a problem with her weight or height.

"Um, when do they start sleeping through the night?" the Fiancé asks. I know he's just asking so it makes us look like we're concerned about something.

"Good question," I say, even though I don't think it's a good question at all.

We hear, for the millionth time, that at around three months the baby should start sleeping through the night.

I slip her back into her used diaper, and we pack her up. I want to hop on the scale again, but the Fiancé drags me out.

"Well, that's pretty good. She's at the fiftieth percentile for her age in weight and height," I say to the Fiancé while he's driving us back home.

"Yes, we have a perfectly healthy, average baby," he says.

"Nothing wrong with that," I say. "Nothing wrong with that at all."

10:15 P.M.

The Fiancé and I have sex. Is it scary because we haven't done it in so long and I am not completely convinced that I'm healed properly? Only a little bit. And afterward, lying together naked, it's nice. Very nice. In a way, I feel like it was celebratory sex. Not just because we were finally doing it after so long, but because we have a perfectly healthy, average baby. What more could two parents hope for?

One week later, my perfectly healthy baby is not.

November 28

"So, when are you coming home?" I ask the Fiancé.

"Soon."

"Like how soon?"

"Soon."

"Okay, it's just that the baby seems to have a really bad cold and I don't know what to do. I'm kind of freaking out here. I really think she's really sick."

It's five o'clock on Friday.

"Well, didn't the nurse who came to our condo give you an emergency number to call if you had any health questions?"

"Right. Do you know where that is?"

"I think it's in the kitchen somewhere."

"Okay, see you soon," I say, hanging up.

I can't stand watching my poor baby. She's so congested that she can barely breathe. It breaks my heart to hear her cry because I know she doesn't understand she just has a cold.

Luckily, I find the 1-800 number that is still in the folder the nurse gave us, full of baby information we had never bothered to read. I dial the number.

"Hi, I have a question about my baby," I say when a woman answers the phone.

"Okay. Have you ever called here before?" she asks.

"No."

"Okay, first I just have to ask you a few questions," she says.

After what seems like twenty minutes of inane questions, like what's my phone number and where do I live and when did I give birth and do I breastfeed, and after biting my tongue to stop myself from screaming at her, "My baby is in trouble! Can't this wait?" the person on the other end finally asks the reason I'm calling.

"My baby has a really bad cold, and I don't know if she can breathe properly," I say. My voice is wobbly. I might cry.

"Is the area around her mouth purple?" she asks.

I look at my baby's mouth. I don't see any purple. "No, I don't think so."

"Okay, what I want you to do is undress her and take a look right under her rib cage, as she breathes," she says.

"Okay, hold on," I say as I unbutton her sleeper and unsnap her onesie. "I'm looking," I tell her.

"Does her breathing seem labored?"

"Yes," I say; when she tries to breathe in, her rib cage rises slowly.

"Well, she could be in distress. I'd suggest you go to the closest emergency room," the woman says.

Distress? My baby is in distress? MY BABY IS IN DISTRESS!

"Okay, I'm going to go right now," I say, and hang up. I call the Fiancé on his cell phone.

"I just called that number and the woman said she could be in distress and we should get to the nearest emergency room," I say. I'm hysterical now, and in tears.

"Okay, I'm just pulling up to our building now. I'll meet you out front. But traffic is really heavy. It's rush hour. Should we wait awhile before going?" the Fiancé asks.

"The baby could be in distress!" I yell at him, and hang up. What the fuck is he thinking wanting to know if we should wait until traffic lessens? Why isn't he concerned? MY BABY IS IN DISTRESS! I'm running around like a chicken with its head cut off. Bottle. Diapers. Health card. Fuck. *fuck*. FUCK!

We're in the car, stuck in rush-hour traffic.

"I can't stand this!" I cry.

The baby is screaming and snorting in the backseat, and I feel a migraine coming on.

"I can't go any faster. I'm going as fast as I can!" the Fiancé says.

"I know," I snap. "You said that already."

"Don't snap at me," he snaps back, and I start to cry.

"Don't talk to me like that! Why are you doing this now?" I

cry out. "Don't be such an asshole now. I'm worried. Can't you understand that?"

"I'm going as fast as I can," he says, hitting the steering wheel.

Finally we arrive, and he drops me off in front of the emergency room entrance. I race inside while he finds a place to park.

I'm still in a line in the emergency room waiting to check in when the Fiancé races in. He does look worried. I can't believe there's such a line. I'm practically shaking. I hand the baby, who's in the car seat, to the Fiancé and walk to the head of the line. I don't wait in line at clubs, and I definitely don't want to wait in line here.

"Well, I have this bad cough and I've had it for a couple of weeks now, but I didn't have time to see my doctor during the week," someone is saying.

I can't believe this. Some dude who's had a cough for two weeks decides to go to the emergency room? Doesn't he know that there are actual emergencies? LIKE MY BABY, WHO IS IN DISTRESS?

"Excuse me," I interrupt. I know there's a fine line between bitchiness and persistence, especially in a hospital where everyone is so overworked, but this is my baby we're talking about. The guy with the cough is lucky I don't punch him. "I have an eight-week-old baby who's not breathing properly," I say in a loud voice. The three people in front of me shoot me a dirty look. "Fuck you all," I think.

It works. Immediately a nurse takes my baby to the back room to take her temperature. She doesn't seem worried. What is wrong with everybody? I was told MY BABY COULD BE IN DISTRESS!

"Well, she doesn't have a temperature, which is good," the nurse says.

In fact, the baby is now sleeping soundly. (It's like when you desperately need a haircut, but the day of your appointment you wake up and your hair looks fabulous. Although this is way more serious.)

"I swear, she couldn't breathe like ten minutes ago! I called a 1-800 number and the woman told me we should come directly here," I explain.

"Oh, we hate those 1-800 numbers. You can't make a good diagnosis over the phone, and they just tell everyone to come here. Just wait over there in the waiting area, and a doctor will see you shortly," she says.

The Fiancé and I take seats. I can't help but look at all the other sick people in the waiting room, wondering what their ailments are. What kind of germs is my baby going to catch while we wait?

"I don't know, maybe we should just go," I say to the Fiancé after we've waited about half an hour. "I don't want her to catch anything worse than she already has."

Just then, we're called in.

A doctor checks out the baby and hands us a blue suction thing.

"She just has a bad cold. Every parent of a newborn should have one of these. First you put saline drops, which you can buy at any drugstore, in her nostrils, then stick this up each nostril and it will suck out all the phlegm," he says, demonstrating.

I have never seen one of these things before.

"Colds for babies can last anywhere from a month to six weeks," the doctor tells us.

Six weeks! "Thank you," I say to the doctor. "Thank you so much. I was so worried. They did tell me she could be in distress."

"Well, it's always better to be safe than sorry. You did the right thing coming here," he says, and I kind of feel like kissing him because I'm so relived nothing is wrong with my baby.

Back at home, I feel like I've been through a war. The baby starts crying, and her nose, once again, is clogged. We stopped on the way home to buy the saline drops.

"You do it," I tell the Fiancé, handing him the suction thing that we're supposed to stick up the baby's nostrils, which are smaller than chocolate chips.

"No, you do it," he says.

"I can't! You do it!"

"Fine. But you have to help," he says.

I hold the baby's arms down, while turning my head and looking away. She's not happy, and I can't stand to see her flailing her arms and listen to her screams.

"I'm like a doctor," says the Fiancé proudly when he sucks out the boogers and the baby can breathe much better again. "And you are *never* to call that 1-800 number again. Ever!"

"She told me the baby was in distress," I say quietly. "And the doctor said it was better to be safe than sorry."

"I know. I know," he says, wrapping his arms around me. I cry again, tears of exhaustion and tears of relief. I don't ever want to feel that worried again. How do mothers deal with the worry?

December 1

Now I'm really sick. I feel like hell. My throat itches. I have a fever. I cough. My nose is running. But at least I know how to use tissues. The baby's nose runs like a nonstop faucet, and it's pretty disgusting.

December 2
Now the Fiancé is sick. He feels like hell. His throat itches. He has a fever and he's coughing now too.

December 3
The baby is still sick. I'm sick. The Fiancé is sick. Our house reeks of germs.

December 4
We're all sick. Even Nanny Mimi is sick.

Babies are very contagious.

December 5
"Okay, we have to divide and conquer this," I say, after days of feeling like I've been swallowing knives. My nose is so raw it hurts. "The only way we're all going to get cured is if we're not with one another in the same room," I tell the Fiancé. "Can you move out?"

"What?"

"I'm just joking. But we can't sleep in the same room. We'll never get better."

Is this how it's going to be from now on? The baby gets a cold, passes it on to me, then I pass it on to the Fiancé, who loves kissing me, which means he's just giving me my sick germs back. Of course, I can't not kiss the baby, which means she's giving me her germs and I'm giving her mine. This could be a never-ending cycle. We could just keep passing this cold back and forth to one another *forever*.

The Fiancé sleeps on the couch. I think our relationship can't possibly deteriorate any more than this. We're now sleeping in separate rooms? I know mothers who breastfeed sometimes sleep in separate rooms from their husbands, so as not to wake them up when they have to feed. But we live in a two-bedroom condo. Even if I would allow the Fiancé to sleep in a separate room from me, where would he go? I guess he could sleep in the bathtub.

December 15

10 A.M.

We're all better. Physically, that is. But something is still wrong with me. I just feel . . . wrong. I can't get out of bed.

11 A.M.

I'm just so tired. I should get out of bed to say hi to the baby. I can't.

1 P.M.

My cell phone has been ringing all morning. I know it's the Fiancé wondering where I am and why I haven't called. I don't want to call him back. I don't want to do anything.

3 P.M.

I've been dozing on and off all day. I should get out of bed. I just can't. My body feels like concrete.

5 P.M.

The Fiancé comes into the bedroom.

"Beck, what's wrong? Mimi says you haven't been out of the room all day. Why haven't you called me? Why haven't you answered your phone? What's happening?"

"I don't know."

"What do you mean, you don't know? Are you sick?"

"I don't know," I respond. I've been in bed all day, and I still feel exhausted. I haven't eaten all day, but I'm not hungry.

"What can I do? Do you want to sleep? Do you need me to get you something?" he asks.

"I don't know."

"Beck!"

"I think I just want to be left alone."

Days later

I can't fight it anymore.

Though I've tried, I'm miserable.

I feel like I'm a failure at everything. I'm failing at my career, which has basically come to a complete halt since I gave birth. I'm failing at being a mother, because I need a nanny. When I do spend time with the baby, I wish she was sleeping. I'm failing at being a good wife, because everything the Fiancé does annoys me, and I annoy him because he knows he's annoying me for no reason and then he gets upset. And I'm just so, so tired.

"Something, uh, something's wrong with me," I cry to the Fiancé. I called him at work. I started crying this morning, and I haven't been able to stop.

"What's wrong? What's wrong?" he asks.

I just feel like I'm a big, fat failure at everything and that life sucks, I *think* that's what I'm feeling, at least. "I think, uh, I have, to, uh, see a doctor. Something is wrong with me," I cry.

For the past few days, I could barely get out of bed. I can't eat or sleep either. I can't stop crying. It's not that I want to kill myself, but I have had thoughts that if I didn't wake up ever again, that would be fine with me. Maybe it's purely exhaustion. Maybe I'm having a nervous breakdown.

"Okay, stay right there. Don't move. I'm going to call the doctor and make you an appointment."

The last time I bawled this hard was when I was four months pregnant and I realized for the first time that none of my clothes fit and I had a party, in honor of my birthday, to attend. I'm crying ten times harder now.

I sit there bawling, waiting for him to call me back. What is wrong with me? Why have I cried for hours every day for the past week? If someone looks at me the wrong way, I cry. Did Gwyneth Paltrow, after she had her baby, cry for hours because she hated her life? Had Courteney Cox not showered for days after she gave birth? Why am I the only mother who feels like a bad mother? I have a good life, I know that, and yet I'm more miserable than I've ever been. Ever.

The Fiancé calls back. "Okay, the doctor can fit you in at one today. I'll come pick you up. Do you think you can wait?"

"No, I think I have to go right now," I say, sobbing.

The Fiancé comes and picks me up immediately and doesn't know what to say. He doesn't understand why I'm so upset, and I can't explain it either, because I don't know why. I just know I've never been so upset in my life. That I'm sad. Very, very sad.

I walk into the doctor's office still crying. I tell the nurse I have an appointment in three hours. Apparently, no one wants to have a bawling woman sitting in their waiting room. They take me immediately.

"I can't stop crying," I tell the doctor.

"Any changes in your life recently?" he asks. "Career? Home life?"

"I had a baby," I say. I don't mention that I'm now living in a new city, with barely any friends, and that I am homesick too. I don't mention that it would be okay if I didn't wake up.

"You don't want to harm your baby, do you? You don't have any feelings like that?" he asks.

I don't. Not at all. Even thinking about harming my baby makes me cry harder. I know I don't want to kill myself—how could I do that to my beautiful baby, the love of my life? I would never do that to her. But if I just didn't wake up one day . . .

"And your home life is okay?" the doctor presses. I'm not an idiot. I know what he's asking. The doctor wants to know if the Fiancé abuses me.

"It's fine. I just, I just can't do anything. I can't think straight. I can't stop crying. I don't know what I'm doing, and I can't do anything right. I sleep for hours and I'm tired. I'm just so tired." I know my parents love me, I know the Fiancé loves me, heck, I'm sure even my baby loves me, but I feel completely alone and unloved.

The doctor explains what an antidepressant is. He thinks it would be good for me. I think it's a good idea too. I'm not the first person I know to be on antidepressants. In fact, I'm practically the last of my friends to go on antidepressants. And many of them have gone on antidepressants after a breakup. This is much more serious.

"When do these start working?" I ask.

"They take about two weeks to fully get into your system."

Two weeks? *Two weeks?* Two weeks seems like an eternity for me to continue feeling like this. I don't know if I'll last. The doctor tells me to come back in a couple of weeks.

I take the first pill. I wait for it to work.

That evening the Fiancé and I have a long discussion about my depression. He feels horrible. He doesn't know what to do. He feels like it's his fault.

"Maybe these pills will help me," I suggest. I feel awful for making him think that I'm so miserable. I don't really have anything to be miserable about, and yet I am. I have a healthy baby, a wonderful fiancé, parents and in-laws who care about me. I have more than most people could ever hope for.

The Fiancé thinks I should book a trip back to my city to visit my friends and family. He thinks I should rent an office, outside our condo, to write in so I have someplace to go each day and something to do aside from sitting around at home all day obsessing over my life, or lack of life, and calling him asking what time he'll be home. He suggests renting a place, too, for two months, somewhere warm and cheerful. He'll do anything to see me happy, and I love him for it. But even knowing that he loves me doesn't make me feel better.

December 22

The Fiancé has been walking on eggshells around me. I have booked an airline ticket home to visit my friends and family in January. I can't wait. I've called everyone to let them know I'm coming back for a visit. Vivian is organizing a baby party for our friends, so she and I can show off our babies at the same time. I'm going to go out with Lena and Heather and Sara because my parents have offered to babysit whenever I want them to. I'm going to get drunkity-drunk-drunk! The Fiancé has also rented a condo, in Maui, for two months for the baby and me. He thinks the sun will help my depression and that it will be easier to take care of a baby in warm weather. For the first time since being pregnant, I feel like there are things to look forward to. But I'm still depressed. I try to hide it because seeing me sad makes the Fiancé miserable and that depresses me even more.

December 23

Tonight, although I don't feel like it, we're meeting two of the Fiancé's friends for dinner at a "family restaurant," which means they serve pop in super-size plastic cups and the menu is as big as a road map. The wife, Tammy, is seven months pregnant. I force myself to try to be happy about going out. Everyone keeps telling me that I should keep busy and that going out will keep my mind off being depressed. I'd rather just stay home and mope and do nothing.

The baby is coming along.

"Should we take the diaper bag?" I ask.

"I don't know. Should we?"

I hate carrying the diaper bag around. It's heavy and I can never find anything in it. "Well, she just shat like an hour ago," I say.

"And we won't be very long," says the Fiancé.

"Screw it, let's go," I say. Just as we're heading out the door, I change my mind. "No, we better take it. I know she'll end up shitting just because we were too lazy to take it with us. We're unlucky that way," I tell the Fiancé. "And I think I'll just go to the washroom again."

We enter the restaurant and see our friends, who are already seated. They coo over the baby, and it brings a smile to my face. I'm proud of her. Even though she doesn't do anything yet but lie there and look cute, I'm still proud to be her mother. Then I'm not smiling. Because I recognize the look that's just appeared on my child's face. It's a look of relief and joy, which is not really a look of relief and joy. It's the "I'm shitting" look.

"Um," I say to the Fiancé, "we have a situation."

"Okay, well, I guess you'll have to go change her," he says.

(Damn restaurants that only have changing tables in the women's washrooms!)

"I will, but can I have the diaper bag, please?" I ask.

"I don't have the diaper bag. I thought you brought it," he says.

"No, I thought you brought it," I say.

"You said that we should bring it."

"I know I said that, but I thought you were going to get it when I went to the washroom."

"I thought you were getting it," he says.

"What's going on?" asks Tammy.

"We didn't bring the diaper bag," I admit, feeling like the stupidest mother in the world. What kind of mother leaves the house without a diaper bag? Obviously, the Fiancé and I were having communication issues. Why would he have assumed that I took it? Just because I said "No, we should bring it" doesn't mean that I'm the one who has to bring it. He has arms. Am I responsible for everything?

"Okay, there's a drugstore across the street. I'll be back in a second," the Fiancé says, jumping up from the table. "It's no problem."

Five minutes later, the Fiancé walks in with a jumbo-size package of diapers, a large container of wipes, and a mammoth jar of Vaseline. He arrives just in time, because I don't think I can last a moment longer with the stench that is coming from the baby. It is embarrassing actually. I am pretty positive the baby is ruining many, many meals around us.

"Wow!" I say. "That's a lot of supplies. Why did you buy ninety-nine diapers?"

"This is all they had. It was this or nothing."

I head to the washroom. I'm not going to ask why the only washrooms with changing tables are the women's.

8:15 P.M.

We're driving home.

"Did you see the look on Bob's face?" I ask, laughing about Tammy's husband.

"I know, he looked mortified," agrees the Fiancé.

"I know. He probably thinks we're the worst parents ever."

After the diaper debacle, the baby had dropped her pacifier on the floor during dinner and I had picked it up, put it in a glass of ice water, swished it around, and shoved it back into her mouth. You learn, after the millionth dropped soother, that not sanitizing it doesn't really matter. Your baby will not die, as you may have been led to believe, by sucking on a pacifier that was dropped on the floor.

"They'll see," he says. It's true. I, too, may have once looked mortified upon seeing a mother place into her child's mouth something that has fallen on the floor in a public venue.

As we're driving home, the Fiancé tells me a story about one of his colleagues whose live-in girlfriend had gotten pregnant and had the baby, much to the colleague's dismay. This guy was forty, a toxic bachelor, or at least lived like one, out at bars until 3 A.M. each night. "I just feel so bad for him," the Fiancé says.

"Why?"

"Because his girlfriend refuses to get any help, so now when he comes home after working all day, she hands him the baby and says, 'It's your turn. I've been with him all day.' And then she'll go to a movie with her sister or friends."

I'm torn over this story. Yes, I have full-time help, and yet I'm still exhausted from even spending three hours alone with the baby. Having a baby is like a full-time job. I understand how hard it is to be a mother of a newborn. At the same time, I understand that his friend has been at the office all day and has also worked and is probably pretty tired at the end of the day. I find it sad that babies have the ability to turn relationships sour. I find it sad to hear about a mother handing over a baby to her partner and saying, "It's your turn."

"Well, I guess they'll work it out," I say. I can't help but add, "At least I'm not like that."

"That's true," the Fiancé says.

"See, you're lucky to have me," I say.

"I am."

Though I am depressed, I've never once said to the Fiancé, "It's your turn."

We put the Dictator to bed and we have sex. We do it very quickly. The baby could sleep for hours or she could sleep for two minutes. You just never know. We have quick sex because we have learned our lesson. We almost had sex a couple of nights ago. We were just getting into it when the baby started to wail. Nothing like a wailing baby to, um, kill the mood.

By the time I had come back to bed, the Fiancé was like, "You still want to?"

I was like, "Um, no thanks."

December 29

Every parent must do the office visit. I tell Nanny Mimi that I want to take the baby to visit the Fiancé at his office. Nanny Mimi bundles the baby up with so many layers, she looks about 150 pounds heavier. It's very cold outside, and the ground is covered in snow. But I'm going to walk over since I have basically given up on exercising at the gym. I've been too tired and too blue.

"Are you sure this is okay?" I ask the Fiancé. "I mean, won't people look at me like I'm weird for bringing the baby to your office?"

"No, it's fine. Come over!" The truth is, he's been asking me to bring the baby to his office for a while.

"Am I fat?" I ask. "What if everyone looks at me and all they think is, 'My God, she's still fat and it's been months since she's given birth'?"

"I think they'll be too busy looking at the baby to look at you," he says.

"Thanks. You're too kind. Do you think I'm fat?"

"I'll see you in an hour, okay?"

It's not an easy walk. First of all, strollers are hard to push over snow—even our stroller, the BMW of all strollers (it only cost one thousand dollars). Second, every time we have to cross the street, not only do I have to lift the stroller over the snow-banks, but I also realize that drivers are friggin' crazy. I no longer run across the street, dodging cars like I used to. I watch all cars driving close to us, making sure they see me and the stroller and that they're going to slow down. God forbid one of them hits my baby!

I'm slightly pissed that the baby has fallen asleep on our walk over. She can't be all cute if she's asleep. What was the point of me dressing her in such a cute outfit so I could show her off, now that she's asleep and I probably won't even take her out of her jacket?

The Fiancé beams as his law partners gather in his office to see our child. At home, the Fiancé is always grumpy and moaning about the baby. But now, while all his colleagues and friends, most of whom are already fathers, come in and ooohh and ahhh, he looks proud.

I smile. God, I love the Fiancé. I'm even turned on a bit. There is nothing sexier, I think, than a man who proudly shows off his baby to his colleagues.

January 2
10 A.M.

The mother-in-law has been on our backs to look at schools for the baby.

"But she's not even twelve weeks old!" I've told her a million times. In fact, I think I remember saying, when the baby was still in my womb and the mother-in-law was asking about schools, "She's not even born yet!"

"Well, I read this article about how competitive getting your children in to school is," she had said.

Of course she had read an article. Argh!

"You have to call the school today," I tell the Fiancé.

"Okay, I will."

"Also, what time are you coming home? Hello?"

An hour later the Fiancé calls me back.

"Well, I called the school," he says.

"And?"

"They laughed at me."

"What?"

"They asked how old my child was, and I said almost three months. Then they laughed at me and told me to call back in two years." Apparently, not all schools are all that competitive to get in to.

"Oh. Well, at least we did it. At least your mother can stop asking us about it now."

3 A.M.

The Fiancé has only one rule, which is that the baby is never to sleep in our bed. He is convinced that if we even once have her sleep in our bed with us, she'll get used to it and never want to sleep in her crib again. Plus, he has friends whose babies have slept with them for, like, five years because they have gotten so used to sleeping with their parents. I wonder how those couples have sex. Anyway. Because this is the Fiancé's only rule, I let him have it. Plus, it's not easy sleeping with a baby. I know, because I've been trying to sleep with her on the couch. Babies make cute but strange noises constantly. She kicks. She moans while sucking on her bottle.

But by 2:30 A.M. I've had enough. I just want to crawl into our king-size bed. I make it another half hour debating, then pick up the baby and head for the big matrimonial bed. Who says the Fiancé owns the bed? It's my bed too. He's not the boss of me.

The Fiancé, amazingly, has fallen asleep. How did he do that? I suppose it's the same as a boyfriend falling asleep after a wicked fight. While a fight could keep a girlfriend up all night, the guy can easily fall asleep. It kind of pisses me off that the Fiancé has learned to sleep through the baby's wails. If I even hear her moan, I'm suddenly wide awake.

"Is everything okay?" the Fiancé asks groggily, hearing me climbing back into bed with the baby.

"Yup, fine. Go back to sleep." He does, of course.

Praying silently that the baby doesn't make any noise, I lie down, with her on my chest.

Next thing I know, the Fiancé is talking to me. I look at the alarm. It's 7 A.M. "How long has she been in here?" he asks.

"Oh, only, like, ten minutes," I answer.

"Oh, I didn't even hear you bring her in here."

Ha ha! Tricked him! Loser!

Maybe I can get away with her sleeping on me in the big bed every night.

January 6

"Okay, don't forget that she needs to wear socks on the plane," the mother-in-law is saying. "And bring diapers."

God, it reminds me of my father, who whenever I said I was going on a trip somewhere warm, would say, "You didn't forget to pack your bathing suit, did you?" Um, I'm going to Jamaica. Why would I forget my bathing suit?

Why does everyone assume I don't want what's best for my baby? Does the mother-in-law really think I'd let my two-and-a-half-month-old baby's feet freeze on the plane? Does she really think that I'd forget to bring diapers? I may not win any mother of the year awards, but I'm not that clueless. I'm sort of offended that she thinks she has to remind me to bring diapers!

I'm slightly nervous, I'll admit. Okay, I'm terrified to go on the plane with the baby. It's the first time that not only will I be traveling with her but I'll be with her alone for a week. I won't have the Fiancé. I won't have Nanny Mimi. It's just the baby and me. I can do this. I can do this, I tell myself. Mothers everywhere, every day, do it.

What I can't do is carry everything. My God, who knew that a nine-pound baby needs so much stuff for the airplane? The diaper bag weighs more than a piano. Seriously, if the plane had to make an emergency landing on a desert island, we could last for three months. I've packed eighteen diapers, four sets of sleepers and onesies, twelve cans of formula, seven bottles, and four pacifiers.

Thanks to a seat sale, the Fiancé and I decided to buy two seats, one for me and another for the baby, who will remain in her car seat—hopefully sleeping—next to me.

We check in super-early, in order to be prepared. The Fiancé came with us to the airport. At the check-in, there's a family in front of us with four young kids. They have ten pieces of luggage, I'm not kidding.

"Can you imagine traveling with four kids?" I whisper to the Fiancé. "Look at how much stuff they have!" They look like they're moving, not just visiting family or going on a vacation.

"That's a nightmare," he agrees.

Just before we go through security, the Fiancé and I have to say good-bye.

"Are you going to miss me?" I ask.

"Yes."

"Are you going to miss the baby?"

"Yes."

"Well, I'm going to miss you too."

It's true. I am. I haven't been apart from him since the baby arrived. But this is what I want, or thought I wanted. Going back to the city I grew up in, to see my friends and family, will remind me that I'm still me, that I have a *life*. I'm still a fabulous person, I just have a baby. That's all. Going back to my hometown will make me feel like a human again, and not just a baby maker. Is it possible to be lifesick, like being homesick and missing your home? I am lifesick. I miss my old life.

"This is a boarding call for flight 123," comes the voice over the loudspeaker. "We invite all those who need extra time getting seated and those with young children to board at this time."

The baby is sleeping and I'm flipping through an *Us Weekly*. Oh! Wait! Right! That's me. I'm now one of those fliers who have young children and need extra time. "This is kind of nice," I think, "not having to line up as I walk to the gate." I push the stroller to the doors, hold the car seat, which weighs, like, a thousand pounds, in one arm, and the diaper bag, which weighs, like, two thousand pounds, and my purse in the other arm. I can barely squeeze through the aisle. I somehow make it to my seat. I'm sweating. I think I may have pulled a muscle in my shoulder. I've definitely bruised my legs.

The baby wakes up—crap!—and I give her a bottle, while the other passengers board. I can see them looking at us as they walk down the aisle. I know what they're thinking: "Please, don't let me have the seat next to that baby!" I was once one of *those* people. I used to think the same way when I traveled. But now these looks kind of piss me off. How dare they wonder if they have to sit beside us? My baby is fabulous. They'd be lucky to sit next to her.

Amazingly, the flight is not full, which means we have all three seats to ourselves. Okay, maybe this four-hour flight isn't going to be bad at all.

The plane takes off, and the sound of the engines immediately puts the baby to sleep again.

I go back to reading my *Us Weekly*. I still have not picked up a book since I gave birth. I used to read two novels a week. But now, well, a book just has too many words for my brain. Plus, now I'm addicted to the celebrity-and-their-babies photographs. Is Coco, Courteney Cox's baby, cuter than mine? How does Courteney manage to look so skinny? And why does Ryder, Kate Hudson's baby, who is younger than my baby, have more hair than my baby?

Two hours later

A baby is screaming somewhere, and the sound is pulling me out of a deep slumber. Whose baby is that? Why won't the mother calm it down? I blink my eyes open and remember that I'm on a plane. I look down beside me. Crap! That's my baby who's crying. I'm jolted wide awake. How long has she been crying for? I look around at the other passengers. Do they look annoyed? Not really. I pick up the baby and cuddle her. She needs a diaper change. My heart is pounding. I don't want to go in the mini-washroom to change her. Even without a baby, I've always hated plane washrooms. "Screw it," I think. She hasn't gone number two. I put her down on the empty seat and change her diaper, only for a second thinking how rude this is. But I don't really care.

We land.

I can't let my parents, who are picking us up at the airport, see the baby looking like this. Now I understand why, when I was growing up, my mother was so crazy adamant about me looking good when we'd go visit my grandparents. When the Fiancé used to pick me up at the airport, when I'd go visit him during our long-distance relationship, I always made sure I'd brushed my hair, put on deodorant, and rubbed some fresh-smelling lotion on my hands before letting him see me. Now I don't care what I look like, or if I smell of airplane. But I do care that the baby looks and smells good. I want my parents to be impressed. I want them to see that I'm a good mother and that my baby is not just alive but alive and thriving. Alive, thriving, and clean, that is.

The baby has somehow managed to get super-dirty, just by drinking formula. And she doesn't smell so, um, fresh. She smells like airplane. In the airport washroom, I change her into one of the many sleepers I packed in the carry-on and put some baby lotion on her face. Perfect. I know my parents love their grandchild unconditionally, but I know they'll love her even more unconditionally when she looks super-cute and smells super-clean.

January 8
3 P.M.

The baby is sleeping at my parents' house for two glorious nights. I have only one plan. I'm going out to get drunk with friends. I know my parents raised four kids, but I can't help but worry about leaving the baby with them. Do they know what the hell they're doing with a newborn? Do they remember what they did three decades ago when they raised my brothers and me? Sometimes it takes my parents a really long time to jot down a phone number I'm giving them. Will this affect them taking care of my baby?

My dad comes to pick her up at my apartment, which I have continued to rent, even though I moved in with the Fiancé right before I gave birth. I'll give this apartment up one day, I'm sure. But not yet.

Although the baby is only sleeping at my parents' for two nights, I've again packed enough clothes and supplies to last her at least a week.

"So, she just ate, but she'll be hungry again in a couple of hours," I tell my dad.

"Okay."

"And she likes to sleep with this animal," I say, showing him the white stuffed sheep.

"Okay. Don't worry!"

"And make sure you sterilize the bottles, and the directions to making the formula are right on the label. Read it carefully."

"Okay."

"And you have to wash her bum really well if she shits and put on a lot of Vaseline so she doesn't get a diaper rash."

"Hey! What kind of language is that?" my dad asks.

I ignore the question. My baby doesn't understand English yet, let alone foul language.

"You have to be exact when you're making the formula, or she'll get sick," I continue.

"Okay, and what's this bag here?" my father asks, pointing to a garbage bag.

"Oh, that's her laundry. And some of mine. Do you mind?"

Just because I'm a mother now doesn't mean I'm not still a kid myself. At least I'm still my parents' kid. They should be happy I still need them—not only to babysit but also to do my laundry.

3:10 P.M.
They're gone. Yippee! Freedom!

3:11 P.M.
Wow. It sure is quiet in my apartment without the baby. What should I do first? Should I take a nap? Should I take a long, hot shower? Should I go get some food and watch some television while eating, a meal I know won't get interrupted with a screaming baby? God, I could do anything now that the baby is gone. The world is my oyster. This is what freedom feels like.

3:12 P.M.
Okay, I'm bored.

3:13 P.M.
Maybe I'll just look at some photographs of the baby. Even though I brought the real thing—the baby—I still packed three rolls of photographs of her.

3:20 P.M.
I've looked at the three rolls of pictures that I've brought of the baby. Twice. I'm bored. It's just too quiet here. I miss my baby. It's so quiet. I have so much time to kill before going out. I'm not used to spare time. I have no idea what to do. I miss my baby.

3:30 P.M.

I call my mother. "Is she there yet?" I ask.

"Not yet. They should be arriving any minute."

"Okay, well, I guess I'll call back later."

"Don't worry. Just go out and have some fun. Take a nap."

"I will, but I miss her."

"You'll see her in two days, and she'll be fine."

I hang up. I don't feel so fine.

8 P.M.

What is wrong with me? I've wanted to go out and party with my friends for months now. I had one plan for tonight—to drink! And now the time is here and I just want to stay in. Even though I had a short nap, I'm exhausted and I could really use more sleep. Still, I force myself to shower and get dressed, and for the first time since I gave birth, I actually try to look good. I straighten my hair and everything. I wear black, because black is slimming and I know my friends will be checking to see what my body looks like. No matter what anyone says, people are always checking out your body, especially after you have a baby.

9:15 P.M.

After calling my mother three more times to make sure the baby is still alive, I meet my single friends—Lena, Heather, and Stacy—at a bar. Sitting down, I go to pull out some lip gloss. Instead, I pull out a pacifier and it makes me miss my baby even more. Why am I here?

I tried to ask my friends if we could meet earlier, but they laughed. How is it possible that at one time I didn't even leave the house to go out until 11 P.M., and now when friends ask me to meet at 9 P.M. I think that's, like, unheard of? Who the hell can stay up and go out at 9 P.M.?

11:30 P.M.

I'm back at home. I am not drunk. Something happened to me after I drank one glass of wine. I realized I didn't really want to get drunk. Well, that's not entirely true. I did want to get drunk, but I couldn't fathom being hungover tomorrow. I may miss drinking, but I don't miss hangovers. What has happened to me? I also didn't bring any photographs of the baby with me. Not that I didn't have a hundred of them in my house, but I thought that my single, nonmother friends would be bored if I handed out photos of my child. It's such a stereotype of new mothers to show off photos. And I didn't want to be one of those mothers who only talks about her baby and passes out photographs to people who pretend to be interested but aren't really, like when people hand out photos of their vacations.

Of course, everyone wanted to see a picture of the baby. You just can't win being a mother who's trying to be cool. But I now think that the only thing worse than bringing pictures of your baby is not bringing pictures of your baby. I make a mental note to always keep at least one photograph of the baby in my bag.

It was fun to be with my friends but weird being at a bar. There really are a lot of single people in the world. I was happy that I wasn't one of them, wanting to meet a man, to get into a potential relationship. It seems like a lot of work. But it also made me sad that I was too tired to continue on with them to another bar.

I know they were thinking that I've changed. I have. It bothers me too that I was too tired to continue the night out. But it bothers me more to know that they're thinking that I've changed. If that makes sense.

January 9
5 P.M.

I've only called my mother seventeen times in the past twenty-four hours. Apparently, the baby is a "joy" and "having the time of her life."

I call Heather. We have plans to meet for drinks later.

"So what time are we meeting?" she asks.

"Actually, that's why I'm calling," I say.

"You're not bailing, are you?" Heather asks.

"I have to. The baby has a fever! I can't leave her."

"I'm sorry. Is she okay?"

"I hope so," I say, sounding worried.

"Well, okay. I guess I'll speak to you later." Heather only sounded slightly pissed. But what could I do? The baby had a fever!

Okay, there is no fever. The baby is just fine and not even with me. She's still at my parents' house. It's just that I want to see the finale of this reality television show I've been glued to for weeks. And I am so tired. Again, I wonder what has happened to me. When did being by myself become more fun than going out to a bar with my friends?

January 10
1 P.M.

The baby should be back by now. My parents said they'd be dropping her off at one.

1:01 P.M.

Okay, where's my baby?

1:04 P.M.

They said they'd drop her off at 1 P.M.! They are four minutes late! Where the hell are they? I miss my baby. I can't wait to see her. I'm practically salivating at the thought of seeing the baby, who I haven't seen in two days. It seems like two months since I last saw her.

1:10 P.M.

Where the fuck are they?

1:14 P.M.

They're here! They're here! My baby is here! I immediately pick up the baby, who is just waking up after falling asleep on the car ride.

"I missed you!" I say, kissing her all over her face, like, a thousand times. "I missed you. I missed you. I missed you! I'm never going to leave you again!"

1:35 P.M.

My parents are gone. What the hell am I supposed to do with the baby all afternoon? I miss Nanny Mimi. But at least my parents did my laundry. Maybe I should have asked them to bring her back later in the day.

1:40 P.M.

I know, shopping! My shopping habits have changed drastically since I had the baby. Because I haven't lost all the baby weight, I refuse to buy anything for myself. I've decided that when I get back down to my normal weight, I'm going to buy myself a whole new wardrobe. So now, instead of shopping for myself, I shop until I drop—for the baby. It's funny, but I get the same high shopping for her that I do when I shop for me.

At Baby Gap, a saleswoman wants to help me. "Oh, he's so cute!" she coos.

"Well, he's a she," I tell her. I'm a little offended. Why couldn't she tell my baby was a girl? She's dressed head to toe in friggin' pink!

"Oh, I'm so sorry. My sister had a baby, and she didn't get hair until she was three years old."

Three years old? No way. My baby was getting hair sooner than that!

January 11
9 A.M.

The baby wakes up and I realize I'm nearly out of formula. I have to go out and buy some. Luckily, there's a grocery store within walking distance. I put her in her stroller. She wails. I get her a bottle. She calms down. I put a blanket on her. She wails. I get her pacifier and stick it into her mouth. I put a hat on her head. She wails. I grab a doll and put it in her arms. She calms down. I race into my room and grab a coat and put it on over my pajamas. I give her a toy. She wails. She's finished her formula, and I make her another bottle with the remaining few ounces. Finally, I get out the door. Preparation time to leave house to go buy formula: twenty-eight minutes. Time to get to the store and back: fifteen minutes.

11 A.M.

I'm going to meet Sara and her baby for lunch at their house. Maybe this is what everyone calls a playdate? Of course, my baby doesn't really move, and neither does Sara's baby, so . . . well, I just know there isn't going to be much playing going on.

A lady stops me in my lobby on our way out.

"What a cute little boy you have. How old is he?"

"Actually," I say, "she's a she. And she's fourteen weeks old."

"Oh, sorry!"

Again, my baby is dressed head to toe in pink. She has a pink blanket on her, and pink booties. Do people actually think that I would dress a baby boy in head-to-toe pink?

Much to my dismay, my baby is bald, bald, bald. Even I can't help but admit she kind of does look like a boy. Which is why I always dress her in head-to-toe pink!

4 P.M.

I need to take a shower, which is something I hadn't thought of before. Not the taking-a-shower part, but how exactly I am supposed to take a shower when I'm alone with the baby. I have just gotten used to showering when Nanny Mimi is around. The baby is sound asleep in her crib, and I don't want to wake her. What if she wakes up while I'm in the middle of shampooing my hair? Then again, what if she doesn't? I'm going to take a shower. I need to take a shower because tonight Vivian is hosting the baby party. I figure the odds of the baby not waking up—50 percent—are pretty good. I make sure all the doors and windows are locked, in case some crazy freak tries to kidnap the baby while I'm showering. I check on her one more time.

I jump into the shower before the water even has a chance to get hot. I soap my body in about fifteen seconds. Just as I put the shampoo into my hair, I swear I hear the baby wailing. I stick my head out of the shower curtain. Silence. Great, now I'm hearing baby screams even when she's sound asleep. I put conditioner in my hair before I even rinse out all the shampoo. Total shower time: four minutes, twelve seconds. I can't even enjoy a shower anymore for fear that she'll wake up and I won't get to her within thirty seconds. The Fiancé is right. The baby is a dictator.

6 P.M.

My friend Lena has stopped by to visit the baby before we head over to Vivian's, where a dozen or so of our friends are gathering for our baby party. Is it awful of me to wonder whose baby will be cuter, Vivian's or mine? It is, I know. I force myself to stop thinking that.

"I've brought her a gift," Lena says, handing over a six-pack of chocolate pudding when she walks into my apartment.

"Um, thanks," I say. "But you do know the only thing she eats is formula? Babies don't eat solids until they are, like, six months, and even then I'm not sure if they eat chocolate pudding."

"Oh." Of course Lena wouldn't know this. She is not a mother.

"No, it's okay. I'll eat them. Don't worry. I love pudding," I tell her.

I ask Lena which shirt makes me look less fat. She picks out the green one.

Lena won't admit that I'm chunky. She's nice that way. Sometimes friends shouldn't tell you the truth, even when you try to force them to.

Vivian's party is super-fun. My baby is passed around like a joint, everyone taking turns holding her. I feel proud. While some of my friends are holding my baby, I head outside for a cigarette. I don't really smoke anymore, but a few friends are going out for a butt and I want to be with them and I really think I missed smoking. I smoke quickly and get dizzy, since I'm no longer used to it. Great. Just another thing that's changed. I'm no longer a smoker. Okay, this is a good thing.

I head back inside and hear my baby crying. I feel awful. I went out for a cigarette, and now my baby is crying. And I reek of smoke. What kind of mother am I?

Still, the party has proved, at least to me, that you can still have fun with your friends at a perfectly reasonable hour, you know, before nine o'clock at night. The only bad thing is that Vivian, who had her baby only weeks before me, is already back into her pre-pregnancy jeans. In fact, she looks skinnier that she did before she even got pregnant. And that makes me feel bad. And what I mean by feeling bad is feeling fat.

January 12
2 P.M.

Ronnie has left her kids with her nanny and stops by my place to see my baby. We decide to go out for a walk.

"Is she crossed-eyed?" she asks me, holding the baby.

"What?"

"She looks a bit crossed-eyed. I have the name of a really good doctor if you want to check it out."

I hadn't noticed that my baby was cross-eyed. But Ronnie has always been super-paranoid about everything. If she gets a cold, she thinks she has the West Nile virus. But, still, now I'm worried that not only does my baby girl look like a boy but that she has crossed eyes!

I tell Ronnie that I'm on antidepressants. I tell her about my crying fits and everything. She tells me the motherhood thing gets easier. "I promise it gets easier. I've been there. I know. It does get easier," she says.

I can't help but wonder if she's telling the truth, like all those people who kept telling me how rewarding a baby would be. Were they telling the truth? Or is every parent a liar?

January 13

1 P.M.

We're on the plane home and the ride is uneventful, which is great. I've started to realize that uneventful is a good thing. I think I remember being single, going to parties, and if nothing ever happened, I'd be disappointed. Uneventful used to be bad.

"What a cute little boy," says the flight attendant when we take our seats.

"Actually, she's a girl." I say. Again, head to toe in pink, and people still think she's a boy. What is wrong with the world?

While I'm waiting for the luggage another elderly lady tells me what a cute son I have. The Fiancé, who has met us by the baggage claim, rolls his eyes. I've been telling him every time someone tells me what a cute son I have, which is about three times a day now.

"Thank you," I say to the woman. "He is cute, isn't he?" I'm sick of telling people SHE'S A GIRL!

I don't know. Maybe I should just be happy that people think she's cute, period. Even if people think she's a he.

January 15

7 A.M.

It's the baby's three-month birthday. She sleeps through the night, which the Fiancé and I don't realize until we wake up. I know something feels different when I wake up actually feeling refreshed. "I can't believe it!" I say. "She slept through the night! She slept through the night!" I start jumping up and down on our bed.

"Halle-fucking-lujah!" he says, and we kiss.

I can't believe that at exactly the three-month mark, to the day, the baby slept through the night. In fact, she slept twelve hours straight. She had fallen asleep at 7 P.M.

"We made it! We made it!" I cry. "We made it to the three-month mark. This is when it all starts getting easier."

January 18

The baby slept three nights in a row, all the way through, for at least ten hours. She's no dictator. She's a joy.

And then she doesn't sleep through the night.

At midnight, just as I've dozed off, I hear her wailing. What the fuck? I thought we were done with all that.

"We have to do the tough-love thing now," the Fiancé says.

"No."

"Yes."

"No."

"Yes. It's been three months, and we have to show her that she can't always be the Dictator around here, and that we're not going to run in and see her every time she screams for us. She has to learn to sleep through the night."

I knew this was coming. The Fiancé has been saying for weeks now that it would soon be time to start training her, if she didn't learn to sleep through the night on her own.

She wails and wails. Every muscle in my body gets tense listening to her screams. After twenty minutes, I sit up in bed.

"I can't deal with this. I can't!" I say to the Fiancé.

"You have to be strong. Don't go in there," he warns.

Ten minutes later, she's still screaming. I start to cry.

"Don't cry. It's hard, but we have to do this, or she'll never learn," the Fiancé says. When did the Fiancé become such a hard-ass? I'm not sure if I'm crying because I'm worried that my baby is in pain, and that I'm traumatizing her for life by letting her scream, or because I am going mental listening to the noises. My tears are half tears of guilt and half tears of frustration. Why was she so good for only three nights? Why is she being bad again?

"I'm going to get her," I say.

"Don't get her."

"I'm going to get her," I say, jumping out of bed. "I can't deal with this."

As soon as I pick her up, she stops crying. "We'll try again tomorrow," I whisper in her ear. I get back to bed at around 3 A.M. I'm mad at the Fiancé because he was able to do the tough-love thing. Is his heart made of stone? Am I living with the Tin Man?

January 19

2 P.M.

I call the Fiancé.

"How are you?"

"I feel like shit."

"Me too. So, when are you coming home?"

It's like we're back at week three again. The baby is not sleeping through the night. The Fiancé is feeling like shit, and so am I. When will this ever end?

6 P.M.

We're at the in-laws' for dinner. The baby is extremely fussy. The mother-in-law picks her up. She won't stop crying. The father-in-law tries to quiet her, to no avail. Even the Fiancé can't calm her down. But as soon as I pick her up, she stops. She must know it's me! I know I'm probably not supposed to gloat over this, but I can't help it. My baby loves me best! And now they all know it too! Of course she loves me best. I'm her mother.

I just hope they all remember this little fact.

January 21
10 A.M.

"Oh, my baby sleeps through the entire night and then naps for hours in the afternoon," Sara says.

I have just complained to her over the phone about my Devil Child, the Dictator. How is it possible that her baby sleeps so well? Her baby is younger than mine! It isn't fair.

"You're so lucky," I moan.

"And she had her first haircut!"

"What? You're joking, right?"

"No, her hair was getting so long it was going in her eyes."

"Well, at least five times a day people tell me what a cute little son I have," I tell Sara. "So I went to Wal-Mart and bought her those headbands."

"You did not!"

"I did!"

"Those things are so hideous."

"I know! But she looks like a boy if I don't put one on her!"

I don't add that Sara's the one who changed her voice-mail message to include a two-week-old baby. What's worse? A mother who puts a stupid headband on her bald baby girl or a mother who puts her two-week-old baby's name on their voice-mail message?

I get off the phone slightly grumpy. I kind of feel Sara was bragging about her baby. It bothers me. We aren't supposed to be the type of mothers who brag about their babies. No, those women are annoying. Then again, these days most things bother me.

January 24
The Fiancé is grumpy because we are at the mall.

We need more onesies and more sleepers. And going to the mall is something to do on a Saturday. We take in all the other parents, pushing their strollers around aimlessly at 10 A.M. I act like I'm okay with this, but I'm not really. I don't really want to be here either. The Fiancé doesn't even pretend to be enjoying himself.

Before the baby arrived, this was our worst nightmare—that we'd become parents who were, well, not cool. It's definitely not rock-and-roll to be buying baby sleepers at 10 A.M. at a mall. I try to get the Fiancé's mind off the fact that he's now a father and is one of those early risers who go to the mall.

"Look at those girls. How old do you think they are?" I say, pointing out a group of preteens standing around a bench. They are showing way too much skin. They are wearing way too much makeup. They look like mini-prostitutes. Prostitots is what they are.

"They look around thirteen," the Fiancé says. I agree with his assessment.

What if one day my perfect little baby pierces her lip and dresses like a hooker? Will I be okay with that? I will not allow that to happen. One day, I start to think, my baby will be hanging around the mall, showing too much skin, with a pierced nose and her hair dyed blue. One day she'll hate me. Oh God, one day she'll be having sex!

It's the first time it hits me that I'm not just raising a baby and that one day I'll be raising a teenager. Now, that's a scary thought.

January 26

I'm starting to realize I'm acting way older than my thirty-one years.

"God, I'm starving," I say, sitting down at the table. The Fiancé and I have met for dinner. The baby has changed drastically in a matter of weeks. No longer does she sleep through entire meals. She can sit in a high chair. Mostly, though, she prefers to sit on my lap, which makes eating out less than relaxing. It is good, however, for my weight-loss goal. (Don't ask. Don't even ask!) I can never finish an entire meal, even if I want to, with the baby sitting on me.

"It's empty in here tonight. Is there some sort of event going on in the city? Where is everyone?" I ask the Fiancé. Usually, this restaurant is packed.

"Beck?"

"What?"

"It's five P.M."

"Really? It's only five?"

We're now eating dinner like senior citizens. "I am not pathetic," I think. "We are not pathetic."

"We're so pathetic," says the Fiancé.

"Hey, I was just thinking that!"

We eat dinner and are home by six-fifteen. This is the wonderful life of being parents.

Though it's been only three months, I can't remember what not having the baby in my life was like. And yet, at the same time, I still don't feel like a mother. I still feel like me. The baby is still not sleeping through the night, and I'm still fighting depression. But the pills are working. I think. I don't cry as much.

At least three times a day I'm still told by strangers what a cute little son I have, the in-laws are still driving me mental, and the Fiancé and I have had sex maybe three times. I have to make a doctor's appointment to get the baby's shots and also to see if she's cross-eyed. My ass, though I have been watching what I eat, is still the size of a movie screen. This whole mothering thing is depressing.

Forget about those statistics and experts who say that the first year of marriage is the hardest. I'm amazed that any couple can make it through the first year after having a baby. And it's only been three months!

Ten Mommy Moments People "Forget" to Mention

1. You will lose your hair.
2. You will still think you're fat.
3. You will accidentally hurt your baby . . . at least once.
4. The "constructive criticism" will not stop.
5. You will start falling asleep earlier than you used to leave to go out at night.
6. You will wonder what happened to some of your "best friends."
7. Boring becomes a good thing.
8. Babies have no manners.
9. You don't want your baby to watch television. Still, you will rerun a baby DVD for two hours.
10. You will look around your home and wonder when it turned into a daycare.

The Fifth Trimester (3 to 6 Months)

I've Lost My Mind.
Now I'm Losing My Hair!

January 30

I'm supposed to be in paradise. But I can't stop feeling I'm also in my own personal hell.

The Fiancé, the baby, and I are now in Maui. Sure, there are palm trees everywhere, soft sand on the beach, the clear blue ocean, the fabulous sun and glorious heat. But the worst thing I've ever been through is happening to me. (Except for that time one of my ex-boyfriends dumped me after he cheated on me, which was, I'll admit, pretty awful.) But what's happening to me now, in paradise, is worse. Much worse.

I'm going bald. That's right. I'm going bald.

This morning, while I was taking a shower, I looked down to discover hunks of hair in the drain. The drain had been completely hair-free when I hopped in. (I always check for hair and spiders before jumping into all showers. I also always check to make sure there are no masked men wielding knives behind the shower curtain.) Then, after my shower, while I was brushing my hair, a bunch of long strands came out into my hands. My shoulder-length hairs, which I have been growing long for years after the bob-cut debacle of 1990, were all over the place. There were hairs sticking to my fingers, in the sink, wrapped in my hairbrush, on the floor, and stuck to my face. Some hairs were even in my mouth. Strands of hair were everywhere, like it had just rained hair.

"Something is wrong with me! Something is wrong with me!" I yell to the Fiancé, racing out of the washroom with only a towel wrapped around me. "Something is really very wrong with me. I think I'm dying. I'm dying!"

"What's wrong?" the Fiancé asks, using a tone that actually implicitly says, "What are you going on about now?"

"I'm going bald!" I tell him.

"You are not going bald," he says, and sighs.

"Yes. I am. I am going bald. Look!" I say, running my hand over my scalp and then placing into his hands the hairs that had fallen out.

"Um, that's, um, very interesting," he says. "Can you please take your hair back? It's gross."

"What do you want me to do? Glue it back on? What is happening to me?"

"Just throw it in the trash," he says. "Maybe you're just shedding because it's so hot here?"

"I'm not a fucking dog!" I yell. Why doesn't the Fiancé seem to care that I could be dying here? What other possible reason could there be for all this hair falling out?

I sob while the Fiancé goes back to reading his GQ magazine.

January 31

Okay, I feel a little better after spending an hour on the Internet researching "hair loss." From my research I learned that this hair-loss-ruining-my-life concern is a perfectly normal hormonal development that many women go through after giving birth. Why? I don't know.

What if I have to get a wig? What if I get bald patches? What if my hair never grows back? I wonder how much hair weighs though. Maybe I'll weigh less with less hair. I'm pretty sure, though, that hair doesn't weigh much. Sigh.

Who else can I complain to about the possibility that I'm going bald but the Fiancé, the one person in the world who is supposed to be supportive in all aspects of my life, at all times, especially when I'm super-hormonal and have been diagnosed, by a professional, with depression. Even my friggin' hair, apparently, is hormonal. "Does my hair look thinner?" I ask the Fiancé, for the fourth time today. It's only 10 A.M.

"No," answers the Fiancé, for the fourth time today.

"Seriously. Take a look. Does it look thinner?"

"No," he says, not looking at me.

"You didn't even look! I'm thirty-one and going bald," I moan.

"You are not going bald."

"Then how come when I brush my hair it falls out in hunks?"

"I don't know, Beck. I thought you said it was normal."

"Fine."

"Don't fine me," he says.

"Fine," I say. "But don't expect me to be supportive when your hair starts falling out."

I've decided not to brush my hair until this hormonal hair-loss thing is over. To lose sleep because of this baby is one thing, so is gaining weight because of this baby. But to lose my hair because of this baby? It's unacceptable. How long will my hair fall out for? What if it never stops falling out? I do feel for the Fiancé, who will now have to listen to me ask, "Do I look thinner?" as well as, "Does my hair look thinner?" every other hour.

Okay, make that every ten minutes. But at least he has hair. Well, he does now. I'll wait ten years and see how he reacts when he starts losing his hair. Then he'll regret not being more sympathetic to what I'm going through now.

February 1

A lot of my single fabulous friends (that is, childless friends who still go out and have one-night stands and drink to get drunk and whose only responsibility is making sure they get their rent paid on time) think I'm very lucky to be here in Maui and are quite envious. They think, "Hey, she's had a baby *and* she gets to go to Maui for two months. She has the best life ever." And it is true. Aside from losing my hair, not having had a solid night's sleep for months, still being more than twenty pounds overweight, and suffering from postpartum depression, I am lucky.

These days, maternity leave in my country, Canada, where it's the law that you can take a year off from your work, is no longer just about having time to bond with your baby.

The Fiancé and I are not super-wealthy. Trust me. The condo we rented here for two glorious months could very well make us bankrupt. But I've always wanted to spend more than two weeks in Maui. This will be the only time I can do this, I argued, when we were debating the pros and cons of renting a condo in Maui while I'm on maternity leave. I'll never again be able to just take off from work for two months to travel—bosses frown upon that sort of thing like they do about employees napping under desks at the office—and I won't be able to take two months off to go anywhere when my daughter is in school, will I? Maternity leave might be the last time in my life—until retirement—that I'll be able to go anywhere for a long period.

So, for the first time in a decade, I have no work responsibilities. I'm on maternity leave! I can just as easily bond with my baby in warm weather, in beautiful surroundings, in a fantastic rented condo overlooking the glorious ocean, can't I? Also, the Baby is not running around yet, or even standing or crawling, so she's at the easiest stage in her life to travel with. She basically slept the entire plane ride here. I thank God for that miracle.

Also, thanks to my depression—the only positive thing about being depressed—the Fiancé thinks getting away will be good for my emotional state. There's nothing like seeing the sunshine when you wake up every morning to put you in a better mood. At least for me.

Before we arrived, we rented a crib, a portable playpen, and a swing from a company in Maui that actually rents cribs, portable playpens, and swings. They delivered them to our condo and set them all up before we arrived. Who knew there were companies out there that did that kind of thing?

The Fiancé is only staying ten days with us (ha ha—he has to go back to work!). Then my parents will be coming for one week. Then Nanny Mimi will stay for one week to help out, and then I'll be alone, for a month, with the Dictator, otherwise known as my baby, before the Fiancé comes back to Maui to pick us up.

I know how lucky I am to be able to spend two months in paradise. It's just that I can't stop thinking about going bald! Trust me, if suddenly hunks of your hair started falling out by the handful, you'd be obsessed about it too.

I remember once making the mistake of telling the Fiancé his hair looked like it was getting thinner on top. He didn't speak to me for two days. Losing hair, for everyone, is a big, big deal.

February 2

The truth is, while my friends are envious of my two months in Maui, I have told almost none of them about the depression I'm experiencing. I now understand why so few people admit to postpartum depression; I admire Brooke Shields for laying it all out in her memoir. I could barely admit it to myself.

Postpartum depression makes you feel like a failure and that something's wrong with you because you can't control your emotions, no matter how hard you try. Everyone expects that because you've had a baby, and because having a baby is such a miracle and "so rewarding," you should be overflowing with joy, feel blessed. And you're supposed to be concentrating on the baby, not yourself.

Once you have a baby, you're supposed to stop being selfish, right? All that should matter is the baby's health and happiness. Postpartum depression is very difficult to explain. You're sad, but you can't explain why. You just are. You cry for hours, and it's hard to just get out of bed some days—yet you aren't sure why you're crying or why getting out of bed seems like climbing Mount Everest in heels. How can you possibly tell your friends and family that you're so miserable after having a baby, supposedly the best thing that's ever happened to you, when everyone is so friggin' happy for you and expects you to be happy too?

Nanny Mimi mentioned to me that one of her friends recently had a baby and was miserable. Her friend would go to the mall every day and cry in the food court. One day she was crying so hard, her husband had to leave work to pick her up from the mall. So I know there are other women out there going through this. But that doesn't make me feel better.

Then there's the Fiancé, who, even when I tell him that I

can't explain why I'm so sad or why I'm crying or why I just want to lie by myself in bed for hours, makes me feel worse because he blames himself and thinks he's the one making me miserable. I don't think I could handle making anyone else sad at this point. I'm already exhausted from feeling guilty about making the Fi-ancé sad about my being sad. So I haven't told anyone really. I just keep taking my happy pill.

Screw Tom Cruise, who criticized women for taking antide-pressants for postpartum depression. He has no idea what it feels like. He's a man and will never know what it's like to have a baby. Just like I'll never know what it's like to have a penis. His views make me never want to see a Tom Cruise movie again. Ex-cept he is a good actor. And I do like his movies.

2:45 A.M.

I can't sleep. I keep replaying in my head what I did to the baby on the airplane ride to Maui. Of course, I wake the Fiancé up to talk about my feelings. It was the first time I hurt my baby.

It was entirely my fault. I had been lifting her up and down over my head and she was enjoying looking at all the passengers behind us, kind of like a game of peekaboo. Once we were in the air, the movie screens came down. But I hadn't noticed the screens had come down, and I continued lifting the baby up and down. It was just my luck that one of those miniscreens came down right over our heads. I lifted the baby up, and BANG! Her head hit the movie screen. It wasn't a gentle bang either. It was a hard bang.

Of course, the baby did what any baby would do while play-ing peekaboo and then having her head bonked on a mini movie screen. She started to scream bloody murder. I cuddled her and kissed her, saying, "I'm sorry. I'm sorry! I didn't mean it!" I felt terrible. I felt more than terrible. I felt like the worst mother in the world. Doesn't the saying go that "a baby is an accident waiting to happen"?

Here I was, her mother, the one who loves her the most in the world and is supposed to protect her from all danger, and I was the one responsible for banging her little head on a movie screen.

I was also so completely embarrassed. I mean, there were only a hundred or so passengers sitting behind us who had seen what I had done to my baby.

"Don't worry, Beck. We're in row four. There are only thirty-five other rows of people behind us who witnessed what you just did," the Fiancé said.

"Thanks. That helps a lot. That makes me feel so much better!" I said to him. The dozens and dozens of passengers in the rows behind us who had seen that I just bonked my baby's head probably all thought what a horrible, careless mother I was. They were all probably thinking that I was not mother material. At the very least, they were probably thinking that I was an idiot.

"Remember what I did to her back at home?" the Fiancé asks sleepily, as I fret to him while he's trying to go back to sleep.

"How could I forget?" I answer. "That was bad."

Two weeks ago, the Fiancé had thought it would be fun for the baby to sit on his shoulders while he walked around the condo. She could finally hold her head up well enough on her own.

I had walked around the condo with her on my shoulders, and she loved it. So I'd told the Fiancé to try it. But unfortunately the Fiancé is about six feet tall. We hadn't noticed, or rather we had completely forgotten, how low the ceilings in our condo are. It was fine for the baby to be on my shoulders, because I'm short. But when the Fiancé lifted the baby up into the air to put her onto his shoulders, her head banged the ceiling. Of course, she did what any baby would do upon having her head banged on the ceiling. She screamed bloody murder.

Even though the Fiancé looked miserable and felt awful about what he had done to our child—he even looked like he was about to cry, that's how bad he felt—I couldn't help but grab her from him immediately, shooting him an evil look that said, "How could you do that?" while trying to calm the baby down. "Oh, poor baby," I cooed. "Daddy didn't mean it."

"I just feel so bad," I moan to the Fiancé, "about bonking my own child's head! How could I be so stupid? I keep replaying it over and over again in my head. I can't stop thinking about it."

"You'll get over it. It happens. You didn't mean it. Go to sleep, please. She's sleeping soundly. Let's be happy about that."

"Do you think she's sleeping so soundly because she has a concussion from what I did to her?" I ask. "Is that possible?"

"Are you crazy? You're being ridiculous. Please go to sleep. Everyone hurts their babies by accident. Good night," said the Fiancé.

Maybe the Fiancé is right. Maybe all parents hurt their babies by accident at least once. I remember my friend Jenna once telling me about the time she was pulling her nephew in a wagon. She kept walking and walking before she realized that she wasn't hearing any sound from her nephew in the wagon she was pulling. She turned around and the baby wasn't in the wagon! He had fallen out and was lying in the middle of the sidewalk on his back a half block away from her.

I heard another story about a mother who was holding her baby and tripped down the stairs. Actually, I've heard a few of those stories.

So maybe I wasn't the worst mother in the world. You have to learn from your mistakes, right? The Fiancé has learned to look for low ceilings when he puts the Dictator on his shoulders. Jenna learned that if she's pulling her nephew in a wagon, she should check behind her once in a while to see if he's still there. Mothers who trip down the stairs while holding their babies, I'm pretty positive, walk down all stairs from then on very cautiously. And I have learned to always look to make sure there are no movie screens above my head when I play peekaboo with the baby on an airplane.

February 3

I wake up and immediately look at my pillow to see how many hairs have fallen out while I've been sleeping. There are at least a dozen strands on my pillow. I'm mortified. I feel like a middle-aged man. Middle-aged men do that, right? Then I immediately go check out my stomach in the mirror. The progress is slow. What can I say? I'm still flabby.

After breakfast, we decide to head down to the pool. It only takes us about an hour and a half to get out the door. We take the stroller, bathing suit for the baby, diapers, wipes, towels, formula—everything we might need, and things we're pretty sure we won't need, but you never know. You can never pack too many backup pacifiers. You can never be too prepared when you have a baby.

It will be the first time I've been in a bathing suit in public since I gave birth. I look at myself in the mirror before we leave the condo. It ain't a pretty sight. I am wearing the same bikini I wore when I was seven months pregnant when the Fiancé and I came here on our last trip as nonparents, otherwise known as our "last vacation before we would have real responsibilities."

Yes, the bikini still fits, and that pretty much says it all.

God, those were the days, when we could just lie out, reading books, and napping whenever we wanted. That's not going to happen today, or ever again, or at least not until the baby turns sixteen. We don't even bring books down to the pool. We're always so tired that our attention span is, like, zero. Our brains have turned to mush. Books with words in them are no good. Magazines with large pictures of celebrities in gowns on red carpets? We can deal with those. Being a parent, I sometimes think, makes you stupid. It's like the baby has sucked out all your intelligence. Plus, we actually now have to pay attention to the baby.

We set up by the pool, basically taking over four lounge chairs thanks to all our supplies. It looks like we've brought luggage for a round-the-world trip. Under an umbrella, I undress down to my bikini. I can't stand my body. I hate how my stomach skin sags. I hate how my thighs rub together when I walk. I hate that even my face still feels bloated. Of course, I hate my ass. I'm convinced other people hanging by the pool are looking at me and thinking, "What the hell is she doing in a bikini? Doesn't she know better?" in the same way I look at women I see in tight dresses or belly-baring shirts who really should not be wearing tight dresses or belly-baring shirts. You know the type.

I put my tank top back on over my bathing suit and only take it off when I go into the pool.

"Am I—" I say to the Fiancé.

"Don't even ask," the Fiancé says. "You're not!"

"Well, am I fat? Do I look fat?"

"You just had a baby!"

"I know, but it's been three months! Victoria Beckham lost all her weight in about four days. So did Heidi Klum. And Vivian lost all hers in a week."

"You ate a Big Mac every day for months and months. I'm pretty sure Posh Spice didn't do that. What did you expect? I really can't talk about this anymore, okay?"

"So what you're saying is that I'm fat?"

The Fiancé doesn't answer and instead picks up an *Us Weekly*. Of course, he would prefer to stare at skinny celebrities than at me!

"I'm fat and I'm going bald and no one loves me," I say.

"I'm going to pretend I didn't hear you, okay?" the Fiancé says while giving the baby a bottle.

I jump into the pool. That's the good thing about pools. You always feel light in water. In the pool, I actually feel skinny again. Even fat people float in water.

February 5

The good news is that I'm starting to "get" the baby. It's like finally understanding a really difficult math problem. Suddenly, after you've been staring and staring at an equation, it makes sense. What I mean is that I'm starting to recognize the baby's cries. And, somehow, I now can hear the difference. She has one cry when she has a shitty diaper (a vicious cry). Another type of cry when she's hungry (a cranky cry). And another cry when she's just being bitchy (an annoying, whiny cry). The Fiancé cannot decipher her cries, and he looks at me with inquiring eyes when she wails, and I'm like, "That's her tired cry. She needs a nap now." I can't help but feel proud of myself that I finally understand this baby. I can't help but gloat inside that I get her, and the Fiancé doesn't. Maybe men don't have an ear for baby cries. Which is amazing. Because when a car drives by the Fiancé can tell without even seeing it what kind of car it is and what year it was made, all by the sound of the engine.

More good news. The baby is not eating and sleeping nonstop anymore either. I don't know, maybe it's true what people say. Maybe it does get easier after a couple of months.

Sometimes I look at my baby and think it's not possible to love someone this much. Maybe this whole having-a-baby-thing *is* rewarding, just like people had told me it would be.

My hair, however, is still falling out. The Fiancé has started to recognize my cries, if not the baby's. Or at least he's getting there.

"Are you crying now because you're worried you're going bald, or because you think you're fat?" he'll ask when he hears my sobs. "Wait! That's the 'I'm so fat still' cry. Am I right? Am I right?"

Usually I'm crying about both.

February 7

"This is so NOT rewarding! I need help in here! I need help!" I scream to the Fiancé.

I'm in the washroom preparing the baby for her nightly bath. While the water filled the bathtub, I took off her clothes and was holding her in one arm, and feeling the temperature of the water with my other arm when I felt something warm and wet on my side. Yep. The baby had peed all over me. I'd been peed on!

"It's so rewarding, isn't it?" the Fiancé asks as I hand him the baby and strip off my urine-soaked clothes, trying not to cry. The Fiancé is trying not to laugh.

Why can't anything be easy? I know it's not the baby's fault that she has no bladder control. I don't want to scare her with yelling, "She peed on me! She peed on me!" It's just slightly disgusting to be peed on. And who knew such a little bladder could store so much urine?

"God, this is so gross," I say. I know some women (and men) like to be peed on for sport, you know, as a sex thing. But I am not one of those women. Not even if it's my own child peeing on me do I enjoy being peed on. I do not deal well with bodily fluids on me, especially bodily fluids that are not my own.

I need to shower for the second time today. I can't walk around smelling like pee for the rest of the night. But all I can think about is that all this showering cannot be good for my falling-out hair. Risk more hair falling out by taking another shower? Or smell like urine for the rest of the night? My two options are kind of like voting for a political candidate. Usually, you have to choose the lesser of two evils. I choose to shower.

7 P.M.

After dinner, when I'm freshly showered and the baby is freshly bathed, we are lounging around the condo. I'm in the kitchen when the Fiancé calls out. "Um, Beck?"

"What?"

"Did you leave the baby on her front?"

"No. Why?"

"Because she's on her front."

"She's what?" I say, racing into the living room, where the baby is lying on one of those colorful mats, with toys hanging down from cushy bars for her to play with. "Whoa," I say when I see her. As the Fiancé said, she's lying on her stomach. She can roll over now. My child can roll over! And I missed it!

Pretty soon, she'll be crawling. God, everything is happening so fast.

Next thing I know, she'll be asking to get a nose ring, and to borrow fifty dollars, and my car.

February 9

I'm obsessed with a woman named Julie Aigner-Clark. This is a woman I had never heard of pre-baby. She is the founder of the

Baby Einstein DVD line. The DVDs feature classical music and pictures of toys. All mothers these days are well aware of the Baby Einstein line of DVDs. Mothers put in these DVDs for twenty minutes so they can prepare dinner or clean up around the house while keeping their baby occupied.

Like most mothers, I don't really want my baby to watch more than twenty minutes of television a day. Yeah, right! I'm just joking.

When we're in our condo, I play DVDs for the baby almost nonstop. Is this wrong?

My one problem with these Baby Einstein DVDs is that they only last, like, thirty minutes, which means I keep having to restart them. At the end of each one, there's Julie Aigner-Clark, introducing herself and her Baby Einstein collection.

Julie Aigner-Clark is a very pretty woman.

I hate her.

But not because she's blond and pretty and has a very soothing voice. I hate her because she has come up with such a basic, brilliant idea, a product that babies and mothers love and that has made millions of dollars. I mean, really, I could have come up with the idea to film toys with classical music. I hate it when people come up with great, multimillion-dollar ideas before I do. Especially when the idea is so friggin' simple. Of course, the fact that Julie Aigner-Clark is blond, skinny, and very pretty doesn't help.

February 10

Our days in Maui are fairly boring, which is nice. When you have a baby, uneventful is a good thing, and so is boring. We get up, we lounge around, we take the baby for long walks, and hang out by the pool. One unfortunate aspect of our days is that although I know it's bad, I like to suntan—who doesn't look healthier with a bit of color?—but with the baby, who I definitely don't want to get skin cancer and whose newborn skin would burn easily, we can't stay in the sun for too long. I had no idea that you can't put suntan lotion on babies younger than six months. I'm really hoping some genius out there comes up with a suntan lotion for newborns. Maybe Julie Aigner-Clark could create one. She's obviously an idea person. Meanwhile, the Fiancé and I have to take turns. Mostly, we try to be in the shade, which isn't so easy, considering we're in a sunny destination.

I also learn that the baby hates hats. I force her to wear them, because everyone knows that babies should wear hats if they're in the sun. And if your kid isn't wearing a hat in the sun, trust me, other mothers look at you, and judge you, and think you don't care about the well-being of your baby. I know this because when I see babies who aren't wearing hats in the sun, I judge those mothers, like I can't help but judge people in yoga who have dirty toenails. But keeping a hat on a baby is a very tricky process, mostly because my baby doesn't like wearing hats. In fact, she hates wearing hats. I put her hat on. She takes it off. I put it on again. She cries and takes it off. I put it on again. She takes it off. We go back and forth like this about a million times a day until finally she realizes this is one battle she's not going to win. I'm bigger and stronger than her, after all.

Along with an adult pool, there's also a baby pool at our condo. I like to call it "the Pee Pool." Because along with the water in it, I'm pretty positive there's a ton of pee as well. How many babies do you know who can control their bladders? And the water is unusually (disgustingly) warm. Exactly.

Along with learning that babies shouldn't wear suntan lotion, I've also learned what "swimmers" are. Swimmers are pull-up diapers non-toilet-trained babies wear in the water. (Another idea I could have easily come up with. Doh!) I have no idea if the swimmers are supposed to go on by themselves or over the diaper. They don't give instructions on the package. Doesn't the company know there are mothers like me who haven't got a clue about these sorts of things? I put the swimmers over the baby's diaper. I'm pretty sure swimmers were really invented to make other people in pools feel better about sharing water with non-toilet-trained kids.

I know I'm going to have to get used to going in Pee Pools now. What choice do I have? It's not like my baby can go in the pool alone. She'd drown. In any case, she has already peed on me. A little pee never killed anyone. I don't think. But the Pee Pool is not just about having pee in the pool. After I took the baby out of the pool, and got her out of her swimmers and regular diaper, which, filled with water, weighed about a hundred pounds, I saw that she had also pooed while we were in the Pee Pool. Take it from me, if you don't have kids, stay away from baby pools. Pee is the least of your worries.

February 11

On our last night here in Maui before the Fiancé returns home, we decide to take the baby out for dinner. On paper it was a good plan, and the baby was sound asleep in her car seat when we arrived at the restaurant. But, now that we've been seated, the Fiancé and I are more than slightly disturbed while overhearing a conversation at the table next to us.

I've always been an eavesdropper—I love listening in on other people's conversations. It's especially fun when you know that the couple at the table next to you are on a first date. You get to guess if the date is going well or not and if they're going to end up having sex later that night.

But, unfortunately, we are not seated next to a couple out on a first date. We are seated next to a family of four. This is the conversation we overhear, between the parents and their two kids, who looked about age four and six.

"So, let's go through the highlights and lowlights of our day," says the father, in the same serious tone I remember my teachers using when I was in high school. "I'll go first. My highlight was getting a good checkup from my doctor. My lowlight was not being able to finish the garden like I had hoped to."

"My turn, my turn!" says the four-year-old boy. "My highlight is going for dinner. My lowlight was school."

"Are you listening to this?" I ask the Fiancé quietly. He looks cranky. Which means, yes, he's been listening.

"My turn now," says the six-year-old girl. "My highlight of the day was going over to Katie's house. My lowlight was not having a long recess."

Is this what happens when you become parents? Your conversations with your children become truly and utterly boring? Is there some sort of book on the *New York Times* bestseller list that advises parents to ask their children what the "highlights" and "lowlights" of their day were?

I leave the restaurant feeling full but depressed. I wonder if Julie Aigner-Clark has such boring conversations with her children when they eat dinner. Does Reese Witherspoon talk to her kids like that? I mean, isn't there anything more interesting to talk about with your children than taking turns announcing the highlights and lowlights of your day? It just seems, so, well, so not spontaneous, so rehearsed.

After putting the baby to bed, the Fiancé and I, because he's leaving tomorrow, have good-bye sex. Afterward, when we're lying together intimately, I ask him, as a joke, "So, what was your highlight of the day?"

"This," he says, grabbing my breast.

"And your lowlight?"

"That awful conversation we had to listen to over dinner. Please, never ever ask me again what the highlight and lowlight of my day was."

"You won't have to ask me twice."

February 12

The Fiancé has left and I'm already a little lonely. I cried saying good-bye to him. The baby just doesn't have the same conversational skills as the Fiancé. She has no conversational skills.

I take the baby for a walk on a path along the beach, where I run into a woman holding a baby who looks about the same age as my daughter. "Oh, he's so cute," I say to the woman. "How old is he?" Now whenever I see another mother with a baby, I always ask how old her baby is. Now I understand what it's like to be in some sort of Mommy Club. Because we all have at least one thing in common—babies. When I'm with my baby, I can't pass another mother with a baby anymore without looking at her and her baby, or having her look at me and ask me about my baby. (Okay, I admit, I also check out whose baby is cuter. My baby always wins, hands down.)

"He's four months," the woman answers.

"I love his outfit," I say, even though it's not really anything special. It's just that there's only so much you can say to a mother you've just meet, after asking how old her child is and what its name is. I know her baby is a boy because he's wearing blue socks. When you have a bald baby girl who is always mistaken for a "little man," you learn to look for the telling signs of a baby's gender. It usually always comes down to socks. Pink socks = girl. Blue socks = boy. Always, always look at the socks.

"Oh, my husband dressed him today. I hate when my husband dresses him because he doesn't know how to match clothing," the woman moans.

"Oh," I say, though I haven't noticed that her baby doesn't match. In fact, I think he matches just fine. When did blue and beige stop matching? And why does this mother care so much that her four-month-old baby doesn't match?

I barely dressed my baby. She is wearing only a onesie, because I was too lazy to throw anything else on top. What would be the point? She's just a baby. She should be comfortable. I can only imagine what this woman is thinking about my baby's outfit, or, rather, her non-outfit.

"So, how old is your son?" the woman asks me. Now I want to hurt her. I do not like this woman.

"She's a girl," I say pointedly. I know this stranger is thinking, "Thank God my son has hair." I just know it.

At least I'm not the kind of mother who complains about how her husband dresses their baby. I never want to be that kind of mother. Or the kind of mother who asks her child what "the highlight and lowlight" of her day was. Or the kind of mother who . . . There are so many kinds of mothers I don't want to be. I just have to figure out what kind of mother I do want to be.

February 13

Heather calls on my cell phone, while the baby is napping and I'm sitting by the pool under an umbrella. I'm happy to hear from her because lately I've realized I haven't heard from very many of my single friends, who are obviously too busy trying to meet men, working, and feeling like productive members of society.

Many of my friends think it's strange that I could take the baby and be apart from the Fiancé for so long.

"So doesn't he miss the baby?" Heather asks.

"Of course!" I answer. I've grown to hate this question. I hate when people assume that I'm being a bad person because I'm not spending all my time with the Fiancé and have also taken the baby away from him. But I'm not sure if it's entirely true that he misses the baby. Yes, the Fiancé's back at work, which must suck. But he gets the condo all to himself, he can go out with friends, and he doesn't have me around asking, "When are you going to be home?" and "Does my hair look thinner?" and "Does my ass look fat?" He doesn't have to worry about getting woken up at 3:30 A.M. to give the baby a bottle. He doesn't have to change any diapers. He can go out, drink up, and have a hangover without worrying about waking up to take care of a baby. From my view, he has it pretty good being apart from us.

And the truth is, babies at four months are kind of boring, like they are at three months, and two months, and one month, and one week.

Sure, babies are cute. But they don't do much. They eat, sleep, pee, and poo. You feed them, you watch them sleep, you dress them, you bathe them, and you change their diapers. It's not like babies can play chess with you or talk about current events. It's not like babies can discuss politics or tell you they like your hair better in a bun. Of course, I don't tell people that babies are boring. No one wants to hear that babies are boring, even though they are.

Plus, I'm the one who had to carry the baby around for nine months. Don't I deserve a vacation, albeit a vacation with a baby, which is not exactly a vacation per se? And it was really boring being back at home, in the cold weather. Sometimes back home the weather was so bitterly cold that we couldn't even leave the house. (A positive of living in Canada is a long maternity leave. The negative is very long, cold winters.) It was like we were being held hostage. At least now I don't have to spend eight hours bundling her up before we can go outside. It's so much easier throwing her into a sundress than putting on pants, a onesie, a shirt, a jacket, hat, and mittens. Getting the baby dressed in Maui takes two minutes. And she can spend most of her time nearly naked, save for her diaper. After the peeing-on-Mommy incident, I don't let her go diaperless for more than one minute.

February 14

I take the baby for a walk. I cover her legs with a blanket and make sure the top of the stroller is all the way down, covering her face, so not one millimeter of sun can touch her body. The heat tires her out, and just like I do back at home, I make up destinations for us so we can kill time. We go to Blockbuster and rent movies (for me). We go to bookstores and buy books (for me). We go grocery shopping. If I have a craving for a slurpie, that turns into an afternoon destination. The most menial tasks—hey, I think we need garbage bags, and one day I'll need more toilet paper—can turn into a whole-afternoon time killer.

A day with a baby can be very long if you don't make plans. I now understand why my friend Sara, who gave birth just weeks after me, is busier than she ever was when she was working. She makes daily plans nonstop for her and her child, just to keep busy and kill the time.

6 P.M.

Come six o'clock each and every night, I become really energized. Mostly, this is because I know the day is coming to an end.

I count down the minutes until I can put the baby to sleep. Because she's always in so much fresh air here in Maui and spends a lot of time splashing in the pool, she's exhausted by the end of the day and sleeps soundly and—yippee!—through the night. I know that come 7:30 P.M. when I put her in her crib, my "work" for the day is done. Did I once count down to getting out of the office like this? I don't think so. Or maybe I did. I don't remember what it's like to work anymore. I do know that I really enjoy those two hours by myself, watching television or reading a book in peace, once the baby is put down. By the way, I really hate the phrase "put down" when it refers to putting kids to sleep. It reminds me of "putting a dog down." And you know what that means. But it just comes out.

February 21

My parents were in Maui for a week and just left. Along with visiting parents comes a shitload of cameras. They even brought a video camera to take "action shots" of the baby. Which is kind of ridiculous. Because the baby's only "actions" are rolling over and sitting up. I'm not exactly sure when she began sitting up by herself. Mostly all I remember of the week with my parents is them saying, "Pose with the baby!" or "Take a picture of me with the baby!" I also remember a lot of "Maybe she needs a diaper change," "Maybe she needs to eat," "Maybe you should put a jacket on her."

It's hard for me to get mad at my parents, who clearly care so much about their first grandchild. That's not to say they didn't get on my nerves with all their "constructive criticisms." At least I know it's not just the in-laws who have the power to bug me. But, on the other hand, it was nice to have two extra sets of hands to help out with the baby.

I also noticed that my parents spoil my baby rotten. I don't care about people spoiling babies. Hey, you're supposed to spoil babies. It makes you feel good. It's just that my parents never spoiled me when I was growing up, so it's weird for me to see them shelling out money for toys and puzzles and clothes for my daughter, without thinking twice about what they're spending. Why weren't they so generous to me when I was a child? I've heard that some grandparents love their grandchildren more than their own children; probably this is because they don't have to deal with them 24/7. I can't help but feel, sometimes, that this is true in my case. If Baby Rowan even looked longingly at a stuffed animal, they'd buy it for her, even though she already has 253 stuffed toys.

I was sad to see my parents go. Mostly because now I'm alone with the baby again, which means hours and hours a day of making up stuff to do, and no more adult conversation. I'm happy, however, that when my parents left, so did the video camera. I'm just not ready to be seen on film quite yet. I don't want any lasting memories of these fat months.

February 23

Nanny Mimi arrived yesterday. Yay! Adult conversation again! I'm getting more comfortable with Nanny Mimi, and I hope she's getting more comfortable with me. And, truth be told, it is a hell of a lot easier having Nanny Mimi around than being alone. She wanted to share a room with the baby, and there was no argument from me. In fact, since Nanny Mimi arrived, I've gotten to sleep in. When I get up, Baby Rowan is already dressed and ready to go. (When looking for a nanny, always ask if they are morning people.) Nanny Mimi will take her for long walks, and I'll be left on my own. I get to work out, take naps, read books, and lie in the sun.

It's weird having Nanny Mimi as a roommate. I mean, she sees me in my pajamas and I see her in hers. I kind of like it. It brings me back to the days of university. Of course, I'm paying Nanny Mimi, and I never paid any of my university roommates. But at least Nanny Mimi can partake in conversation. And that's a refreshing break from my usual one-sided talk with the baby, which goes something like "Are you hungry? Do you need a diaper change?" and "You're cute." I get no response from the baby.

March 2

The time has come for Nanny Mimi to leave. She's happy to be leaving. This is not because she doesn't love the baby or Maui, a place she'd never been to before, or because she hates me. She's happy to be leaving because she confided to me she has a serious boyfriend. She loves him, and they hate spending time apart. Who knew? I had no idea that Nanny Mimi had a love life. Which is ridiculous of me. Of course she has her own life outside of our home. Of course she should have a boyfriend. Why shouldn't she? She's an attractive, kind, grown woman. A woman I know once told me that it's always better to get a nanny who doesn't have many friends or a boyfriend, because then you know they'll always be available when you need them. But I'm happy to learn Nanny Mimi has a boyfriend. Now I have another woman in my life to complain to about relationships.

March 4

The Fiancé, thanks to one of his friends who once spent time in Maui with his children, found a nanny service in Maui. He had been bothering me about getting a part-time nanny once Nanny

Mimi and my parents left, even if only for a couple of hours a day. He didn't think I could handle being with the baby 24/7, day after day after day. I was a little offended when he suggested this to me. I know he was worried about my depression. But I told him of course I could manage to be with my own baby by myself for a few weeks. Stay-at-home mothers do it all the time. Who did he think I was? Some bad mother who was incapable of taking care of a baby? Did he think that I couldn't handle hanging out with my own baby? I love my baby.

Okay, he was kind of right. Being alone with a baby, for days on end, can be exhausting. And boring, especially with no friends around. I mean, there are only so many trips you can make to Blockbuster before you realize you've seen all the movies you've wanted to see and some you don't.

Also, when I'm alone with the baby, I can't work out. For some reason, she doesn't find it fun to sit in her car seat while watching me run on a treadmill. Go figure. I can't work out when she's asleep because I'm always too worried that as soon as I start, she'll wake up. Which always seems to happen. She could be sound asleep in her car seat, and I will have just put on my workout clothes and running shoes, and that's exactly when she'll wake up. It's like Murphy's law or something. I certainly don't feel comfortable with her sleeping while I do laps in the pool. What if she starts screaming and I'm underwater?

So I give in and call the number of the highly recommended nanny service and tell them that I'm looking for a nanny for three hours every morning. I tell them I want someone outgoing, because Nanny Mimi is very outgoing and the more happier, noncynical people the baby is around, the better.

I can work out, attend spin classes at a nearby gym, and do some water-aerobic classes too. The nanny starts tomorrow.

I know I am fully capable of taking care of my baby. But

there's nothing wrong with some alone time either, is there? That's what I'm telling myself.

March 5

A very sweet older woman shows up at my door at 8 A.M. exactly, introduces herself, and immediately picks up the baby. The agency has done background checks on all the nannies they employ. This nanny tells me she's raised two kids and has two grandchildren, whom she often takes care of. I take this as a good sign. If she's a mother and a grandmother, then she knows how this whole keeping-a-baby-alive thing works. But I feel awful leaving the baby for the first time with this woman I've just met. How much do I really know about her? I explain what the baby needs to eat and when. I show her where the diapers and supplies are. I leave her my cell phone number in case of an emergency. What's the worst that can happen? The baby could scream for three hours, I suppose. Or she could sleep for three hours. Who knows? Like I said, there's no rhyme or reason to this kid.

All I know is that I have a spin class to get to. My ass isn't getting any smaller while I sit around worrying about leaving my baby. After hiding out, spying on them from behind a tree through a window for a few minutes, I leave. I'm not the type of woman who would get a secret camera put in a doll to spy on a nanny, but I will hide out behind a tree for a few minutes. I'm only human after all.

Noon

When I get back, the baby is napping soundly in her crib. I find the sweet older nanny lying on the couch watching my *Sex and the City* DVDs. I'm not sure how I feel about this. She just looks so, um, comfortable in my condo, almost like a teenager loung-ing around after school. Of course, the baby is sleeping, so what else is this nanny supposed to do? But who knew that sixty-five-year-old nannies could appreciate the humor of *Sex and the City*? I'm just thankful I didn't find this woman in my washroom, tak-ing a bubble bath and drinking a glass of wine. Could you imag-ine?

The rent-a-nanny tells me the baby was a perfect angel. To which I say, "Are you talking about my baby?" I'm just joking. I don't say that. I only think it.

"I've rubbed baby oil on her cradle cap," the nanny tells me. "It was getting really bad. It's practically gone now."

"Oh, you did! Wow! I had no idea how to get that off. Thank you." I'm really happy about this. I hadn't really known what to do about the very dry, scaly skin on the baby's scalp. It was dis-gusting. And now this woman has gotten rid of it. I don't mind rent-a-nanny, even if she lies on my couch watching *Sex and the City* DVDs while my baby sleeps. Hey, at least she isn't watching porn. I would definitely have a problem with that.

March 10

By seven-thirty each night, the baby goes to sleep. I'm in bed by nine-thirty. For the first time in what seems like years, I'm actu-ally starting to feel healthy again, physically and emotionally. The spin and water-aerobics classes make me feel like I'm on my way to losing weight. Unfortunately, or fortunately, I don't have a scale here, so I can't weigh myself. I can't believe I'm now falling asleep at 10 P.M., after reading a book for half an hour. I feel like an Olympian in training. I don't even remember what it was like to leave the house at 10 P.M. to go out and party and not get home until 2 A.M. It's sad, maybe, but you really do feel better when you go to bed early night after night. You do feel happier in the morning. I can't believe these words are coming out of my mouth. Who am I? Have I really changed this much?

March 11
7 A.M.

Argh. Okay, I might now enjoy going to bed at an early hour, but I am definitely still not a morning person. I've never been a morning person. Even when I was six years old, I liked sleeping in like a teenager. Will I ever be a morning person? The baby wakes up at the ungodly hour of 7 A.M., and I give her a bottle and put her in her portable crib in the living room, placed in front of the television, so she can watch a Baby Einstein DVD. Thank you, Julie Aigner-Clark!

Maybe I should send her a thank-you card.

I fall asleep on the couch. If the DVD runs thirty minutes, that means thirty minutes more shuteye for me. My baby loves these DVDs. For her, watching toys on television is the most fascinating thing in the world. She watches these DVDs like men watch dancers at strip clubs. I don't feel bad about plopping her down in front of the television. Hey, it's not like she's watching *Girls Gone Wild* or anything.

I recently found out that Disney bought Julie Aigner-Clark's Baby Einstein company for millions and millions of dollars. So now I kind of hate her even more. I'm really jealous that I don't have a business Disney would want to buy for even ten thousand dollars. I have to think of some idea for babies so I can become the next Julie Aigner-Clark. Yes, I am way too obsessed with this woman. But at least I know who to blame if my child turns out to be a television addict. I'll blame Julie Aigner-Clark, that's who. She's the one who came up with the idea to film toys. My child's television addiction will have nothing to do with me. Nothing at all.

March 15

"You sound sad. Is something wrong?" the Fiancé asks, calling me on my cell.

"My hair! It's still coming out!" I moan. I'm pretty sure I'm going to have bald patches soon. "You don't understand how much hair is falling out!" I continue. "I thought it would have stopped by now."

"Beck, you're not going bald. Are you taking your medication?"

Asking someone if she's taken her antidepressant is kind of like asking a woman if she's having her period when she's in a bitchy, unreasonable mood. I find the question annoying and stupid. "Yes," I answer.

"Do you think it's working?"

"I think so. I don't mind getting up in the morning now."

"That's a good sign."

It is. The happy pills must have started to work. I still feel slightly sad sometimes, but it is certainly getting better. Life no longer seems devastating and pointless.

After I hang up, I decide to call Ronnie. Though I have told her about my postpartum depression, I know she didn't suffer from it herself, so she couldn't entirely understand, even if she wanted to. But I know she'll at least understand my paranoia about my hair loss. She has three kids. So she must have lost a lot of hair in her lifetime.

"Oh my God. You don't understand how much hair I lost," she says when I ask her about it.

"Really? Tell me. How much?"

"Tons. And it came out for months and months."

"Months? Months and months?"

"I clogged the drain in the shower. Seriously. We had to get a plumber to come in and unclog it."

"Fuck."

"Don't worry. It will grow back. And then you'll have these really ugly tufts of hair by your hairline when it does."

"Fuck!"

March 16

The baby is lying on her back on her colorful play mat. She's making the cutest sounds in the world, like "Gaa goo goo gaa gaa." I race to grab the phone because someone else—aside from me—should hear these adorable, albeit slightly weird, sounds coming out of her. I call the Fiancé first, and his voice mail picks up. Oh sure, when something amazing happens, he's not around.

"Rowan," I tell my daughter, holding the phone to her mouth when the message beeps. "Make those sounds again now." She remains silent, looking at me like "What the hell are you talking about, Mommy?"

"Hi. I swear she was just making the cutest sounds. You snooze, you lose. Bye!" I say into the phone.

Just as I put the phone down she starts making her goo-goo-gaa-gaa sounds again. So I call my mother, who, thankfully, picks up and gets to hear. She thinks it's adorable. It is. It is the most adorable sound I have ever heard. I wonder what they hell she is trying to say. It's like looking at a dog and wondering what it's really thinking. You just never know.

March 17

It's amazing what you learn to do when you're alone with a baby day after day. I've learned that I can undo my pants, pull them down, sit on the toilet, and pee, all while holding the baby in my arms.

The baby doesn't like when I put her down on the floor while I pee. This afternoon I took her to a restaurant I had wanted to try out and I had to go to the washroom. I couldn't very well leave the baby by herself in the restaurant. I'm not that clueless. So I took her with me. I managed to hold her in one arm, and unbutton my shorts and pull them down with the other hand. It wasn't easy, but I did it.

Lunch, however, was a disaster. The Dictator was cranky. Apparently, she wasn't in the mood to go out for lunch. As soon as my meal arrived, I had no choice but to ask for it to be wrapped to go. I was getting evil stares from all the other customers, who were trying to enjoy their peaceful lunches. I swear I heard a collective sigh as I was walking out the door.

March 20

I can't believe it happened again! Again, I almost killed my baby! She almost choked today, and it was all my fault!

I was talking on my cell phone, holding the baby in one arm, preparing to put her into her car seat, so we could go for a drive to the grocery store. I had given her the car key to hold to amuse herself and was yapping away to Ronnie. Because we have rented a car here, the key ring has a piece of paper on it with the license-plate number.

Still gabbing, I glanced at the baby, and realized there was only half of the piece of paper left on the key ring. "That's weird," I thought to myself. "Where did the rest of it go?"

Then I looked at the baby, who was making all these funny faces. I opened her mouth, looked in, and saw chewed-up paper all the way at the back of her mouth and on her tongue. I immediately dropped my cell phone and stuck my finger into her mouth, hooking the paper and getting it all out. She could have died! All because I was too busy gossiping to my friend and not paying attention to my baby, who, of course, puts everything in her mouth. I should know this by now. I feel like I almost had a heart attack, that's how much my pulse was racing. I also think I'd better learn how to do CPR. The only good thing was that it was pure maternal instinct that made me stick my finger into her mouth to get the piece of paper out so she wouldn't choke. Who knew I had that in me?

I checked the baby's mouth again, just to make sure it was all clear, and put her into her car seat.

Just as I was about to drive out of the parking lot, my cell phone rang.

"What happened? Did you hang up on me?" Ronnie asked.

"I had a little issue over here. My kid almost choked on a piece of paper."

"Is she okay?"

"Yes, she's fine. I'm not so fine though."

I was actually sweating buckets. I realized that if my baby really had started to choke, I wouldn't have had a clue what to do. I really have to start paying more attention when I'm gossiping.

March 22

10 A.M.

My baby is ignoring me. Yes, that's right. Only five months old and she's already ignoring me. If she's in front of a Baby Einstein or Barney DVD, she doesn't move when I wave my hand in front of her face. She doesn't even blink. I can rub her arms and she pretends I'm not there. Maybe television is more interesting than me. I'm starting to wonder if Baby Einstein DVDs are like crack. And if my baby is now an addict. She does look completely stoned when she watches. Her eyes get glassy. Or maybe she's just memorizing. In any case, isn't she not supposed to start ignoring me until she turns twelve? I can't help but admit my feelings are a little hurt that she would rather spend time watching television than, you know, pay attention to me. Have I really become that boring that even a five-month-old thinks it too? I decide to turn off the Baby Einstein DVD.

Noon

I turn back on the DVD, so I can prepare myself lunch. Baby Einstein has turned into a great babysitter, what can I say? Who am I to fight a multibillion-dollar business? Who am I not to let my baby do what she wants?

March 23

My sweet-natured baby has turned into the Devil Child. She's cranky and crying for no reason. I don't know what to do. I feel like I'm losing my mind. So I call my mother and tell her that the baby is being bitchy. (I didn't use the word "bitchy." I said, "super-cranky." I'm thirty-one and still not comfortable using swearwords in front of my mother.)

"She could be teething," my mother says. Right! I forgot about that possibility. I open her mouth and look at her gums. Sure enough, the bottom gums look a little swollen, as if something—a tooth—could pop through any day now.

"You're right! She's teething," I tell my mother.

Although it can pain me to do so, I have to admit that sometimes mothers are right. They do know more than we do about this thing called parenting.

March 24

It's raining today, so I take the Dictator to a mall. It's all fine and dandy until we're on our way home. During the car ride, the Dictator screams for half an hour nonstop. I don't think I'll make it home. At least I don't think I'll make it home without killing her or myself. There is nothing worse than a screaming baby in a car, while you're driving. It's enough to make you want to check yourself in to a mental institution. Usually, when I take her in the car, I give her a bottle. But while I was getting her into her car seat, I dropped the bottle and it rolled under the car. After buckling the baby in, I looked under the car, but the bottle had rolled right under the center of the car. Even if I were skinny, there was no way I could fit under the car to reach it. Driving home, I so regret being lazy and not trying everything to get it. Because now I have a baby screaming bloody murder in the backseat of my car and she won't shut up and there's nothing I can do to settle her down because I have to pay attention to the road. It is quite possibly the worst car ride in the history of car rides.

"What do you do when your kids scream in the car?" I ask Ronnie later that night, after popping three Advils for the second time since getting back.

"Um, I turn the music up really, really loud," she says.

"Oh. That's it?"

"Well, I'd buy her some baby CDs. They like listening to those," Ronnie suggests.

Ah, I have a plan—a destination time killer—for tomorrow. I'm going to buy the Dictator some CDs.

March 25

I see a tooth! I see a tooth! I'm excited but the baby is miserable. I've bought Infants' Tylenol—bumble-gum flavor—and I give it to her every six hours. She seems to like it. And, I must admit, it does smell yummy. Some people don't believe in giving drugs to their children. But hey, it's Infants' Tylenol, and why should I let my child be in pain if she doesn't need to be? I believe in pain medication for pain.

I also give her frozen tooth rings to suck on, which she does, for about thirty seconds.

"So, how long does this teething thing last?" I ask Ronnie, whom I have started to call now daily with mothering questions. She is so much easier than a parenting guide. And, like most mothers, she's only too happy to share her experiences.

"Oh, about a year."

"A what?"

"About a year."

"You've got to be joking!"

"No. That's how long it takes for all their teeth to grow in," she says. Ronnie suggests I give her watermelon rinds to suck on. I do. And it seems to work well.

This whole teething thing just seems unfortunate because she had just started being kind of good—well, not good, but not bad. The Dictator had started to act bearable and seemed happy, and now she's teething and she might be bitchy like this for an entire year? A year seems like a very long time. A day with a cranky baby can seem like a year. So, if I do the math, a year of baby teething will seem like 365 years.

March 26

I can't stop thinking about my friendships. I still talk to some of my friends on the phone, all the time, but I feel myself trying hard not to talk about the baby, at least to my single friends. "Oh, she's so cute" is all I'll say when they ask how she's doing, because I'm not sure how much, or how little, they want to hear.

My friend Vivian says she never talks about her baby unless people ask her first. Sometimes, some of my friends, in thirty-minute conversations, don't ask at all about the baby, which I find hurtful. I ask all about their dates and the parties they go to, and about their careers. Why can't they ask about the most important thing in my life? But, on the other hand, I am becoming closer to Vivian, because she is a mother. I'm becoming closer to all of my mother friends, because mothers love hearing about your child and their progress, and I love hearing about their children's progress.

So, as some of my friendships are getting stronger, I can't help but feel the distance growing between me and some other friends. It makes me sad, and I wonder if this happens to every woman after having a baby.

"It happens," says my friend Debbie, who recently got married and has a baby. "It happens even when you just get married. Suddenly, your single friends drop off the earth. Now that I have a baby, I don't even get spam e-mails from some of my closest friends anymore. And these are friends I used to talk to every day."

Maybe there really is a great divide between those who have children and those who don't. I've now realized I'm on the parent side. There's no fighting it. I'm on a different team now.

March 27

The Fiancé is back in Maui! It's good because I've missed him. It's bad because my two-month "vacation" is coming to an end.

"You look really good," says the Fiancé when he walks into the condo. I had planned to pick him up at the airport, but his flight was delayed, and waking the baby, putting her in the car seat, and driving half an hour to the airport seemed like a lot of work, when he could just as easily jump into a cab to get here. What's the point of having a baby, if you can't blame not picking someone up at the airport on the fact that your baby's sleeping?

I have been swimming laps and doing spin classes every morning since I hired the rent-a-nanny. I have also been taking long walks every afternoon with the baby. The baby weight has finally come off. It was hard work, but I did it. Not as quickly as Vivian or Posh Spice, mind you, who lost all their baby weight in, like, two hours. It took me a few months, but it's finally gone! And it was very weird how it happened. Although I have been working out, for the longest time nothing was happening, even after numerous spin classes and swimming laps for hours and eating a protein-only diet. Then, one day, I woke up and the weight had just disappeared. Not only that, but under the fat that I had lost, there were muscles. I look more toned now, in fact, than I did pre-baby. The Fiancé told me I look "hot." I've never felt happier (save for the day the Dictator was born).

Now I like looking at myself in a mirror again. At night, once the baby is sleeping, I try on all the new clothes I've bought myself. I don't feel silly doing this. It's like looking at a whole new person.

And I can have sex again, and not worry about suffocating the Fiancé under me. So we do. The Fiancé and I have great sex.

For the first time in fourteen months, I feel sexy. Plus, how could I not fuck his brains out after he told me how hot I look?

March 30

I can't believe my month alone with the baby is over and we're at home. I've learned a lot. Mostly I learned from being alone with the baby for a month that being a single mother is hard work. I really respect single mothers. I have spent days upon days here not talking to any adults—except for "Can I get that sushi to go?"—which was hard.

The plane ride home was painful. The baby spent practically the entire six hours screaming. Just as I'd settle her down in her car seat, she'd start screaming again, so I'd have to pick her up. I'm not sure if it was her teething, or what. It was an overnight flight too, so added to the pain that was her screaming was the guilt that all the other passengers, who were trying to sleep, couldn't because the Dictator wouldn't shut up. And the lights were off, so it was impossible to find all her supplies. Try pouring a can of formula into a bottle in the dark. It's messy, at best. I drifted off a few times but could never get comfortable, because the baby would only sleep lying on my chest.

The Fiancé had given up trying to settle her down after ten minutes. I didn't blame him. I knew if I could barely calm her down, he'd never be able to.

By the time we landed, she and I both smelled foul, like a mixture of urine and formula. Even her usually sweet-smelling breath reeked.

"Why is she being like that?" the Fiancé asked on the plane.

"Teething," I answered.

When we got off the plane, we found the elevator that took us down to the luggage area. We got on with a couple with newborn twins, who were also on our plane. (Once you travel with a baby, you always take note of the other babies around.) The twins were both sleeping soundly, and the parents, while they did seem a little tired, certainly didn't look like they'd been spit out of a hurricane, like we did. I hated them.

I notice this a lot actually. There are a lot of mothers who look good and put-together out in public with their babies. I wonder how these mothers have it in them to brush their hair, let alone put on makeup, and look not only presentable but ready to walk down a red carpet. How is it possible for them to look so tucked-in, while I look so crappy? There must be some secret they're not sharing with me. Maybe there are some mothers who exist solely to make you feel bad.

Ten Mommy Moments People "Forget" to Mention

1. You will blame every cry on "teething."
2. You will forget the diaper bag. Your will need it when you do.
3. You will become the world's best tipper.
4. You will find yourself participating in "baby-offs."
5. You will lose these baby-offs.
6. You will get offended when someone doesn't think your baby is the cutest.
7. Your baby will say her first word. You think.
8. Your baby will start to eat smelly baby cereal.
9. You will feel guilty about wanting to go back to work.
10. You will wonder if you can give it all up and be a SAHM (stay-at-home mom).

The Sixth Trimester (6 to 9 Months)

My Baby Is Better Than Yours,
Nanana-boo-boo!

April 15

I have rented a cheap office space to work from. I'm just not cut out to be a stay-at-home mother, though I think about being one often.

I used to play the "what if" game with the Fiancé, before I was pregnant. "What if," I'd ask him, "Brad Pitt asked me out on a date? Would I be allowed to go?" Then, when I was pregnant, the "what if" questions became "What if I go into labor and you're on the golf course and can't pick up your phone and I have to deliver the baby all by myself?" Now the "what if" question has become "What if I decide to be a stay-at-home mother? Would you let me?"

"You could never do that," the Fiancé always answers.

"I could too," I always profess.

"You'd last a week. You'd get bored."

It's not that I don't understand mothers who want to stay at home. Actually, I'm a bit envious of them. Not about the fact that they don't work (because I know now that raising children is the hardest work in the world) but because they actually can get through day after day after day with their babies and not seem to mind the tediousness of it all. Is something wrong with me that I get bored and don't know what to do with the baby after three hours?

I read somewhere that it's not the amount of time you spend with your children that matters but the quality of time. But it's something I repeat to myself often to make myself feel better about leaving home to go to my office to work. It's not the amount of time; it's the quality of time, I say over and over in my head, every morning when I walk out the front door.

You just can't win being a modern mother. I remember a woman I worked with at the newspaper who had twins on top of already having a three-year-old. She was back at work within three weeks of giving birth. I couldn't help but judge her. What kind of woman goes back to work three weeks after giving birth to twins, especially since she has the option to take a year off? But now I understand where she was coming from. If you really care about your career, you can't help but wonder what you're missing out on by not being in the office.

You can't help but become paranoid, believing that someone is going to take over your job and do better at it than you ever did. You can't help but hate yourself for having spent all of your twenties working so hard at a job, only to suddenly give it all up because you had a baby.

I also judge myself for wanting to work. In the big picture, what is taking a year off from my career? Why don't I want to stay home with my baby? Why haven't my priorities changed? Shouldn't my baby come before my work? One minute I do think my baby is more important, but the next I just want a career.

I feel guilty no matter what choice I make. I'm constantly

judging myself nowadays, and every decision I make seems like the wrong one.

8 P.M.
The baby is freaking out.

"Why is she being like that?" the Fiancé asks.

"Teething," I answer.

April 17

I meet my friend Tammy for lunch. Tammy is one of my new mommy friends I met through the Fiancé (her husband was the one who looked mortified when we met them for dinner and I put the pacifier that had fallen onto the floor back into the baby's mouth). Tammy gave birth a couple of months ago. Like me, she has only a few mother friends. She also has a hard time being at home with her child every day and went back to work almost immediately after giving birth. It made me happy to know there were other mothers like me out there, some of whom I even knew personally. Yippee!

After lunch, we decide to get a coffee at Starbucks. On our way there, her cell phone rings. "Okay," she says into the phone. "That's fine." She hangs up.

"Who was that?" I ask.

"That was my nanny. She was telling me they're going out for a walk around the block."

"Oh. She calls you every time she leaves the house?" I ask.

"Yes, she has to tell me where she's going. Why? Your nanny doesn't do that?"

"Um, no," I admit. In fact, I have never called Nanny Mimi even once after I leave the house to see how my baby is doing. I never ask Nanny Mimi to call and let me know where she's going with my baby either. Unlike Tammy, who has told her nanny where and when she can go, I've never told Nanny Mimi how she should spend her time with the baby.

Which means I'm either the coolest, most laid-back, most trusting mother in the world, or I'm the worst. I'm not sure which is true. I do know I trust Nanny Mimi entirely. So why should I call? And why should she call me unless there's some sort of emergency?

Also, I'm not even sure I *could* ask Nanny Mimi to let me know if she's heading out for a walk. I'm still worried about being a good employer. I don't want to be overbearing, but I also don't want Nanny Mimi to think I don't care about what she does with my child. Oh, God. Maybe I should call her once in a while from my office, just to check in.

I also hate to admit it, but once I'm working I rarely think about my baby. Yes, occasionally her face pops into my head, and I miss her in my gut. And, yes, I have made a photo of her my screen saver. But mostly, I'm too busy trying to get back into the swing of working to remember her or miss her. I feel guilty about that too.

8 P.M.
"Why is she being like that?" the Fiancé yells at me, over the baby's wails.

"Teething!" I yell back.

May 1
"This is the last time I'm going out to dinner with her *ever*," the Fiancé is saying. "I mean it, Beck. We are not taking her out for dinner anymore."

The good old days of the baby just sitting there or sleeping through dinner are long gone. Now she loves throwing everything she gets her hands on off the table. She throws salt and pepper shakers off the table. She throws knives and forks off the table. She throws napkins off the table. She throws her bottle off the table. Fun for her, maybe, but not so fun for me and the Fiancé, who must bend down and pick up everything off the floor every two seconds. She also won't sit still. She's always squirming around.

"It wasn't that bad," I say after we finish our meal in fourteen minutes. I think we may have eaten in record time. Although I do have a migraine and I am still starving, after spending most of my time picking up shit the baby threw off her high chair onto the floor, I don't know if it's possible for us to never go to a restaurant again. Which sucks, because I'd always thought the baby would fit into our lives, which means eating out with us.

"That's the last time!" the Fiancé says again. "That was the least relaxing meal I have ever had."

"Well, she's teething," I say, sticking up for the baby.

"You say that every time she acts up!" the Fiancé says.

"Well, she is! She's teething!"

"I don't care. That's the last time!"

"Okay, I already heard you," I say. "That will be the last time we take her out."

As if.

9 P.M.

"Why is she crying?" the Fiancé asks.

"Because she's—"

"No, don't answer! I already know what you're going to say," he says.

"Don't worry. We only have another 320 days like this. It will go by like this," I say, snapping my fingers.

Right.

May 15

"Happy seven-month birthday," the mother-in-law says when she calls.

Oh, my God. The baby is now seven months old. Wow. I hadn't even realized it. Of course, I have more important things to worry about, like the fact that it's time the baby got off formula.

The baby is now eating baby cereal. Most parents introduce their baby to baby cereal when they turn four or five months, but we let it go while I was away in Maui and decided to get her on it as soon as we got back. Baby cereal is pretty disgusting actually. It comes in powder form, and you mix it with formula and try to get your baby to eat the resulting mush. It's messy business, because my baby loves sticking her hands into the mush. It's really hard to explain to a baby that it's only supposed to go into her mouth. Also, most of the time, once it gets into her mouth, she spits it out. And, trust me, baby cereal does not smell like roses. Whatever is the opposite of roses, that's what baby cereal smells like.

5 P.M.

"Come on," I tell the Fiancé, "it's her seven-month birthday. Let's go out to dinner and celebrate with your parents."

"With the baby?" he asks.

"Of course! It's *her* seven-month birthday!"

"Fine," he says, sighing loudly.

8 P.M.

"I mean it. That was the last time we're taking her out for dinner," the Fiancé says in a déjà vu moment.

"Okay."

"I mean it this time. I really mean it."

"All right. I heard you. You think I enjoyed being covered in Diet Coke?" The baby spilled my entire glass of pop all over me while we were eating. Let's just say she needs to work on her hand-eye coordination.

The problem is, neither the Fiancé nor I know how to cook. We're take-out, eat-out kind of people. And the truth is, taking the baby out for dinner is a time killer. It's just something to do. And we have to eat. It's killing two birds with one stone.

"I don't think that Chinese restaurant is going to let us come back anyway," says the Fiancé.

"Why do you say that?"

"Um, Beck, she broke three ceramic spoons and threw a bowl across the room!"

"Right."

I call Vivian when we get home, once the baby is in bed.

"So, you never take your baby out for dinner?" I ask her, after she tells me her family never eats out. I couldn't believe it. She used to eat out all the time.

"Never," she says.

"Oh."

I like going out to eat. I don't want to stop going out to restaurants just because we have a baby in our lives now. I'm sure my baby wasn't the first to ever break a few spoons and whip a bowl across a crowded restaurant, and I'm sure she won't be the last. And, really, no one got hurt. When you think about it, it could have been much, much worse.

May 16

"So, what are we doing for dinner tonight?" I say when I call the Fiancé.

"I don't know. What do you want to do?"

"Do you want to go out for dinner?" I ask.

"I guess so." See? I told you the "this is the last time—ever—we're going out with her" wouldn't stick. The Fiancé can be a pushover.

Dinner is another disaster. Babies are not good customers in restaurants, which is why the Fiancé and I are now officially the World's Best Tippers. Our tips are in proportion to how messy and misbehaved the baby is. The messier and more misbehaved she is, the bigger the tip we give. We've tipped waiters up to 50 percent on really bad outings. In fact, I don't understand why waiters don't like having people like us, people who bring children, coming in. Sure, babies make huge messes and dump entire bowls of rice on the floor. But in return, the waiters get huge tips.

We stay home the following night, ordering in Thai food.

We both feel a bit like inmates serving a jail term. It might be six years before the Dictator behaves well in a restaurant.

Maybe we should send her to etiquette classes. I wonder if there are any etiquette classes for babies less than a year old out there. You know, "Throwing bowl across room is bad. Putting napkin on lap is good."

May 17

It's my first Mother's Day, and I'm super-excited!

I've been talking up the importance of Mother's Day for, well, since the baby was in my stomach. I had even wondered if

I was going to get a present while I was pregnant. The Fiancé told me when he had proof, you know, when there was a baby in my arms, that's when I would be a mother and get a Mother's Day gift. So, no, I didn't get a gift while I was pregnant, even though I tried to convince him that I was a mother because a baby was growing inside me. The Fiancé didn't agree with my logic.

Of course, the greatest Mother's Day present would be something like a daylong spa experience. But I want to spend Mother's Day with my baby, who has not a clue what Mother's Day is. I don't care though.

The Fiancé has bought me a Prada purse as a gift, and I love it. Proof of being a mother? Good Mother's Day gifts. And even though the Dictator has definitely not been on her best behavior today, all I have to do is look at my new Prada purse and I feel better about being her mother.

There is only one thing that bothers me.

"So, I shouldn't be upset?" I ask Ronnie, when I called her this evening to brag about my new bag, wish her a happy Mother's Day, and explain to her why I'm upset.

"No. You're being overly sensitive," she says.

I had called the very few mommy friends I have to wish them all a Happy Mother's Day, and they wished me the same. But none of my friends who don't have babies called to wish me a happy Mother's Day. I had asked Ronnie if I was being too sensitive about this.

"Before you had your baby, did you call me on Mother's Day?" Ronnie asks, to prove her point.

"I don't know. Did I?"

"No."

"Oh. Well, I'm sorry. I should have. Happy Mother's Day!"

It's like a good friend forgetting your birthday. I know it

doesn't matter in the big picture that none of my nonmother friends remembered my first Mother's Day, but it still kind of stings.

May 26

"Da," the baby says.

"Did you hear that? Did you hear that? She said 'Dada,' " I tell the Fiancé.

"She did not."

"Da," says the baby again.

"She did! Didn't you hear that? That was her first word! Her first word was 'Dada'!"

"It was 'da,' " says the Fiancé. "Not 'Dada.' "

The Fiancé always has to be so pessimistic.

"I'm telling you. I'm her mother and I know what she's trying to say. I understand her better than anyone. She's trying to say 'Dada.' "

I'm only slightly offended that her first word wasn't "Mama." Aren't all babies' first words supposed to be "Mama"?

Or is that a lie too?

Noon

We're pushing the baby in her stroller and walking to get some dim sum. The baby looks up at a stop sign and points at it.

"Da!" she says.

"She wasn't saying 'Dada.' She just looked at a stop sign and said 'da,' " the Fiancé cries out. "I told you she wasn't saying 'Dada'!"

I pretend not to hear what he just said. The baby said her first word—"Dada"—and I'm sticking to it.

"I'm telling you, she's saying 'Dada,' " I insist.

"Nice try," says the Fiancé.

God, why does he make it so hard for me to try to make him feel good and special?

May 29

Okay, maybe the Fiancé was right. Maybe the baby wasn't trying to say "Dada." She looks at plants and says "Dada." She looks at chairs and says "Dada." She looks at a tube of toothpaste and says "Dada." She even looks at me and says "Dada."

Of course I'm not going to mention this to the Fiancé. I'm going to let him think that I'm convinced the baby's first word was "Dada." That's because I'm a nice person.

9 P.M.

"Why is she like that?" the Fiancé asks.

"Teething."

"You still think she's teething?"

"I have no clue," I say.

"So why do you always answer 'Teething'?"

"I don't know. It sounds good to say it."

This whole teething experience is good for one and only one reason. Whenever she acts up in public, I just tell people that she's teething. Everyone feels sympathy for parents going through the teething process. People just nod and say, "Oh, it must be so painful." They have no idea.

June 1

I'm back in my hometown visiting my parents, who were yearning to see their granddaughter. It's been a couple of months since they saw her last. It's also a great excuse to see some of my friends with whom I've lost close contact. My parents are waiting for us at my condo when we arrive from the airport. One of my two younger brothers is also there. The baby loves this brother, her uncle. It's amazing, because this brother is super-shy and not exactly a superstar when it comes to making conversation. But he loves the Dictator. I never would have pictured him as someone who likes babies, but he does. One of the amazing things you realize once you have a baby is that the people you think would be most comfortable with babies sometimes aren't and are so awkward and nervous if you ask them to hold your baby. But the people you'd least expect to like babies, or feel at ease holding a baby, actually do like babies and enjoy holding them.

My brother hands the Dictator a five-dollar bill. It's a nice gesture. I know he's only trying to be a good uncle and make his mark as the uncle who gives my baby cash. But eight-month-old babies don't need money. I take the bill from him and tell him I'll make sure to put it into her piggy bank. Of course, what I'm really planning is to pocket the money myself and buy coffee with it tomorrow. It will save me a trip to the ATM. Hey, she's my baby. What's mine is hers and what's hers is mine.

One strange thing about babies is that sometimes they just don't like certain people. My baby hates my other brother, who is possibly the nicest guy in the world. But every time she sees this uncle, the nicest guy in the world, she starts screaming. I don't understand it. My parents don't understand it. My brother certainly doesn't understand it.

I wonder if the baby knows something that I don't. Then again, she gets excited at stop signs. I don't think we can take too seriously what she thinks about anything or anybody just yet.

June 6

I'm in the worst mood ever. I just got into a fight with my friend Jenna. Last time I was in town, she took a photo of my baby with her nephew. And now she brought the photo over for me to see.

"Your baby looks so weird in this photo," she said when handing it over to me. "She looks like an alien. But look how cute Jack is!"

I don't believe I have ever been so offended by anyone in my life. Yes, it was kind of true, I'll admit. My baby wasn't looking her cutest in the photo. Yes, it was kind of true, I'll admit, she did kind of look like a creature from outer space. But how dare this friend think her nephew is cuter than my baby! Even if she thought it was true, even if it was true, she should know better than to ever say something like that aloud, especially to the baby's mother. And I told her so. She apologized, but I don't think she really understood why I had gotten so upset. She's not a mother after all. She doesn't understand that all mothers think their child is the cutest, most beautiful child in the world and that you are never supposed to say that their baby looks "weird." When she has her own baby, she'll understand that there are certain things one should never say to a mother, like "My baby is cuter," "Why can't she talk yet?" and "My baby is a genius." It's common sense.

June 7

I go to Sara's house to visit her and her baby. I'm making the baby rounds. Sara puts on a baby-music CD, and her baby starts to wobble back and forth, like an uncoordinated dancer.

"Oh, she just loves to boogey to music," Sara says.

Hey! I thought my baby was the only one who did that when she hears music! It was just like when I was pregnant, and kind of thought I was the only one in the world who had ever been knocked up. I also thought all the cute things my baby does—like clap her hands, or play peekaboo, or boogey to music—were things only she did. Apparently not. Apparently all babies do most things every other baby on the planet does. Sara's daughter has hair that reaches her shoulders. My daughter, who is older, is still very bald. Sara can put her baby's hair in ponytails, while my baby girl is wearing a T-shirt I found that says I AM NOT A BOY!

Trust me, it's my favorite shirt she owns. I just hope my baby gets some hair before she grows out of her I AM NOT A BOY! shirt. Because I still hear, at least once a day, that I have such an adorable son.

June 15

Oh my God! I just experienced my first baby-off!

I have started using the phrase "baby-off" when it comes to competitive parents who think their child is way more advanced than everyone else's. Baby-offs are the equivalent of playoffs in hockey. Like hockey, parenting can be very competitive. There are mothers all over the place who check out who has a better stroller, or whose children are wearing cuter shoes or designer clothes. There are mothers all over the place who tell you their five-month-old baby can sign the word "milk," and mothers who tell you that their child started sleeping through the night starting at a month of age, and mothers who tell you their eight-month-old baby can read Tolstoy. (Liars! All of them!)

I run into an acquaintance while out for a walk. She, too, is pushing her baby in a stroller. (My stroller is better! Ha ha!)

"Hi! How's it going?" she asks, her eyes taking in my daughter's outfit as well as what I'm wearing.

"Fine," I say. "Your baby is so cute."

"Thanks. Isn't he? Did you know that he already speaks in full sentences?"

"No, I did not know that." How the hell would I know that?

"It's because we've been taking him to five classes a week. He just loves them all. What classes do you take your baby to?"

"Um, none?" I say. This acquaintance looks at me like I am a freak of nature. "Well, I got to get running," I say, because I know this conversation isn't going to get any better. I know that whatever comes out of her mouth will only make me feel worse. She is probably going to tell me next that her child has already been accepted to Harvard Law School.

"Give me a call," she says. "We can get our babies together and swim in my pool. He just loves swimming. He's like a fish in water. He's so good at it."

"Sure," I say, thinking, "It's so never going to happen."

"Do you have my number?"

"I think I do," I say. I'm pretty sure I don't.

I've clearly lost that baby-off. I must start bragging about my baby more. I just don't think, when it comes to baby-offs, that I could ever win by saying, "My child says 'Dada' when she sees a tree. But I still have a better stroller, nananana-boo-boo." Of course, her son has more hair. But my daughter has nicer eyes. And on and on the baby-offs go.

June 20

I'm back with the Fiancé and we're out for dinner, just the two of us. It's like we're on a date. The in-laws are babysitting. We are having sushi. It was a long day with the baby, who is still teething. (What is it now, only four more months of hell to go through?)

We are seated next to a table with a baby. I realize now that the world is more of a baby/family place than a single woman's place. There are babies everywhere. I want to ask if we can move tables but don't. That would be rude. But would it? I can't help but think that the Fiancé and I are finally away from our baby for a night, and now we're stuck sitting beside someone else's baby. It's like God is punishing us. Can't we ever get a break?

It's true that since I've become a mother I am way more patient with other people's babies. I no longer judge mothers when I see their children having temper tantrums. But, I admit, this baby who won't stop banging his sippy cup, over and over again, on the table annoys the crap out of me. If I wanted to go out for dinner and be annoyed by a baby, I would have brought my own, thank you very much.

June 21

Great news! My friend Grace is pregnant! Now when I hear news of my friends getting pregnant, I am super-excited. I want more and more of my friends to move over to *my side*—the mommy side. The more of us on the mommy side, the better. Strength in numbers is what I always say.

"If there's one piece of advice . . ." I hear myself saying to Grace. Argh! I hated when people said that to me when I was pregnant. People were constantly offering up their advice, even when I never asked. "Oh, forget it," I said to her. "Don't listen to me. Congratulations. You're going to love being a mother. It's so rewarding."

She is overjoyed at being pregnant. And, yes, the reason, at least partly, is because she hates her job and will have a maternity leave.

June 22
7:20 P.M.

I'm pissed off, and getting pissier by the minute, waiting for my friend Faith to show up. We said we'd meet at 7 P.M. for dinner, and she's late. I used to be the one who was always late.

"I can't believe you're on time!" she says when she finally arrives. "I'm sorry I was late. I couldn't get out of work."

"On time? I was right on time! In fact, I think I was early," I say. I want her to feel bad for being late.

"Okay, who are you?" she asks.

"I know. Pathetic, right? It's just that having a baby really changes you." She gives me a bored look, as if she knew baby talk was coming. "No, don't worry. I'm not going to bore you with baby talk. I just mean that you end up planning every minute of your day."

How can I explain to a nonmother that ten minutes makes all the difference in the world? Post-baby, ten minutes is the difference between having a shower and not having a shower. These twenty minutes waiting for Faith I could have spent hanging out with my baby, instead of sitting alone at a table, feeling like a loser whose friend may have stood her up.

Faith and I have a nice-enough meal. We gossip. She tells me about the people she's been dating. But, for some reason, the gossip doesn't interest me as much as it once did. And this upsets me, because I usually love gossiping. Now that I'm a mother, I suppose, I'm just not as interested anymore, unless it's gossip about someone getting pregnant.

June 28

We just never learn. We've decided to go out for dinner to a Chinese restaurant. Again. With the baby. After we finish eating, I feel like the worst mother in the world. But what could I have done? The baby took a shit while we were eating. Like we do 80 percent of the time, we had forgotten the diaper bag, but at least we had supplies in the car, and the Fiancé ran out to fetch them. There was no way we were going to put her in the car with her dirty diaper. We would suffocate from the smell.

I took the baby to the washroom only to find that there was no changing table there. I didn't even have a blanket or anything to lay on the floor, which was so dirty and grimy that I didn't even feel all that comfortable walking on it in shoes. But I had to change her. What the fuck could I place her on? There weren't even paper towels—the washroom had automatic hand dryers. I had no choice but to lay the baby right on the disgusting tiles. This restaurant, although it has wonderful spring rolls, was definitely not the cleanest place in the world.

She screamed when she felt her head against the cool tile, and I knew I was going to have to give her a bath when we got home. I changed her disgusting diaper and picked her up. The garbage bin had no lid, and the baby's diaper managed to smell up the entire restroom. I was glad no one had come in while we were in there.

Not only had I lain my baby directly on the dirty floor, but I threw the dirty diaper and wipes into the trash bin and raced out.

"We have to get out of here right now," I tell the Fiancé, explaining the situation.

"Oh God," he moans.

"There was nothing I could do!"

He throws down some cash, including a 40 percent tip, and we race out.

"We can't go back there, can we?" I say.

"Beck, there are now about a dozen restaurants in this city who would love it if they never saw us again."

When we get home, I immediately give the baby a bath. I make a mental note to start keeping a blanket in the trunk.

July 4

The in-laws are over and the Fiancé is furious.

"No more big toys!" he yells at his parents. "You want her to have big toys, you keep them at your place! Stop bringing them over here!"

His parents had bought Baby Rowan a tent. Yes, a tent. Sure, it's a tent with Disney princess characters on it, but it's still a damn tent. And it's not a small tent either. It's a big tent. Four people could sleep comfortably in this tent. We live in a two-bedroom condo. I'm less angry than the Fiancé is about this tent. I understand where he's coming from. We can't walk anywhere in our condo now without tripping over a toy. But I like the Disney princess tent. It's pink and it's cute and the baby thinks it's fantastic.

The tent is set up in the middle of our living room. There was no other place to put it.

Well, according to the Fiancé, there was. He would have loved it if we had put it in the garbage bins in the parking garage.

July 7

I force the Fiancé to go out with one of his guy friends. I'm too tired to go anywhere at night. I can't even remember having fun out at a bar anymore. But the Fiancé was always very social and, pre-baby, went out with friends a lot.

He's tired too, after working a long day and then coming home to deal with the often cranky baby, who is forever teething. I know he misses going out with his drinking buddies. I practically force him to make plans with a friend, a barfly, who has also recently become a father. His friend is having a hard time adjusting to fatherhood. You know, having responsibilities aside from making sure you can grab a waiter to get you that final drink before last call.

The Fiancé gets home at midnight, which is early for him. At least it would have been pre-baby. I'm still awake, flipping through a magazine in bed.

"So, what did you guys talk about?" I ask. I always ask the Fiancé when he goes out with friends what they talked about.

"Oh, we talked a lot about work and golf," he says.

"Did he say anything about his child or girlfriend?" It has always pissed me off that the Fiancé doesn't remember conversations with friends in great detail. Like most men, he never asks the right questions.

"Um, I think he said something like 'Having a baby is turning out to be the worst decision we ever made.' "

"Oh my God. That's bad," I say.

The couple doesn't have a nanny. I'm not sure if the girlfriend would want a nanny anyway. Unlike me, she's one of those mothers who thinks the more time you spend with your baby, the better, the more classes you join, the better.

"You don't feel having a baby was the worst thing we've ever done, do you?" I ask the Fiancé. How can I not ask him?

"Do you?" he asks me.

"I asked you first," I say.

"Well . . . it's definitely hard," he says. "It's changed every-thing. . . ."

One of my male friends, who is the father of two kids, once told me that he could easily imagine not having kids. On bad days with the Dictator, I can understand this. But she's become such a part of my everyday life that I really don't think I can imagine life without her. Having her may have been a big deci-sion, but I don't feel it was a bad decision. I don't feel it was "the worst decision I've ever made." Trying on a pair of skinny jeans only two months after giving birth, still thirty pounds over-weight, was the worst decision I've ever made.

Maybe it's different for girls than it is for guys. After all, the baby did grow inside of me. She was a part of me.

It's funny when you talk to some parents about their babies and hear what they say about them. One colleague had a two-year-old. I had asked her, way before I got knocked up, what it was like to have a baby. Her answer was "I love my baby, but sometimes I feel like throwing her out the window." At the time, I couldn't believe those words came out of her mouth. But now I understand what she meant. Babies are hard work.

The Fiancé never answers my question.

Ten Mommy Moments People "Forget" to Mention

1. You will be guilted into joining a Mommy & Me class.
2. You will drop out.
3. You must learn to cook, if not for you, then for your child.
4. You will miss the days of bottle-only feedings.
5. You will realize you never have enough friends with children in your social circle.

6. You will throw a birthday party, even though you know your baby doesn't understand the concept of a birthday party.

7. You will realize your child becomes like a mini-adult.

8. You will dread big toys, like a disease.

9. You may have to move into a bigger place.

10. This does not mean you are allowed to get a dog.

The Seventh Trimester (9 to 12 Months)

We Can't Live Like
This Anymore!

July 15

I can't fight it anymore. Every mother I know, which, granted, isn't that many, has signed her kid up for some sort of baby course. My mother told me about her friend's daughter who signed her baby up for a class every day of the week. I'm not sure if my mother was trying to tell me something like "Don't you think you should be a good mother and sign the baby up for something?" or if she's just telling me about that to make conversation. In any case, I have become a bit worried that my baby spends most of her time with Nanny Mimi, the Fiancé, the in-laws, or me and not enough time socializing with other pint-size humans.

I have picked up brochures featuring kids' programs from various places around the city. I call and sign her up for a music course at a school that's a five-minute walk from my house. It couldn't be more convenient. Like when you have a gym close to where you live, there would be no excuse not to take her.

After I sign her up, I feel like the mother of the year. At least I took the first step. Now we just have to go.

July 20

We head to our first music class, which, even though it takes place so close to our condo, is a pain in the ass. It is the first time I can remember that we actually have to be somewhere on time. But we make it. Sure, I have to wake her up, feed her, dress her, and then dress myself, all in thirty minutes, but come hell or high water I am going to this Mommy & Me music class, even if I have to go in my pajamas.

The instructor is very nice and plays instruments for the babies. We have to sing along with her. I feel stupid, because I don't know any of the songs, while every other mother at the class does. I guess they are regular Mommy & Me music-class goers. The Dictator doesn't cry at all. I take that to mean she is enjoying herself.

July 27

A week later, we're Mommy & Me music-class dropouts. The baby was sleeping this morning and I had to make a decision. Do I wake her so she can go to class, or do I let her sleep? I let her sleep, because I wanted to sleep more too. Is it worse to be a beauty-school dropout or a Mommy & Me music-class dropout? Argh. Thank God my child's memory is zilch. I mean, it's not like she's going to wake up and say, "Mommy, you didn't wake me and we missed music class today. Thanks a lot!"

I make a promise to myself to at least put on a CD and dance around the condo with her later.

August 1

The baby has started to eat real food. Though "real food" might be an exaggeration. She now eats mashed peas, mashed corn, mashed everything and anything. Nanny Mimi tells me she's going to make homemade food for the baby, because it's healthier. She makes it in the blender (I didn't even know we had a blender. "I found it under the sink!" Nanny Mimi announced) and spoons the mashed food into ice-cube trays to freeze. Nanny Mimi, who must think I'm an idiot, has labeled all the trays—peas, corn, and squash. All I have to do, she explains, is microwave a couple of cubes and feed them to her.

I thank her for making all the homemade food, thinking, "Seriously, is this *Little House on the Prairie* or something?"

5 P.M.

"Where are you?" the Fiancé asks, calling me on my cell phone.

"I'm at the grocery store with the baby," I answer.

"What? Why?" he asks, as if I've just told him I was in space. Sure, I'm no cook—not that this is something I'm proud of—but boiling a pot of water to sterilize bottles was a big deal for me. So is going to the grocery store. In fact, I go very rarely, which is why the Fiancé sounds so stunned when I tell him where I am.

"So, why exactly are you there?" he asks.

"I'm here because there's no way I'm going to be making homemade baby food."

"What are you talking about?"

"Nanny Mimi made all this homemade baby food and she told me how to make it and I'm not going to do that. You know how I feel about blenders. They should only be used to make milkshakes. So I'm buying jars of baby food." Even taking out frozen cubes of mashed food and putting them in the microwave seems like too much work, especially since all grocery stores offer organic everything now, including baby food. If jars of organic baby food are good enough for other babies, then they are certainly good enough for mine.

"Hey," I say, "what time are you coming home?"

"I'll be home when I get home."

"So around what time?"

"As soon as I can get out of here," he says.

He should at least be happy I'm no longer asking him if I'm fat. And yes, my hair has stopped falling out.

Now, like Ronnie warned me, I have ugly tufts of hair growing at my hairline. But at least it's growing back in. Now, if only the Dictator's hair will start to grow, I'll be really happy.

7 P.M.

The Fiancé has arrived home.

"What are you doing?" he asks. I'm hiding the jars of baby food that I purchased at the grocery store in a back cupboard above the stove.

"I'm hiding the food because I don't want Nanny Mimi to see that I've bought jars of baby food after she told me homemade food is better for babies and she spent so much time making it and explaining to me how to make it myself."

"You're ridiculous. Do you think she'll really care?" he asks.

Maybe I am being ridiculous. But I don't want to hurt Nanny Mimi's feelings. I figure, on weekdays the baby will eat Nanny Mimi's homemade food. But on weekends she'll eat the jars of baby food. Nanny Mimi will be none the wiser.

August 15

Feeding the baby is the longest process in the world. I have little patience for feeding this baby. I've watched Nanny Mimi feed the baby, and sometimes they sit there for almost two hours. I don't sit down anywhere for two hours, for any reason, except for *American Idol* specials. And the baby hates wearing bibs now. I'm sorry, but if you're eating mashed blueberries and mashed squash and you're eating it with your hands, you kind of need a bib.

The baby doesn't understand this. So we get into battles every mealtime. But, just as she fought me over wearing sun hats in Maui, I'm still stronger than she is, and bigger too, so I always win the bib wars.

September 15

"Why is she being like that?"

"Teething!"

"Man, you're really going to have to come up with something else soon," the Fiancé says.

It's true. My baby's teeth are almost all in.

What will I blame her crankiness on next? I'll have to come up with something.

September 17

The baby is no longer a baby. Or is she? She can walk on her own. She's like a mini-person now. Sometimes I look at her and think, "How is it you came out of me?"

October 1

I tell the Fiancé we have to do something to celebrate the Dictator's birthday in two weeks.

"Do we have to?" he asks. "It's not like she understands what a birthday is."

"I know. But it's not really for her. It's for your parents and our friends. I mean, we have to do something. That's what parents do. They celebrate their kids' birthdays and have parties."

"Who would we invite?" he asks.

This is a good question. The baby doesn't really have any friends. We made it to only two out of the eight Mommy & Me music classes, so, needless to say, I didn't make any friends there and neither did the Dictator. "Don't worry about it. I'll figure it out," I tell the Fiancé.

"I know what that means," he says. "I know I'm going to have to end up doing everything."

"Come on! It will be fun," I say.

Or it might not be. But you have to have a birthday party. You just have to. That's what parents do. You have a kid and you throw birthday parties for her. They're like mini-weddings. You don't do it necessarily for yourself. You have them to show off.

October 15

The baby is one year old today, and we're having her birthday party. I can't believe one year has gone by. It's seems like the time went so fast but, at the same time, took, like, seven years.

We're pretty sure, since she giggles looking at plants and stop signs, that she doesn't understand what this day means. We're pretty sure she has no idea she's been with us for 365 days. But still. How could we pretend today is just any other day? I had made a list of people to invite. There was Tammy and Bob and their newborn. There's my gym trainer, a single mother, who is bringing her two-year-old over (you know you're really desperate to invite people with kids when you're inviting your personal trainer and her kid to your daughter's birthday party). And that's about it for kids. (Mental note: I must make more friends with children.) We've also invited a number of the Fiancé's colleagues and their wives. Basically, this one-year-old birthday party has turned into an adult cocktail party—with three kids on the invite list, one of them the birthday girl.

We hold the party at four o'clock, in hopes that people will leave by six. We've laid out plates of pâté and cheese and crackers.

At four o'clock the first guest arrives. It's one of the Fiancé's colleagues.

"What the hell is that?" I ask, opening the door for him and taking a box the size of a refrigerator he's holding in front of him.

"It's the baby's birthday present," he says, laughing, like I'm an idiot.

"No, I mean what exactly did you buy her?"

"You'll see," he says.

The Fiancé and I look at each other. It is possibly the biggest box in the world. And it's heavy.

"What is it?" I ask again.

"Open it and you'll see," says the Fiancé's colleague. I grab a knife and start ripping open the box. Inside there is a kitchen. Yes, a full-fledged plastic kitchen. My immediate thought is "Fuck, this is going to take three years to put together." My second thought is "Where the hell are we going to put this thing?" My third thought is "Well, it is kind of cute."

About twenty friends and relatives, plus the two kids, arrive to celebrate. As far as children's birthday parties go, it is a success. Mostly because all the adults get tipsy. Well, at least it's a successful cocktail party.

The three kids have a great time playing with the huge box the toy kitchen came in. We don't even need the kitchen itself. The Fiancé's colleague could have just bought the Dictator an empty box and she would've been just as happy. In fact, the Fiancé tries to convince his colleague to take the gift back. This kitchen set is bigger than the tent.

We put candles in the cake and take the absolutely must-have photo of the baby putting her hand in the cake. It has to be done. Most of the adults leave happy (that is, tipsy), and the Dictator got a crapload of gifts.

"This is great," I tell the Fiancé once everyone has gone. "We won't have to buy her another toy for like a year." This is why, I'm convinced, people have birthday parties for babies who don't understand what birthday parties are. It's all about the presents.

"You just like the idea of presents," the Fiancé says.

"So?"

"I'm going to kill him," the Fiancé says of his colleague who bought the mammoth toy kitchen. "Look how big this thing is."

"Well, the baby seems to love it," I tell him. It's true. After the party, the Fiancé's father and Nanny Mimi put the new kitchen together. It takes two and a half hours.

The Fiancé sits staring at the toy kitchen with a look on his face that says, "The world is against me."

October 16

"This is not how people live!" the Fiancé complains, walking around the condo and shaking his head. "It's like Gymboree in here!" (I had no idea he even knew what Gymboree was. I'm impressed.)

It doesn't bother me so much that our condo is now overrun with a mammoth toy kitchen and tents and puzzles and children's books and swings and stuffed toy ponies and diapers and wipes. But the Fiancé is freaking out about how messy our place has become. I decide to be helpful and do some organizing.

An hour later he finds me hovering over a black duffel bag that has been sitting in our hallway for months.

"What's that bag?" he asks.

"It's the duffel bag from when I went to the hospital when I gave birth. I never unpacked it," I tell him.

I can't believe what is in the duffel bag when I ruffle through it. There are three pairs of pajamas, dozens of pairs of socks and underwear, and a hardcover book that hasn't been cracked open. What had I been thinking, packing all that stuff? It looks like I packed to go on a vacation instead of to the hospital to have a C-section. Was I really so naïve that I thought I could read a book in the hospital right after giving birth? "I can't believe I brought a book. What was I thinking?" I say to the Fiancé.

"We really had no idea," the Fiancé says. "Did we?"

"No idea," I say.

I stop looking through the bag and head to the living room to watch some television. It's only been twelve months since I gave birth. What's the hurry to unpack now?

October 17

The Fiancé has tripped on a jumbo-puzzle piece in the hallway.

"I can't stand this anymore!" he yells. "We have to move!"

Our entire condo is now a playroom. The dark, masculine shades of the bachelor condo have been replaced by bright-colored toys, the ExerSaucer, the play kitchen, baby blankets, toy cars, balls of all shapes and sizes. Oh, and how could I forget? The tent. The damn tent! No longer is this place a bachelor pad. It's Romper Room. It seems that every time I take a step, my feet land on some battery-operated toy that makes a noise. Living like this is starting to drive me crazy too.

The Dictator has really, really taken over. She's not only taken over our lives, she's taken over our home.

"We have to move," the Fiancé says again. "I can't stand it.

I'm losing my mind. I'm going to start looking at houses tomorrow."

"Yes, we have to move," I finally agree. "Hey, if we move into a house, can I get a dog?" I love dogs.

He walks away muttering something under his breath. I think he said, "Yeah, that's all we need."

Sheesh. You'd think I'd just asked him if we could have another baby or something.

Ten Mommy Moments People "Forget" to Mention

1. Your baby will have a better wardrobe than you.
2. You will find Cheerios in your underwear.
3. You will still feel clueless about mothering.
4. A portable DVD player is one heck of a great invention.
5. There are professional male babyproofers. Who are hot.
6. You will be guilted into babyproofing your entire house, including your bath mat.
7. Strollers will break.
8. You will not like when others dress your baby like a mini Britney Spears.
9. Reading a newspaper will become a painful experience.
10. Your baby will hurt herself falling on her face. Or be just fine.

The Eighth Trimester (12 to 15 Months)

Babyproofers, Electronic Babysitters, Busted Bugaboo Frogs

December 15

6 P.M.

"Where are you going?" asks the Fiancé.

"We're going to see Santa," I say, holding the cell to my ear while driving.

"Beck! Didn't you just go see Santa yesterday?" the Fiancé asks.

"Yes. But you saw the photo."

"And?"

"Well, you could practically see the snot coming out of the Dictator's nose she was crying so hard."

"And?"

"Well, it was a bad picture! I don't want a picture of my child—our child—sitting on Santa's lap with snot on her face. Do you?"

I drove to the mall only yesterday to have the baby's photograph taken with Santa because (a) Santa can be found in an indoor mall and it's freezing outside, and (b) getting a photo taken with Santa is something to do with the baby.

I have started to find the hours between 4 P.M. and 9 P.M., the time from when Nanny Mimi goes home to when the baby goes to bed, very l-o-n-g.

Now that the baby is actually more like a human being—she can walk, she's starting to talk—she gets bored. She's no longer happy playing on the bed while I watch Oprah and reruns of *Friends*. She needs to be moving, all the time, and I like tiring her out, because she falls asleep so much faster when she's had an action-packed day.

I know it's pathetic that we're visiting Santa again, especially since we're Jewish. But I want a picture of my child sitting *smiling* on Santa's lap. Every mother needs to have her child sit on Santa's lap, and get a photo of the experience, at least once. Plus, Santa is nondenominational, isn't he?

The line to sit on Santa's lap, once again, is longer than any line for any ride at Disney World. I try to remain calm and think of the positive reasons we're here for a second time. It'll teach the baby patience, for one. You get free candy canes (that's for me). And one day, Santa will teach the Dictator the difference between good and bad.

After fifty-five minutes, we reach Santa. The Dictator doesn't cry when I plop her on his lap. Well, not immediately anyway. But just as the elf is about to shoot the photo, I see the baby's face crunch up as she holds her hands out to me. I know what's coming and I know what she wants. She wants me. She wants me to sit on Santa's lap too, and if I refuse, she'll start bawling. So I also sit on Santa's lap. The elf photographer clicks. We are finished in fifteen seconds. I look like crap in the photograph. In fact, we both look grumpy. The Dictator has this evil look on her face, like "Why the fuck are we here again?" And the look on my face says, "How the hell did I wind up here again?"

No worries. We'll just come back tomorrow and try again. I'm going to keep on dragging the Dictator back, until we get the shot I'm happy with. No, I'm not obsessive. Not at all.

This must be the reason Santa Claus hits the malls December 1. It's not that there are so many children. It's because all parents take their children to see Santa numerous times until they get the good photograph.

We get home at 7:30 P.M. I feed and bathe the baby, and it's bedtime. See how time flies when you have a plan?

December 19
10 P.M.

"What is that?" whispers the Fiancé.

"What is what?" I ask, also whispering.

I'm sorting through the baby's clothes. It's hard to see what I'm looking at and what I'm packing. The only light in the room is from a dull Elmo night-light. A birthday candle would give off more light than this night-light.

As I continue to pack, I can't help but ask myself, somewhat bitterly, how the baby got a larger wardrobe than mine. It doesn't seem fair. I've found shirts and pants that the baby has worn only once. In fact, there are items in her closet—including a really cute pink raincoat and a beautiful white knitted sweater—that still have the price tags attached and are now way too small for her. She's growing out of clothes before she even gets a chance to wear them!

The baby also has fourteen pairs of shoes. Seriously. When did that happen? How did I allow that to happen? If anyone in this family should have fourteen pairs of shoes, it should be me. It definitely should not be a one-year-old.

I think it's time for me to get new clothes and new shoes. The

Fiancé is nattering away about something, so I can't escape into my daydream about coming home with twelve bags of clothes and five shoe boxes.

"Hello? Earth to Beck! That thing over there. Are we taking it or not?" the Fiancé whispers again.

We are, if you haven't figured out, in the baby's room. The baby is sound asleep. We do not want the baby to wake up, because we want to go to bed ourselves soon. There is nothing worse than finally getting into bed, only to have the baby wake up. Nothing.

"You mean the Diaper Genie?" I whisper. "Of course we're taking it." Duh.

"Oh. Why are we taking it? Have we even used it yet?" he asks.

I look at him like he's crazy, but I don't think he can see my expression in the dark room. "No, we haven't used it yet," I whisper.

"So, why are we taking it, then?" he asks.

"Because we just are," I say, slightly annoyed. I always get slightly irritated when I'm reminded of, or asked about, the Diaper Genie. That damn useless Diaper Genie I've become so attached to seeing.

"Okay," he says. "We'll take it. If you insist."

"I insist. We're not going to have a garbage chute anymore, you know. We might need it," I explain. "Or else we'll be running out to the garage with the baby's dirty diapers seventeen times a day."

I've long given up trying to figure out how the stupid Diaper Genie works. But that doesn't mean I want it out of my life entirely. The Diaper Genie has become something akin to a birthmark. You might have hated it growing up, but it becomes a defining part of you as you get older, so you don't want to get rid of it. Plus, like I said, we're not going to have a garbage chute at our new house.

"Okay, but it seems silly to take it with us if we haven't used it and we've had it for more than a year," the Fiancé says. "Are you sure?" God, he can be such a lawyer.

"I will figure out how to use it," I say, sounding more confident than I feel. "I will."

"Sure, Beck. Sure you will. And you'll also start putting the cap back on the toothpaste and stop leaving wet towels on the bed."

"I will!" I say loudly.

"Shh! You don't want to—"

"I know, I know, wake the baby."

"Let's go to bed. We've done enough, I think. Ah, thank God, the Dictator is still asleep," he says. We've been calling the baby "the Dictator" more and more often, because as she gets older, she gets more and more demanding. Yes, it's all about her. We are her slaves.

I am very tired. It's been a long day.

But we're finally moving. We found a house that both the Fiancé and I could agree on. Meaning the architecture is modern (which the Fiancé wanted) and I got good vibes from walking around the house when the real estate agent showed it to us. Which surprised even me after we found out why the owners were selling the beautiful house, and wanted it to sell quickly. They were going through a nasty divorce, according to our real estate agent. They wanted to split the money from the sale of the house and get it over with, the quicker the better. (I also try not to think that the Fiancé and I are a lot like Brad Pitt and Jennifer Aniston. Pitt was all about the aesthetics of their house, and Jen just wanted a comfortable couch to sit on. And we all know how that marriage turned out, don't we?)

But the Fiancé and I will not turn out to be just another Brad and Jennifer. So what if another couple ended their marriage in this house? We're not even married yet.

Our new house has four bedrooms, four washrooms, a kitchen, a living room, and a finished basement with a fifth washroom/shower and bedroom. It's definitely a house you could raise more than one child in.

I did not mention this little fact to the Fiancé during the buying process. I know the suggestion that we might want to make our family bigger isn't something the Fiancé would like to hear.

It's because of the Dictator—and all her crap—that we had to move to a bigger place in the first place. The Fiancé could have happily lived in his very male-decorated condo for the rest of his life, if it weren't for the Dictator.

Another great thing about this house, aside from the fact we can now throw all of the Dictator's toys into the basement, so they're out of sight and out of mind, is the fact that the Dictator will not be in the room beside us, separated only by a glass door, as she has been since she was born. Sure, being separated by only a glass door means we have easy access to her. But it also means that if she even turns over in her sleep, sneezes, or moans, we can hear her. Needless to say, the Fiancé and I haven't had a good night's sleep in, um, well, since the baby was born a year and three months ago. Not that I'm counting or anything.

In our new home, there are three doors separating her bedroom from ours. Yippee! Of course, the Fiancé and I will never close any of those doors, because we do need to hear the baby crying out at night. We're not that cruel. It's just nice knowing we have the option. It's like having the option to do all your banking online. You might not feel comfortable doing it, but it's nice knowing that if you want to, you could.

After two months of renovations—making the kitchen area

a little larger, getting new marble countertops, new wooden floors, upstairs carpeting, and new appliances—we are now ready to actually move in to the house, which we tell ourselves will never look like Romper Room, the way our condo had begun to look, because we have so much more room.

We hired a decorator, who did a fabulous job. She had wonderful ideas, which were sometimes very extravagant. I said, "Uh, thanks but no thanks!" to the chandelier she suggested for the Dictator's room. It was a beautiful chandelier, no doubt about it. It was also eight thousand dollars. No doubt about it, there was no way we were going to shell out eight thousand dollars for a chandelier . . . especially for the baby's room. The Fiancé agreed 100 percent. What kind of one-year-old, who loves putting two fingers in her nostrils as a joke, needs an eight-thousand-dollar chandelier in her bedroom? We are definitely not a royal family, though the Fiancé has started to call the baby "Princess" as a term of affection. (I am only slightly miffed that he has started to use this pet name for the Dictator. He had been calling me "Princess" forever. I just don't think there is any non-psychotic way I can bring it up. What could I say? "You used to call only me 'Princess,' but it seems you call everyone you know 'Princess' now"? I've even heard him call his mother "Princess.")

Anyway, we have now spent an incredibly long day packing. For us, that means throwing a lot of clothes and books into garbage bags. Hey, whatever works, right? The movers will do the rest.

I hear the Fiancé brushing his teeth and getting into bed as I check on the baby one more time, to make sure she's still breathing, a habit that I haven't broken yet. I don't think it's necessarily a bad habit, like smoking, which I have, mostly, quit. The baby looks so peaceful when she sleeps. It almost erases any of the bad thoughts I had about her while I was trying to get her to sleep only hours ago. I leave her room with a warm feeling in my heart. Sleeping babies have that effect on you. You love them a lot when they're sleeping.

I wash my face and brush my teeth. The lights are still on when I walk into our bedroom and sit on the bed. The Fiancé is already under the covers. First I take off my grungy packing clothes, starting with my army pants and ratty T-shirt. Then I take off my bra and underwear.

I once was so embarrassed for the Fiancé to see me getting undressed. It's funny how things change. Maybe it's because the Fiancé has now seen me at my very worst (with the catheter bag hanging from me after my C-section, never a pleasant sight).

I've noticed that he's definitely more used to doing things he once considered private in front of me. Yesterday, for example, he clipped his toenails in bed. I wasn't as grossed out as I thought I would—and should—be. It actually felt kind of nice, realizing he now felt that relaxed around me. Unless clipping his toenails in front of me means he really no longer cares what I think about him. Argh!

I will not be paranoid.

"Nice," the Fiancé says, laughing. I turn to look at him and see he's gawking at my ass. It's all right by me for him to gawk at my ass and say "Nice." But it's most certainly not all right for him to gawk at my ass, say "Nice," and then break into laughter.

"What? Please don't make fun of my ass," I moan to him. I'm in no mood for any stupid ass comments or jokes—or any discussion about my ass for any reason whatsoever. I don't want to go on and on about my ass, but it still isn't the same as it was pre-pregnancy, when I used to participate in at least three spin classes a week.

Nowadays my butt is much closer to looking like a pancake than melons. I should really, really start getting back into spin classes. It's just that I'm always so tired. I'm starting to think that my friend who had said my ass would never be the same after having a baby was right.

The Fiancé won't stop laughing.

"What is so funny about my ass? Tell me!" I demand.

"You have two Cheerios stuck to your left cheek," he says, and hoots, as if this is funnier than any movie starring Vince Vaughn.

"What? Where?" I ask, reaching my hand around to feel my butt. He's right. I peel off two Cheerios and look at them with awe.

It's astonishing where baby food ends up.

How did two Cheerios get from the baby's high-chair tray into the back of my underwear, sticking to my ass the entire day? I only remember the baby eating Cheerios at breakfast.

And that's not the only thing.

Yesterday I found a sticker on my left boob when I got undressed for bed.

Earlier in the evening the Dictator and I were playing sticker book, where she points to a sticker and I give her the sticker and she puts it in a book. But how did a sticker of a balloon manage to get stuck on my boob, which not only was under my bra but under a shirt too? It's just so odd.

"Come on! It's pretty funny, Beck," says the Fiancé, chortling as one can only chortle when one is *not* the one with Cheerios stuck to one's butt. In principle, since the Fiancé has way hairier butt cheeks, the Cheerios should be sticking to his ass, not mine. My ass is really smooth (the one thing it has going for it these days).

"Shut up!" I say.

I like Cheerios. And I am already in bed. What else am I supposed to do with them? I pop them into my mouth.

"You didn't seriously eat them, did you?" the Fiancé asks.

"Yup!"

There's nothing wrong with eating a food that you find on your own behind. That's my theory, and I'm sticking to it.

December 23
9 P.M.

When I think about it, I realize that a lot has changed very quickly over the past couple of months. Not only did we find a new house, but the baby has learned to walk. She is still slightly unsteady, but she's definitely walking. While I don't always walk beside her, I'm definitely always going, "OW, OOH, EEE, watch it!" whenever I'm around her. She falls often. I try not to make a big deal out of it when she falls, but sometimes I think she's very close to giving me a heart attack. It's almost enough for me to wish for the days when all she knew how to do was sit. But I do kind of like that I don't have to hold her every minute of the day.

Babies are more durable than I'd ever imagined. Sometimes, when she falls and hits her head, I expect her to scream and cry so loud that social services will hear her and come take her away. But even though the bang on her head echoes throughout the house, I swear, she actually giggles. She can smack her head on the corner of a glass table and not cry one tear. Then the tiniest bump into the wall can make her wail like Ozzy Osbourne in his heyday. Once again, there's no rhyme or reason to this baby of mine.

One thing that has definitely not changed in our lives, however, is the baby's bottles. She's still using the same bottles and nipples we bought for her before she was born, during our whirlwind "let's-get-everything-we-could-possibly-ever-need-for-the-baby-so-we-don't-have-to-come-back-to-this-store-ever-again" shopping sprees. Which I thought was fine. But then tonight we met Tammy, her husband, and their baby, Zack, who is five months younger than the Dictator, for dinner at a Vietnamese restaurant. "What nipple is she on?" Tammy asked, out of the blue. I've realized that mothers can ask you anything, like "So is she breastfeeding?" or "What nipple is she on?" as easily and breezily as if they were asking you to pass the salt. No question is too personal when you're a mother talking to another mother.

"What do you mean?" I asked.

"What number nipple is she using for her bottle?" Tammy asked.

"There are different-number nipples?" the Fiancé asked Tammy. Thank God, he asked exactly what I was thinking.

"Yes! Of course there are! Zack's on nipple number three," Tammy said. "Let me see her bottle," she said, grabbing the Dictator's bottle and looking at the nipple.

"Oh my God." She laughed. "There's only one hole in this nipple. You're still on number one! Zack's on number three already, and he's five months younger!"

I grabbed Zack's bottle and looked at the nipple, and sure enough, there were three tiny holes, as opposed to the one tiny hole in the Dictator's nipple.

How was I supposed to know that there were different stages of nipples for bottles? Had we been starving the Dictator? No wonder it took her, like, three days to finish one bottle. I was disappointed in myself. I couldn't figure out how to use the stupid Diaper Genie, I had postpartum depression, and I'd had no idea there were different nipples. I was clueless when it came to this mothering thing.

"Don't worry, we'll get some this weekend," the Fiancé said to me quietly, sensing my distress.

"Okay," I said, knowing that this would be one more thing we would never get around to doing. We'd just write "Buy new nipples" on our Things to Do list, which I'll one day start.

How is it that Tammy knew about the different nipples, and I didn't? When it comes to being a new mother, I always feel like the last person to get in on a secret.

December 24
2 P.M.

Not that I didn't have to go shopping for things. When you're a mother, shopping takes on a whole new meaning. Shopping— gasp!—becomes a chore.

The Fiancé and I are Jewish, so we don't celebrate Christmas. We barely celebrate Chanukah either. But we do have to buy one very, very special Christmas present for Nanny Mimi, who is Catholic. Christmas is a big deal to her. But buying her a gift is harder than it would seem.

Nanny Mimi is definitely one of the most important people in our lives. How could she not be, when she takes care of the most important person in our lives? And, to a certain extent, we have to show our appreciation by what we buy her for Christmas. It's not like some other kinds of jobs, where a boss can give you a better title to placate you. Unless we call her Executive Nanny. No, I don't think that would make her any happier. She needs gifts.

The Fiancé and I had the following conversation late last night.

"So what should we get her?" I asked him.

"I don't know."

"Me neither."

"Okay. I'll leave it up to you," he said.

"Well, we definitely have to give her a Christmas bonus like last year."

"Right. Do you remember how much we gave her?"

"No."

"Me neither."

"Was it a thousand?" I had asked.

"I think it was $750."

"Wait. I think it was $850, because I remember talking about it and how we thought $1,000 was too much but $750 too little," I told him.

"Right. So how much should we give her this year, $850 again?" the Fiancé said.

"Don't we have to give her a bit more this year?"

"Do we?"

"I don't know. Do we?"

"I don't know. We should also get her something from the Dictator," I said.

"So, how much should we give her if we also get her a present from the Dictator?"

"Maybe we should give her a thousand."

"Why?"

"Because she works so hard, she's never asked for a day off, she's never been sick, and I trust her entirely to take care of the Dictator."

"Right. Okay. A thousand it is."

"Or do you think that's too much?"

And on and on it went. Really, we spent less time talking about the car I got than we did talking about Nanny Mimi's Christmas bonus. I wish I knew more about the etiquette of Christmas presents for nannies.

But here I am at the mall, on the worst shopping day of the

year, to buy a present for a holiday we don't even celebrate. I rush around the department store like crazy, picking out clothes I'd like for me.

I don't want to suggest that Nanny Mimi is like Jennifer Jason Leigh in the movie *Single White Female* (we're not single roommates; she's Filipino), but I've noticed that her fashion has changed since she first began working for us. When I first met her, she was wearing jean overalls, very strong perfume, and her hair was in ponytails. Let's just say that when I bought a puffy winter coat, she then bought a puffy winter coat. I started wearing my boots over my jeans, and then so did she. I had highlights. She got them too. It kind of makes me feel good though. Imitation is the sincerest form of flattery, they say. I just never imagined that it would be a nanny who imitated me. But it does make last-minute shopping a heck of a lot easier, that's for sure. I know that whatever I like, she'll like.

I get home exhausted.

"So, I'm just writing out Mimi's bonus check," the Fiancé says. His office closed early today. "What did we decide to give her again?"

"I don't know!"

Argh!

January 4
3 P.M.

I call and tell my mother about the greatest invention since tampons and individual-size warm lava chocolate dessert cakes: the portable DVD player. It really has changed my life for the better, especially since Nanny Mimi had taken some time off (stupid Christmas holiday and all).

We first saw another couple with a portable DVD player at a restaurant. Their toddler was actually sitting quietly watching a DVD and—gasp!—the couple was doing the impossible. They were eating! We knew that we had to get one. We like to eat when we go to out to, um, eat. So we bought one and have since taken the portable DVD player to many, many restaurants and plopped it on tables. The Fiancé and I have actually had real uninterrupted conversations at restaurants while the Dictator sucks on a sippy cup or a bottle and watches her DVDs. In fact, last night, the Fiancé, the Dictator, and I met Tammy, her husband, and Baby Zack for dinner. Zack watched his *Bob the Builder* DVD on his own portable DVD player and Rowan watched *Dora the Explorer* on her portable DVD player. It's kind of like having a babysitter for forty-five minutes, without having to pay anything.

Other parents who see us eating always come up and ask us about the DVD player, where we got it, and then profess it's such a great idea that they're going to get one. Young waiters and senior citizens stop by our table and ask what the portable DVD player is. I am so pleased with the results of the portable DVD player (not only can we have conversations, but the Dictator is too distracted watching DVDs to pour all the salt and pepper out of their shakers onto the table) that I want to spread the news about them, like juicy gossip.

"You should get one for Michael!" I say excitedly to my mother. Michael is my older brother, who lives in Israel. He's planning to visit my parents with his baby and wife soon. (Hey, it's only a twelve-hour flight. They're not going to need to distract their baby at all! Yes, I'm being sarcastic.)

"I told him about them. But he doesn't believe in them," my mother tells me.

"Doesn't believe in them! What's not to believe in?" I ask, shocked. "So what, then? He believes he's going to read books to his baby for twelve hours? That's so ridiculous," I scoff.

"He refuses to even let me buy one for him as a present," my mother says.

I mean, not believing in God or right-wing politicians is one thing. But how could somebody not believe in portable DVD players? I feel like I don't know my brother at all.

I should really know by now that you can never, ever, assume what people believe in, and what they don't, when it comes to how they want to raise their children.

January 6
11 A.M.

I have to keep reminding myself that our new home, which we have finally entirely moved in to, is a grown-up house. I tell myself I will not allow the Dictator to put stickers on the fridge in the new house like I let her at the old condo. Another thing I have to remind myself of is that we now have two flights of stairs. It's not a lot of stairs for us. But it's definitely a lot of stairs for the Dictator, who, after all, only recently learned to walk and hasn't ever been around stairs before.

"We need to get this place babyproofed," I tell the Fiancé. He's at the stove making us eggs. He's still on winter vacation. The Dictator is snacking on Cheerios and watermelon slices, watching her portable DVD player.

We didn't have any trouble with the Dictator during our first night at our new house. She fell asleep quickly, as if she'd always lived here. I took that to be a good sign.

"Do we really need to?" the Fiancé asks, almost whining.

Then he mentions some friends of his who have two toddlers and have never babyproofed their house.

"I know they didn't, but we're not them," I say, sounding much too mature, and much too much like an overbearing mother, than I want to sound. In fact, I am one step away from actually saying, "Just because your friends didn't babyproof doesn't mean you don't have to. If your friends tried crack cocaine, would you?" Argh!

The Fiancé is very much into decorating and art, which means he very much cares about the aesthetics of our house. To ruin this newly renovated, modern house with safely gates would destroy the whole "mood" and "feel" of the house, in the Fiancé's opinion.

"Listen," I say, like I'm explaining the benefits of brushing your teeth, "we have two flights of stairs now. She's never lived with stairs before. Do you want her to tumble down them and break a bone? And she could lean over the railing upstairs and fall over and kill herself. Then you'll regret not babyproofing. Plus, the gates won't be here forever."

I think the whole "The Baby could kill herself" argument changes his mind. It's really hard to argue with that, even when you are a lawyer.

January 7

Obviously, we need a professional to help us babyproof. We couldn't put the damn Diaper Genie together, and it took us four weeks to assemble the stroller, after all. Both of us together can barely change a lightbulb. There's no way we could put up gates and do any other babyproofing that needs to be done. (Hey, we're talking about the woman who had no idea you were supposed to switch bottle nipples as babies get older.) Luckily, Tammy, who owns an art gallery, is also very into the home aesthetics and didn't like the idea of ruining the look of her house by babyproofing either. She told me about a professional babyproofer who comes to your home, tells you what you need done, and comes back and does it all for you. And supposedly the baby gates aren't white and ugly; they're black or silver and almost cool-looking. All we have to do is call the babyproofer, get him over here, and sign the check.

"He's also so hot! He's a god, that's how good-looking he is," Tammy said when I called to get the babyproofer's number, like she was talking about Jake Gyllenhaal or Johnny Depp. (I didn't mention this part to the Fiancé. I just told him I found a very highly recommended babyproofer.)

I called and made an appointment for this supposedly gorgeous babyproofer to come over.

Who knew there was such a career as a professional babyproofer? Who knew there were men who were super-hot who were professional babyproofers? How much does a professional babyproofer make a year? How did he become a professional babyproofer? A hot male professional babyproofer is kind of fascinating, when you think about it. Have you ever met one at a cocktail party? It's really one of those careers you only realize exist after you have a baby.

January 10
10 A.M.

Three days later, the male oh-so-hot professional babyproofer arrives at our house. The Fiancé, although he usually goes to the gym on Sunday mornings, decides to stay home for this appointment. (Was he worried because the babyproofer was male? Is it now "in" to have an affair with your professional babyproofer, like it once was the stereotype to have an affair with your plumber or gardener?) As soon as I open the door, I realize Tammy was right on the mark.

This isn't just any male professional babyproofer. This is the Calvin Klein underwear model of professional babyproofers.

The Fiancé and I follow him like lost puppies through the house, as he checks each and every room, and each and every nook, for places and things that should be babyproofed. The Dictator follows us from room to room, mostly wanting me to carry her, because she's being shy. (Like most girls do in front of Calvin Klein model–type men, she's acting all coy.) "I'd definitely get a gate here, and here, and here, and here," the oh-so-hot professional babyproofer says, looking at our stairways.

When we enter the Dictator's room, I plop the Dictator down on the floor. She's not as light as she once was. Or am I not as strong as I once was? I make a mental note to call the trainer and ask her to make me work on my biceps. You hear how new mothers' arms are so strong and buff because they're always carrying their babies and strollers. This hasn't happened to my arms, just like my hair never got shiny during pregnancy, just like a lot of things never happened that people said would.

"And this window here," continues the oh-so-hot professional babyproofer, turning his attention to the floor-to-ceiling window, which opens at the floor with a knob and looks out onto a large concrete patio in our backyard. "I'd get a lock on this window, because she'll be able to turn the knob and open it. And if she opens it, then she'll be able to push through the screen, and you don't want her to fall out the window and land on the concrete," the oh-so-hot professional babyproofer says.

"Oh, I don't think we need that," I say. "She doesn't even

know there's a window in her room. She's never even touched the window, let alone the knob."

The oh-so-hot professional babyproofer walks over to the window and kneels down on the floor. He tries turning the knob, which opens the window. "This knob is very easy to turn," he says.

At this point, I start to kind of, maybe, think that this oh-so-hot professional babyproofer is trying to scare us into giving him more money. Now I'm kind of expecting him to tell us to babyproof her washcloths. After all, the entire baby industry, I have realized over the past two years, is based on taking advantage of a parent's fears. That's why there are video baby monitors, a million types of lotions for babies' skin, and hundreds of books that should be titled "How Not to Kill Your Baby in Week Number 20." (You've got to wonder, if a baby born in a hut in a Third World country can live without a video baby monitor and special baby creams, is it possible your baby can too?)

Just as I finish saying that we don't need to babyproof the window, the Dictator crawls up to where the oh-so-hot professional babyproofer is kneeling and starts playing with the knob! Doh!

If the oh-so-hot professional babyproofer hadn't pointed it out, I'm sure she would still be oblivious to the knob and window in her bedroom! Thanks to the oh-so-hot professional babyproofer, the Dictator now knows all about the stupid knob that opens the window! Thanks a lot, Buster!

"Oops! Sorry!" the oh-so-hot babyproofer says. Sure you are. Right. Whatever.

I'm starting to think that this is what an oh-so-hot professional babyproofer does. He comes into your home and basically shows babies all the things that could hurt them, so the parents are forced to babyproof everything. I was on to this oh-so-hot professional babyproofer! Yes, I'm on to you, Buster!

Still, what can I do? The Dictator now knows about the knob, and I am now paranoid that she'll fall out the window onto the concrete patio below.

I write him a large check to babyproof almost everything in our house, including the windows. I don't ever want to think, "I should have listened to the oh-so-hot professional babyproofer!" about anything.

Plus, how often do you get a Calvin Klein underwear model coming over to your house? He says he can come back tomorrow to set it all up. Too bad I won't be around. I'll be at my office working. Nanny Mimi will just have to be the one to enjoy looking at him as he works.

January 11
10 A.M.

I've been back at work full-time for a while now. And I'm back with a vengeance. Or at least I'd like to be. I've been trying. I'm still depressed, not so much on the outside, but sometimes I can feel "it"—the sadness—pulling at me, tugging at me, like a pesky younger brother you're trying to shake off so you can go play with your friends.

I try not to think of the depression and that it seems to be lasting longer than I thought it would. I know if I keep my mind occupied, there's a greater chance I won't be sucked in, at least not to the great depths of despair I used to feel.

I have not told any of my bosses that I'm suffering from postpartum depression. Any kind of depression, no matter how widely discussed in the media, is a hard thing to admit to and explain, especially to work people. I am pretty sure no one at my job would understand what I'm going through, and I'm pretty sure I can't explain it to people as clearly as I want to.

It's not completely fair to say my bosses wouldn't and couldn't understand. I guess I don't know how they would react. But I don't plan on telling them. I feel that admitting I'm suffering from postpartum depression will make them believe I'm not up to working hard, which is not exactly the case. Though I am often depressed, thankfully I can still get out of bed most days (though it is sometimes hard). I can still drive to my office and work. Keeping busy helps keep my mind off the sadness. So I especially want to keep busy at my job. In my industry (or is it the case in most industries?) there's always someone ready to take over your job in a second, which is why most career women who have babies can't stand being away on maternity leave. There's this paranoia that even though the law protects women on maternity leave, their job won't be there for them when they get back. I want to work hard. I want to work this PPD right out of my hair.

It's difficult though, because even though I want to work hard, it almost seems to me that because I'm a mother, my bosses won't let me work as hard as I once did. Am I being paranoid?

I try not to feel paranoid, not to feel as if suddenly my editors think that I'm no longer as valuable as I once was because I had a baby. The problem is, I don't think I'm being entirely paranoid. Some of them, I'm convinced, are treating me differently. And not in a good way. Suddenly, I no longer get calls to do the good stories, or stories that would require travel out of town (not that I would necessarily take those assignments, but it would be nice to be asked. You know, the whole isn't-it-better-to-be-asked-on-bad-dates-than-on-no-dates-at-all thing?). It's almost like I'm starting back on square one at work. Although I don't have to prove I'm worthy because all the editors know me, I feel I do have to prove I'm still worthy since I've become a mother.

Some days I want to shake some of my editors and scream, "There are laws! You can't treat me differently! There are laws!" Why is it people believe that just because you've had a baby, all your attention is now on the baby and that's all?

But then I also start to think that maybe my paranoia is all because of my postpartum depression. My thoughts go round and round in a vicious circle.

Why hasn't having this beautiful baby made me prioritize what's important in my life? I know the Dictator is more important than anything. She is definitely more important than work. So why am I not thinking, "Well, who cares how things are going at work right now? I have a beautiful baby"? Why am I thinking, "I am still *the same* person I was—skinnier even—before I gave birth"? And "I am still that same hardworking, overly ambitious writer who always got her work in by deadline"? And "Why does the baby being the *most* important mean work issues should be *un*important?"

I have discussed these feelings endlessly with the Fiancé. I rant. And rave. And rant and rave some more. And then some more. And then even more. "Can you believe in this day and age women are still treated like second-class citizens when they come back from maternity leave? It's because most of the editors are *male* and the women I have to work with never had children, so *no one* understands!" I'll cry. Or "Why aren't there more women with babies who work in newspapers?" The Fiancé tries to tell me that I've always been self-sufficient and that I'll make them remember how good and hardworking I am and that maybe I should take more initiative on my own. Maybe he's right. He usually is.

So I decide to pitch some story ideas, which go something like this:

1. Yoga classes for babies: There are so many of these classes now, and so many stores have yoga clothes for babies. Why it's important, what type of women go, and how much does dressing your baby for yoga cost?
2. Sign language classes for kids: Apparently, you can teach your kid to sign, "I want a boob. I'm hungry!" Debra Messing, of *Will & Grace*, taught her little boy to sign.
3. Designer jeans for babies: They can cost up to $250 a pop. Now four-year-olds know what Seven jeans are. What this means for modern mothers.

My story ideas, I realize, are so different from the ones I used to pitch. In fact, all I want to do is write about mothering and babies. Babies and mothering are really all I'm interested in now. While I used to want to be up to date on all the latest designer jeans, now all I want to do is be up to date on all the designer *children's* jeans. I'm pretty excited about my pitches, until I get an e-mail back from an editor at the paper.

"We already did that story a couple of months ago," this editor writes about the yoga classes for babies. The e-mail feels like it was shot out of a gun, it seems so terse. I've been in this business for a long time. I know this editor must be thinking, "You haven't been reading the paper! It's your job, being in the newspaper business, to read the newspapers!"

"I guess I was on maternity leave when it was published," I shoot back in an e-mail. "Sorry!"

The truth is, I find it nearly impossible to read newspapers now, even though they are my bread and butter. It's just that newspapers are always filled with horrific stories. There are bad mothers out there, who leave their two-year-olds alone for five days so they can party with boyfriends. There are fathers kidnapping their children during awful child-custody battles. There are children born with severe deformities and others dying at age fourteen, in gym class, for no apparent reason. There are house fires that kill children while their mother is out of town. There are twelve-year-old gang members, and teachers sleeping with students. I never noticed how many awful stories about children there were until I had a baby. Now my eyes are drawn only to these stories. I can't control it. The only thing I can control is whether I pick up the paper at all, or at least whether I look at the news pages. So that's what I do now.

Now when I read the newspaper, I try to only read movie and book reviews, which do not make me feel bad, sad, and worried about the Dictator's future and house fires. I really don't know how parents can deal if their children die before them. I wonder about these parents who are mourning these terrible tragedies. I don't know them. But their stories make me really, really sad. I can't help but feel so relieved that nothing like the terrible stories in the newspapers has happened to the Dictator. I also don't want to be reminded that bad things could happen, that one day she could join a gang, or be kidnapped. It makes me sick to think about it.

Again, I can't help but wonder if it's postpartum depression that makes me feel like this, or if all mothers feel this way about the news section of papers. Surely some mothers out there read the news pages. Or maybe all mothers just read lifestyle stories. Nice, light, lifestyle stories about dog shows.

January 13
11 A.M.

Being back at work, with not so much to do, also means I get to procrastinate again. I'm thinking about which friend to call when, just that second, my cell phone starts to vibrate. It's my friend Marci, who moved to take on a new job in a different city than mine.

"How are you?" I ask excitedly. "How's the man?" The last time we spoke, she had been boasting about a new guy she'd been seeing for three weeks. It had seemed promising, as most relationships do at the beginning with Marci.

"He broke up with me!" she says immediately. "I think."

"You think?"

"Yes, I think. He turned out to be such an asshole," she says miserably.

"Are you okay? Are you okay?" I ask. "Tell me what happened."

She explains the situation. As breakups go, it's not an original, by a long shot. Basically, this guy, after three months of blissful dating, went AWOL on her. He won't return her calls. He won't respond to her e-mails. She has even dropped by his house and heard him rummaging around inside. He didn't answer the doorbell, though she rang it seventeen times. He has numerous belongings of hers held hostage.

I try my best to cheer her up, saying the usual things: "You deserve better." "He's such a jerk." "Men are tricky." "You'll meet someone when you least expect it."

She sighs and says, "I know. I know," like she's heard them all a million times before. Which she probably has.

It's at times like these, hearing stories like this from my single friends, that I am reminded it's nice to have a partner and a child. It's nice not having drama. It's nice knowing that I'll never be in the situation where I'll fall in love with a man who holds my belongings hostage.

"Are you sure you're okay? Really? Are you sure?" I ask her. I can't believe the tone of my voice. God, when did I start talking to grown women in a baby voice? I'm asking her "Are you sure you're okay?" in the same tone I use for the the baby when she walks into the countertop.

I remember one of my colleagues, a mother, telling me that when she went to meetings, she found herself asking others, "Are you hungry? Do you want something to eat now?" in the same tone she used with her three-year-old. I guess it happens to the best of us. I almost ask Marci if she would like to put her head in my lap and have me run my fingers though her hair.

1 P.M.

I decide to call Lena, my best *single* and very outrageous friend. Lena and I do talk quite often. She's definitely the one single friend who has made a point of keeping in regular contact with me. She's forty years old but looks thirty. She's just never met the right man so has never really "settled" down in the traditional sense. I feel bad for her sometimes because when she goes out, and meets a potential, she feels the need to tell him her age. She thinks it's not fair, because she looks so much younger than her actual years, not to let men know how old she is. This is because she wants to make it clear that it may be very difficult for her to have babies, in case they're looking for a woman to be the mother of their child. This can be very awkward because she also tells them the reason she's telling them her age—the possibility that she will not be able to conceive. Funnily enough, many men, upon hearing talk of babies, even talk of the possibility of no babies, run for their lives. But some don't. And Lena has a very active social life, which sometimes makes me jealous, even if the men don't last.

Lena is working on a book and has decided to give up on men, at least for the time being. "You know, it's like having a baby. You think about it all the time, you slave over it, and it takes years to turn into something you love," she tells me.

I don't tell her that at least her book doesn't require diaper changes. And you can go out and leave a book unattended. And a book can't pick up a crayon and write all over your walls. I do tell her that I've done something very stupid.

"What? What did you do?"

"I sent an evil, stupid, very mean e-mail to my boss, telling him that I wasn't being treated properly and there were laws that protect me after coming back from maternity leave. I'm so stupid."

"No, you're not."

"Oh, yes. Yes I am. I'll probably be fired."

"What exactly did you write?" Lena asks.

"I don't even know. I swear, after I sent it I deleted it in my sent file so I couldn't reread it. I regretted it the minute I sent it. All I know is that I went on a rampage about how some of my editors weren't treating me the same. I couldn't stop myself!"

"Well, if that's how you feel."

"It's not that simple. I'm not quite sure they are treating me differently. It's just this feeling I get."

"Well, you're usually right with your feelings. That's what's so great about you. If you don't like how someone's treating you, you let them know."

"Yeah, I guess. I just know nothing is going to come of it. It's a losing battle."

"Well, you never know."

"Oh, I know."

Stupid e-mail. I contemplate sending another one to the editor explaining that I have been diagnosed with postpartum depression and I'd like to take my previous e-mail back. But I don't. Like I said, I don't want pity. I just want to be treated like I was before I gave birth. I look at my screen saver, a beautiful photograph of the Dictator, and feel a little better about life. Fuck my editors. I have a beautiful baby.

3:30 P.M.

Guess what? My beautiful baby is . . . just below average! A round of drinks for everyone, on me! Did you hear the news? My child is just below average!

"Our child is not a genius, not advanced, not even average! She's slightly below average," I say to the Fiancé, who is at work.

"What are you talking about?" he asks. He sounds flustered, like he has a lot of papers on his desk and a lot of work to do. I hate him for having a lot of work to do. Well, I'm a little envious of him, because what I had just done was pretty ridiculous. Even more ridiculous than sending that rant of an e-mail to my boss.

"I did one of those baby-IQ tests," I tell him, which is what one does when one most certainly does not have a lot of work to do. It's so funny to think that when you have a lot of work to do, you hate it. But when you don't have any work to do, you also hate it.

"Why did you go and do that?" he asks.

"I don't know. I was bored. I found it on the Internet. They ask questions like 'Can your child point to objects you point out?' and 'Can your child build a tower with blocks?' " I explain.

"And then you add up the results and it will tell you if your baby is a genius, or, in our case, just below average."

"You can't trust a baby-IQ test on the Internet," he says.

"Why can't you?"

"Because she's too young to be tested for IQ. Shouldn't you be working?"

"Thanks for reminding me," I say. "I should be working. I'm getting paid to be working. But my work, apparently, doesn't need me anymore. I don't have anything to do," I moan. "Which is why I am doing IQ tests for the baby!"

"Beck, did you pitch stories?"

"Yes, I did. I guess I'll just wait until I hear back from them. But waiting for them is depressing me. It really feels like they are treating me differently," I tell him for the millionth time.

"We can talk more about that later at home. Why don't you enjoy yourself, then? Go get a massage or something."

"Maybe," I say.

"Good. I'll speak to you later. I have a ton to do. And stop playing with the Internet!"

"Yippee for you," I think. "It's so much easier being a man," I also think. He didn't seem worried at all about our child being below average. I don't really care either. In fact, we have often talked about what kind of child we want. We both agree that we want a sweet, nice, happy child above everything else. We also want her to be smart, but not necessarily a genius. We want her to be good-looking but not too good-looking. I once said to the Fiancé, "I kind of hope she turns out to be the geeky book type. That way, I won't have to worry about her staying out all night and missing her curfew and having sex."

"Well, geeky book types do have sex," he responded. Right. Of course they do.

January 13

7 P.M.

The Fiancé is royally pissed off. You'd think it was his car that had a tire slashed, not the baby's stroller. Somehow, one of the tires on our Bugaboo Frog—the Porsche of all strollers—has been puntured. For the past few days we've been using a crappy twenty-eight-dollar stroller.

Nanny Mimi told me about the tire more than a week ago. But because the Fiancé and I are not good at that whole "getting right on it" thing, Nanny Mimi had to remind me about it again a couple of days ago, and then again two days ago, and again yesterday. It was definitely time to take action. There is nothing worse than being reminded, over and over, that you haven't done something that really does need to be looked after. Nanny Mimi, for the past week, has been unable to take the baby for long walks, thanks to the flat stroller tire. (You get a backache using the twenty-eight-dollar stroller, because the handles are so low down, you have to bend to push.) "What happened?" I remember asking Nanny Mimi last week, when she first told me about the tire. I remember thinking, "Do I have enemies who would really slash the tire of my baby's stroller? Does the Fiancé? Does Nanny Mimi? Does the Dictator have enemies?"

"I think I pushed it over a broken beer bottle," she said, just as I was imagining an envious knife-wielding mother running around the park looking to slash stroller tires.

Anyway, the Fiancé spent two hours yesterday, leaving early from work, trying to find a replacement wheel for the Bugaboo Frog. This is harder than you'd expect. I, too, had called a number of stores, with no happy results. Having a slashed Bugaboo Frog tire is almost like having a Porsche and the dealership saying, "We can fix your engine, but because you have a Porsche, we'll have to order the parts from overseas and it will be ready in three weeks."

Of course, it's not like there's a rental-stroller place. If Nanny Mimi wants to take the baby anywhere that requires a long walk, we need to either find a new wheel or get a new stroller.

The Bugaboo Frog didn't come cheap, so we really didn't want to buy a new stroller. The Fiancé ended up taking it to a bicycle store and an employee somehow patched up the tire. The Fiancé feels he wasted enough time finding someone who could fix a stroller tire, so he was happy when I called him this morning at work to tell him the patched tire was working out great.

He is far from happy when I call him again, a couple of hours later, to tell him that it's no longer working and that we have another flat. (Seriously, flat stroller tires? What is happening to our lives?) The Fiancé, like I've said, is not good at fixing things and gets even more annoyed when something is fixed but doesn't stay fixed.

"We'll get a new stroller," he finally says. "That's it. I don't want to hear anything about the fucking broken stroller anymore."

We go shopping after work. Nanny Mimi stays late with the baby. We end up shelling out another $850 for another Bugaboo Frog. It is Nanny Mimi, in fact, who, when we said we were going to get a new stroller, insisted we get a Bugaboo Frog. While it may be a status symbol these days for new parents to have the "in" stroller, it is just as much a status symbol for the nannies who push the strollers around. No joke. Though he would never tell her so the Fiancé is pissed at Nanny Mimi for being so adamant that we buy another Bugaboo Frog. I'm not thrilled about it either, but I want to keep Nanny Mimi happy, because she is a really good nanny, and she's the one pushing the stroller every day. I don't want Nanny Mimi to get mad at us for any reason, because the Fiancé and I would be royally fucked if she decided to quit on us.

"Well, it's because Rowan takes her nap in the stroller, so we need a good one," I tell the Fiancé, sticking up for Nanny Mimi.

"And that's wrong too," the Fiancé argues. "She should be napping in her crib, so she'll get used to it. She shouldn't be getting used to napping in her stroller!"

"Well, can you mention it to Nanny Mimi? She doesn't listen to me," I tell him. I very rarely, if ever, tell Nanny Mimi to do anything.

I agree with the Fiancé that the baby should nap only in her crib. Nanny Mimi doesn't mind walking and pushing the baby around for two or three hours every afternoon while she sleeps, but the Fiancé and I do. It's been a pain in the ass for us recently on weekends, because the baby screams when we try to get her to fall asleep—I mean, put her in her crib—in the afternoon. This is because she's so used to Nanny Mimi letting her nap in the stroller. We want the baby to get used to napping in her crib so we can watch television when she sleeps.

"Why do I have to say something?" he asks. "Why can't you?"

"I have! Trust me on this. She listens to you way more than she listens to me. She still gets nervous around you, and she's been with us for more than a year!" I've noticed that the odd time the Fiancé is still home when Nanny Mimi arrives at 8 A.M., she's always super-friendly to him and overly eager to please, rushing around, scrubbing the counters or folding laundry. I guess she knows who writes her check, or she thinks she knows. I mean, it could just as easily be me who pays her. I work. I make money. (It's not me who pays her . . . but it could be.) Maybe Nanny Mimi is really just old-fashioned this way, and thinks the man wears the pants in the house. (If only she knew. I also think she *should* know better by now who wears the pants in the house. I mean, she has been with us for a year.)

He agrees he'll mention it to Nanny Mimi again.

I pick out the red Bugaboo Frog this time (instead of the black one we bought last time) as the Fiancé grumbles, "This is the last time we're getting a stroller! If this one breaks, too bad."

I rub his lower back as he throws down his platinum card. I know, because I am a woman, that this will calm him down. Sometimes you have to baby your husband so he won't have a temper tantrum. It works on one-year-olds, and it works on thirty-something-year-old men.

January 14
6 P.M.

"What is she wearing?" the Fiancé asks, appalled, when he walks into the house and sees the baby and me in the kitchen. I asked Nanny Mimi the same question, in the same what-the-fuck tone, two hours earlier, when I arrived home.

The baby is wearing a jean skirt, with rhinestones, a matching button-down jean shirt, also with rhinestones, and a red velour turtleneck underneath. Maybe this sounds cute. But it's not. Unless you are Christina Aguilera, five years ago. In fact, this outrageous outfit is actually quite offensive to the eye. She looks like a badly decorated Christmas tree.

"This is one of the outfits your mother bought," I say to him. "From their trip to Palm Springs."

"Oh," he says.

"Yeah. I know."

You can tell whose clothes the Dictator is wearing quite easily. If she's dressed like Britney Spears, circa 2002, that means the in-laws have bought the outfit. They gravitate to clothes that the baby would wear if she were in a child beauty pageant or a formal event. If she's dressed in a knitted sweater, my mother has made it. If she's wearing jeans or sweats, I've bought them. Most of the time, Nanny Mimi dresses the Dictator in the comfortable clothes I buy for her. But sometimes she has fun with the baby, or thinks she should dress her up for special occasions ("special occasions" is a very loose term because, for the baby, a "special occasion" can be art class at the Y). Sometimes Nanny Mimi dresses her in clothes that even someone visually impaired could tell don't match at all. It's sort of funny, in a very tragic way.

You realize when you have a child that what you think is appropriate and cute for a baby to wear is different from other people's version of cute or appropriate for a baby.

"Maybe you should start to lay out what she should wear?" the Fiancé suggested the other day when he arrived home to find the Dictator dressed in pink pants, an orange top, a blue vest, green socks, and brown boots. She looked like a clown.

I had actually laughed out loud when I came home and saw her that day. "What is she wearing?" I had asked, not even caring if I was hurting Nanny Mimi's feelings. My child looked ridiculous. And, being her mother and all, I'm supposed to think she looks beautiful in everything. But, no, she looked like a clown.

"Oh, she just has so many clothes, and I wanted her to wear them, at least once, before she grew out of them," Nanny Mimi had said, explaining why my child was dressed like a psychedelic light show. Apparently, wearing all her clothes at least once could mean wearing them all at the same time, even if they don't match.

I call Tammy and ask if she ever tells her nanny what she'd like Zack to wear, or if she lets the nanny pick out his clothes.

"Usually I just let her do it. But sometimes I'll say, 'Dress him cute.' And her version of cute and mine are usually very different. Once, I suggested to my nanny that he wear these cute green pants. I came home and he was wearing the green pants. And he was also wearing green socks, and a green shirt and a green jacket. He looked like the Green Giant!"

"Hey," I say, "you should come over and check out how my child is dressed today! You'd think Mimi was on drugs when she dressed her."

If we weren't laughing so hard, we'd probably cry.

Ten Mommy Moments People "Forget" to Mention

1. No matter how cute and small your baby is, the smells it can make are unimaginable.
2. Children's performers, like Barney, become celebrities.
3. No matter how large your home is, your child's toys will take over.
4. Portable DVD players will break.
5. Men do not get excited over artwork done by their babies.
6. Mothers get very excited about artwork done by their babies.
7. You will be ecstatic when you miss changing a dirty diaper.
8. You will wonder what happened to your sex life.
9. Even though you are a mother, your mother will still treat you like a baby.
10. Babies do not mind sleeping in their own shit.

The Ninth Trimester (15 to 18 Months)

Shit, Shit, and More Shit

January 18
9 P.M.

I'm walking upstairs when I first inhale the disgusting scent. It's like nothing I have ever smelled before. As I reach the top floor, the smell becomes overwhelming. I have never smelled anything so vile in my life. What could possibly smell that horrific?

"Get up here!" I yell to the Fiancé.

"What?" he says, taking the stairs two at a time. "What's wrong?"

"Um, do you smell that?"

I watch him sniff the air. "Oh, God. What is that?" he asks.

"I don't know. I have no idea."

"God," he says. "That is one very bad smell."

We follow the smell, which is so overpowering we have to hold our hands over our noses and breathe through our mouths. The scent leads us directly to the Dictator's room, where she's sound asleep.

"I'm going to puke," I say. "I think I'm going to puke and then I'm going to faint."

It's obvious the baby has pooed in her sleep. The Fiancé is practically gagging.

"Well, do we change her, or let her sleep?" he asks.

This is a very good question. We're usually so grateful when the baby is finally asleep that we will do anything not to wake her, aside from rescuing her from a house fire. And, yes, sometimes we know she desperately needs a diaper change in the mornings—how could she not after sleeping in her urine for eleven hours?—but we'll wait until she wakes up.

But those are only pee diapers I'm talking about.

This is different. It is a whopper of a diaper, I can tell. This, I know, is not just any poo diaper. This must have been an explosion. "We have to change her," I say. "We have to. We'll be very careful not to wake her."

"How can she just sleep in her shit like that?" the Fiancé asks.

"I don't know. She really doesn't seem to mind though. She can even sleep through the stench!"

I pick the baby up gently, trying not to gag. How is it possible that someone so cute and small can make such a big mess and disgusting smell? The Fiancé and I work quickly together. We now have a rhythm to this diaper-changing thing, which happens after you've changed 6,036 diapers together. He holds her legs up while I take off the dirty diaper and clean her bum with the wipes. I always have sheets of wipes prepared before we undress her. It's strange, but sometimes when she poos, it doesn't smell at all, and it is a complete shock to see the dirty diaper. Not this time.

"Oh! Oh! Oh God!" the Fiancé says when I open her diaper. "Oh my God!"

"What the hell did she eat today?" I ask, gagging. "This is revolting!"

Poo is all over her butt, inching up toward her back. It becomes clear she'll need to be changed into new pajamas as well.

The funny thing is, we're still not quite used to the dirty diapers. It's the one thing that doesn't get better. I hated changing her first poo diaper, and I still hate changing poo diapers. As soon as her bum's wiped clean—it takes nine wipes—the Fiancé grabs a plastic bag and I throw in the dirty diaper along with the dirty wipes. We put on a new pair of pajamas.

Thankfully, the Dictator barely knows what has happened and I place her back in her crib while the Fiancé races down the stairs with the plastic bag of dirty wipes and the diaper. He puts it in the trash can in our garage in the back of the house.

I sit on the bottom step, trying to get over the drama of what just happened—the nastiest diaper ever. I feel like I just swam through an underground sewer system, no joke, and somehow got out alive.

You're probably wondering about the Diaper Genie. Well, the Diaper Genie did move with us, and is now in the baby's bedroom. But I still haven't figured out how to use it. It's become part of the décor really, and nothing more.

"It smells so bad in this house," the Fiancé says when he's back inside.

"I know! I left her door open to air out her room, but the entire upstairs reeks! I think it was the peas she had for dinner. She's not allowed to eat peas ever again," I say.

"I'll second that," the Fiancé says. "You'd think we'd fed her Indian food for dinner. How can one dirty diaper stink up the entire house? It even smells downstairs."

"You know, it's times like these I really miss the garbage chute."

"Why do you care?" he shoots back. "I'm the one who always takes out the trash."

Okay, he has a point. What can I say?

He's a man. Along with never having to worry that his bosses will treat him differently after he has a baby, like women do, he also will most likely always have to take out the trash.

January 20
8:30 P.M.

I turn on the television and look to see what TiVo has recorded for me. I am excited to find that an episode of *Supernanny* has been recorded. I hope it's not a repeat. I'm sure I learn things watching *Supernanny*, not that I remember any of her lessons, aside from "The Naughty Chair." But mostly I like watching *Supernanny*—and hearing her say with her British accent, "That's unacceptable!"—because I get such a thrill knowing there are worse children out there than the Dictator, and that these unruly children are not mine. The Fiancé and I will watch *Supernanny* together (he watches only because I make him), and neither of us can keep quiet.

Usually, I'm the type of person who will not let anyone speak, except at commercial breaks, if I'm watching shows like *The L Word* or *The OC*. I need to hear every word the characters say. But with *Supernanny*, even I can't refrain from talking. "Can you believe that that kid just slapped his mother like that?" I'll say. Or the Fiancé will say, "That father is even lazier than we are!" Or I'll say, "The Dictator is so much cuter than those babies." And then he'll say, "What is wrong with these parents? How did they let their children turn into such nightmares?"

But most often, we find ourselves saying to each other, "I really hope our baby doesn't grow up like those kids."

"You never know. It could happen to us!" is how I usually respond. I should probably try to be optimistic. After all, I know all about the Naughty Chair, and I'll use it if I have to. It's just that I know I can't see into the future. I'm pretty sure all the parents featured on *Supernanny* never imagined their kids would turn out so bad.

January 24
6 P.M.

I'm trying to have a civilized conversation with Ronnie, which is impossible. What was I thinking, calling her at dinnertime? I've never had a civilized conversation with Ronnie while she is at home, and mealtimes are the worst.

If she's driving, sometimes we can have a civilized conversation. When she sneaks out of the house for a smoke, we can have a civilized conversation, but only for seven minutes, which is the amount of time it takes to finish a cigarette. I know this because I used to be a smoker, and now I'm not a smoker (well, I am now a "social smoker," which is really much better than being a smoker).

"STOP TALKING TO ME!" Ronnie yells.

"Are you talking to me?" I ask.

"No. Wait. I'VE HAD IT!" she screams.

"Okay, I'm going to go. Call me back later," I say and hang up.

Thank God my child doesn't really speak yet. I love Ronnie and her three children. But her house is so crazy loud all the time, I would go mental. And it will be even louder soon enough.

Yes, Ronnie, who already has three children under the age of five, told me last week she's pregnant with her fourth child. To which I said, "No fucking way." And she answered, "Yes fucking way."

I'm happy for her, thrilled even. But after her fourth baby is born, I wonder if I'll ever be able to get her on the phone again.

Also, Ronnie tells me she already spends most of her time in her car, driving her kids to school and to classes. I can't help but wonder why the heck she wants another.

6:30 P.M.
Ronnie calls back.

"Hi," she says.

"Hi," I say.

"That's GOLD!" she screams.

"What?" I ask.

"No, not you. I'm talking to my son and he's refusing to eat his steak. YOU EAT THAT STEAK RIGHT NOW! IT'S GOLD! GOLD!"

"Ronnie! Call me back later!"

"Why?" she asks.

"Because I don't like to be yelled at," I tell her.

"OKAY, NOW YOU EAT YOUR SPINACH!" she screams.

"Ronnie, just call me back when you're not busy," I tell her.

"I just want to know if you're going to be in town next week."

"No, why?"

"I'm having a birthday party for Poppy. She's turning three. Kyla's coming."

"Kyla? Who's Kyla?" I ask.

"You don't know who Kyla is? How could you not know who Kyla is?"

"I just don't," I say, thinking, "Please dear God, let Kyla not be someone who's always featured in *Us Weekly*, because if I don't know all the names mentioned in *Us Weekly*, then it means my life has really, really, really, changed."

"Kyla's a singer and a guitar player for kids. She goes to all the children's birthday parties in town. She's famous!"

"Famous for what?"

"Famous for playing at kids' parties around town," says Ronnie.

I laugh. Phew. Kyla is famous for playing at children's birthday parties in the suburbs? It actually says more that I've *never* heard of her than it does if I had heard of her. It means I'm still kind of cool, doesn't it? "She's famous for kids' parties around town? Whatever!" I say to Ronnie.

"Well, she is famous," says Ronnie.

"At kids' birthday parties!"

"I know, I know," she says. "So will you be in town?"

"No, sorry, though I hate knowing I'm going to miss the famous Kyla."

"Trust me, the kids love her," Ronnie says. "You will be missing out. She even has CDs!"

"Hey! I know who Barney is!" I say.

"Everyone knows who Barney is! Even people who don't have children know who Barney is!" says Ronnie.

"Yes, that may be true. But can they sing off by heart every Barney song known to man? Because I can."

"Wow. I'm impressed," says Ronnie.

"I know. Me too. Sorry I can't come. I guess I'll have to catch the very famous Kyla some other time," I say.

"Your loss," she says.

God help me.

January 27

8 P.M.

Somehow, our plan to keep all of the Dictator's toys in the basement, so we can have some semblance of a nice home, hasn't worked out as we had planned when we moved in.

The baby's shit is everywhere (I'm talking figuratively, not literally).

The Fiancé is stomping around the main floor saying, "Her shit is everywhere!" Every five steps or so, he'll kick a toy that's lying on the floor.

The house, it's true, is a mess. There are flash cards and books and mini grocery carts and mini plastic barbecues and plastic balls and dolls on every available surface in the kitchen, living room, and television room. I don't understand how this happens. How did she get so many toys?

When I get home every day, at around 4 P.M., the house is spotless. The toys are where they should be, in the basement, which is the toy room, or in the cupboards in the kitchen. Somehow, Nanny Mimi manages to keep the house neat and tidy with the toys out of sight, as well as taking care of the Dictator. I don't know how she does it. Nanny Mimi leaves at around 5 P.M. By the time the Fiancé arrives home, around six-thirty or seven, the house is a disaster.

All the Dictator's toys have somehow managed to get upstairs and out of the cupboards. I find it hard to follow the whole "before we start on something else, we clean this up first" rule. The baby's attention span is shorter than a flea's. I can't keep up with all the toys she plays with from minute to minute. I can't seem to watch her and play with her and change her diapers and feed her *and* keep the house spotless. I'm just not that type of person.

"I'm going to have to get the housekeeper to come in two days a week," says the Fiancé. "I can't live like this anymore."

"Don't you think that's a little excessive?" I ask. We're lucky to have a housekeeper come in once a week.

"Either we get a housekeeper twice a week, or I'm moving out," he says. "I can't live like this."

"Fine. We'll get her to come twice a week."

"I thought we wouldn't have this problem once we moved to a house," he says grouchily.

Space is like money. The more money you make, the more you spend. The more space you have, the more toys you have. Or, as the Fiancé likes to say, "The bigger the house, the more shit you have." Sometimes bigger is not better.

January 30
3 P.M.

"I'm going to kill you," Tammy says when I pick up my cell phone. "I'm so mad at you."

"What? What did I do?"

"I am so mad at you," she says.

My heart sinks. Tammy does sound mad. I try to think of what I could have done to upset her, between last night and now. We had dinner over there last night, and everything was fine. I really don't know Tammy all that well. We are just starting to become close friends. Did I not thank her for dinner? Was I rude to her? Did the baby leave handprints on her mirror?

"You taught my son how to play ring-around-the-rosy, and now he wants to play it *all the time*. He won't leave us alone! We've played it, like, a thousand times today," she moans. "I can't stand it!"

Oh, right. Last night at Tammy's house, I had taught Zack to play ring-around-the-rosy because the Dictator wanted to play. Since Zack really isn't walking yet, we just stood in a circle and sang the song.

"He liked it!" I profess. "He loved it!"

"He won't leave us alone!" yells Tammy. "We played it twelve times in a row as soon as he got up!"

"I'm sorry!" I say, trying not to laugh. I find this hilarious. It's hard not to, especially since Tammy is truly mad about this. "Well, now you understand what I have to go through," I say to her. "The Dictator has wanted to play ring-around-the-rosy about a hundred times a day for a month already." It's true. And it bites. But you don't hear me complaining, do you?

February 2

7 P.M.

I enter the in-laws' condo. I had gone to a yoga class and Nanny Mimi dropped the baby off at their place at 4 P.M. The Fiancé went there after work. I give him a kiss hello.

"You are so lucky," he says.

"What?"

"You don't understand the diaper you just missed."

"It was a real doozy," says the father-in-law. "We just changed her three minutes before you walked in."

I smile.

"You seem happy," says the Fiancé. "You must have had a nice day."

I didn't really. Work still sucks. I never heard back from the editor I sent the nasty e-mail to. I'm always tired. Heather, my oh-so-very-good friend, hasn't called me in weeks, and it seems like I haven't had any real fun in a very long time. All this makes me depressed. However, it makes my day when I just miss a dirty diaper. It's like winning five bucks on a scratch-and-win lottery ticket. It's not that big a deal, but sometimes that's all you need to feel like you have a little luck left.

February 7

I'm visiting my parents with the Dictator and Nanny Mimi. Nanny Mimi and I have actually started to become friends. We have also started to get the whole packing a carry-on for the baby on the airplane down to a science. Now, instead of the Dictator's carry-on weighing eighty-five pounds, it weighs only seventy-five pounds.

We had a minor freak-out yesterday afternoon, when we realized that the portable DVD player wasn't working. There was no way we were going to take a four-hour plane ride without the portable DVD player. The baby and I are both addicted to it.

"I think she may have spilled water in it," said Nanny Mimi.

"Why do you think that?" I asked.

"Because she was shaking her sippy cup of water all over it this morning. I caught her and told her to stop, but it may have been too late."

Great. I raced out and bought a new one. The Fiancé wasn't impressed.

"We need a new one already? We've only had the other one for, like, a month?" he had said when I asked him where I could buy one.

"I know, but what can I say? It's broken. We need a portable DVD player!" I couldn't imagine life without one.

"Okay, but that's it! No more. She breaks this one, we're not getting another," he had said.

Going through security with a baby—and all the crap we need to take because of the baby—is still not fun. We have to take the baby out of the stroller, then put the stroller through security, as well as all our carry-ons. I also have to take out all the electronics I'm bringing along: my laptop, BlackBerry, cell, and now the portable DVD player. Nanny Mimi and I are both sweating buckets after we get through, that's how arduous it is.

5 P.M.

I'm also visiting friends on this short visit home, and today I've scheduled a playdate with my friend Sara and her baby. I'm to meet Sara at her office, we'll go to her daughter's daycare to pick her up, and then we'll all go back to my place to hang out, for the playdate part. I'm eager to see the daycare Sara's daughter attends and to see what I'm missing by having a nanny. Sometimes I think it would have been better to send the Dictator to a daycare. She would get to hang out with a lot of other kids, and that would be good for her.

We walk into the school-like building and I'm amazed at all the noise. And I thought Ronnie's house was loud. This place is ten times worse. "This is nothing. There are six daycare classes in this building," Sara says as she expertly navigates the maze of hallways until we reach the room where her daughter's daycare is.

The staff, while friendly, seems a little scared of Sara. I'm not sure why. They tell Sara that her daughter was good today, that there were no problems, and they hand her a piece of paper. Sara picks up her daughter and thanks the staff, and we all head to the car.

"What is that?" I ask, pointing to the piece of paper.

"Oh, they give a report card each day for all the children," she explains.

"Cool! Let me see," I say, grabbing the piece of paper. "Wow, this is fascinating. She had her diaper changed at 10 A.M., 1 P.M., and 3 P.M., a snack at 10:30 P.M. and 2:30 P.M., and was very good at art today. Aren't you happy?"

"Oh, I'm so happy!" she says sarcastically.

I wonder if I could get Nanny Mimi to make me a daily report card about the Dictator and put sticker stars on it, like Sara's daughter has on her report card. It would be kind of nice.

"I had to yell at her teachers the other day," Sara tells me as she expertly puts her daughter into the car seat. She does it so flawlessly, I'm amazed. I still get nervous every time I put the Dictator into her car seat, fearing that she'll have a fit, or I'll not do up the seat belt right—and I've been doing it for more than a year now.

"I noticed there was something odd. They seemed kind of scared of you," I say. "What happened? Was it juicy?"

"They should be scared of me! She came home with bite marks the other day," she says.

"Bite marks?"

"Yes. It was the third time. There's this other kid in her day-care who bites everyone. In fact, he's known as 'the Biter.' After I yelled at them, they now have one teacher solely dedicated to following him."

"I would have done the same thing. Hey," I say, looking in the backseat at her daughter, "she can eat Cheerios all by herself, holding the container, without spilling anything?"

"God, yes. She's been doing that for months!"

"Oh, we still have to hand-feed. It sucks. Feeding her can take over an hour!"

"Oh, I just throw down food on her tray and she gobbles it up. I figure she either eats it or not, but I'm not going to feed her myself."

Hmmm. Maybe I should do that with the Dictator. I mean, the Dictator should learn that I'm not always going to be the one picking up her food and putting it into her mouth, right? We drive in silence. Hearing about the Biter kind of makes me glad I have a nanny. Sara also tells me her daughter has already had pinkeye, and the chicken pox, and three colds in the past two months, because of other kids in the daycare.

"That's so annoying," I say.

"I know. Some parents send their kid to daycare if they have a fever, or if they have pinkeye, because they don't want them to stay at home. It's so rude."

"It is rude," I agree.

"Well, the good news is that it builds up their immune system," she says.

"That's true. Can you imagine being the parent of the Biter and not knowing that every other parent calls your kid that?" I ask, and we laugh.

We drive to my place and walk into my apartment, where Nanny Mimi is reading one of my trashy celebrity magazines. I love that Nanny Mimi enjoys the same magazines as me. Sara plops her daughter onto the floor, where there are toys strewn everywhere. In fact, my two-bedroom apartment, which I refuse to give up just yet, looks very much like a mini-daycare, like our old condo had before we moved out.

I've bought those soft alphabet flooring tiles, and a Dora the Explorer bath mat, and the fridge is covered in stickers. If the Dictator wasn't just over a year old, you'd think that she was the only one who lived here, that's how much she has taken over my apartment. The Dictator and Sara's daughter each play with their own toys, while Sara and I catch up. We mostly talk about mothering things.

I wonder why people call gatherings with babies "playdates." They so do not play with each other. In fact, our babies barely notice each other at all. I'm not going to get into how much I hate the term "playdate." I've realized I can't fight using the word because every mother in the world now uses it. It's so ubiquitous that if I ever said, "Let's get our kids together," I'm not sure any mother would know what I'm talking about.

February 8
6:30 P.M.

The Dictator and I head to my parents' condominium for dinner.

I cannot believe what I see—or rather don't see—on my parents' fridge when we arrive. There are four shots of my nephew, my brother's son, and only three of my daughter. I'm pissed. There should be more photos of the Dictator on this fridge because she's older, or at the very least there should be the same number of photos of her as there are of her cousin, right?

I stick another photo of Rowan up on the fridge to make things even and lecture my mother for playing favorites with her grandchildren. I say this in a joking way, but I am so not joking. Is it possible for grandparents to love one grandchild more than another? I realize, for maybe the very first time, how protective I am about the Dictator and just how far I'll go to fight for her—even if it's over how many pictures there are of her on a fridge door.

I also realize that even when you become a mother, your own mother still sees you as a baby.

"Do you have to go to the washroom before you go home?" my mother asks me.

"No," I say. "But thanks for asking!"

"Are you sure that coat is warm enough?" she asks.

"Yes, I'm sure."

"You didn't bring a hat?"

"Mom!"

Please, dear God, don't let me turn into my mother.

February 9

The baby and I go to Ronnie's house for dinner. My baby is tired and cranky. Ronnie's three-year-old daughter throws a temper tantrum and is sent to her room. Her eldest son throws a piece of spaghetti against the wall and is sent to his room. Her middle child refuses to eat. Let's just say it isn't the most fun evening out I've ever had. And Ronnie sits there, rubbing her growing bump of a stomach, saying over and over, "I don't know how I'm going to handle another one."

I have a wicked headache, swallow three Advils, and go to bed at 10 P.M. I don't know how Ronnie does it. I really don't. And she's having another?

I will not get pregnant again. I will not get pregnant again. I will not get pregnant again. Going to Ronnie's house for dinner is possibly the best birth control anyone could ever hope for. She should open her home for sex-education classes.

February 10

We're on the plane home. I didn't see Heather on my visit. Lena dropped by to see the baby one afternoon. And one morning the baby and I hung out at Vivian's house, with her baby, and Vivian and I had coffee.

Though I am very happy I saw my three mother friends and my parents, I can't believe I didn't go to one bar during my visit. It's amazing, but I realized during this trip that I would rather stay home with the Dictator, and be able to kiss her good night, than hang out at any bar with anyone. "I've come a long way, baby," I think to myself. I'm not sure this is something to boast about. It's just that I feel incredibly guilty if I'm not home to kiss the Dictator good night.

February 11

1 P.M.

Occasionally, I will read parenting advice. I usually do this when I'm supposed to be working. The Internet just makes information so accessible. After twenty minutes of reading online parenting sites, I remember why I don't like reading parenting

advice. In only twenty minutes, I've learned that I should probably take my kid to the dentist. That we're late on her vaccina-
tions, that I should be protecting her against carbon monoxide
poisoning, and that I should know what to do if she ingests a
poison. I've learned that I should make sure my house does not
contain unsafe levels of asbestos too. Reading online parenting
advice is more depressing than reading the newspaper. There are
just so many "shoulds." I even read that I should take my child
bird-watching. Bird-watching! As if.

I remember being pregnant, and being freaked out by all the
stuff that could go wrong when you're pregnant. It's déjà vu, only
a year later.

I also learn that at around this time, children "crave boundaries," so that I should start to be strict with the Dictator, because she now understands the concept of right and wrong, good
and bad. I'm not good at setting boundaries. I'm just not. I can
barely set boundaries for myself. I can't stop at one chocolate, I
stay up much too late watching television, and I spend way too
much time talking on the phone. The Fiancé and I sometimes
talk about discipline and boundaries. It's something he's worried
about and rightly so.

"She's going to hate me, because I'll be the one setting all the
rules and getting angry at her when she does something wrong,"
he'll say.

I don't disagree with him. I don't have it in me to battle. I
find myself saying "I'm going to choose my battles" when the
Dictator throws her food on the floor, or splashes too much
when she takes a bath, or refuses to wear a hat outside.

I mean, if she asks if she can have a guy sleep over on the
weekend when she's fourteen, I will say no. But is it really worth
the effort to get mad at her for splashing too hard in the bath
when she's one? Is it?

February 15

5 P.M.

I am picking the Fiancé up outside his office. His car is in the shop, and he had a partner at his law firm drive him to work this morning. I pull over to the curb where I see him standing. He opens the car door, looks in, but just stands there. He just stares at the inside of my car, like he's staring at a growth that has suddenly appeared on his skin.

"Well, are you getting in or what?" I ask.

"Beck?"

"What? Get in! We're holding up traffic here."

"Your car is disgusting," he says, reaching in and shoving all the papers and magazines and other crap, which is lying on the passenger seat, onto the floor. This annoys me. Yes, it is crap, but it is my crap, and he's shoving it onto the floor like it doesn't matter. "Oh my God," he says, looking at the backseat and the floor in the back.

"Well, she's very messy!" I say. "I can't help it."

"Don't blame her," he says.

"It's true. It is mostly all her mess!" I protest. When all else fails, blame the child.

The truth is, about 60 percent of the mess is the Dictator's, which is still more than half. There are spare diapers lying on the car floor, along with pacifiers, old Cheerios, empty boxes of crackers, crumbs, and more than a few pieces of baby clothing.

The Fiancé does not have a car seat in his car. It's a sports car—damn him for having an early midlife crisis—and we've only recently found out they do make Porsche baby seats. Can you believe it? If we take the baby anywhere, it's always in my car, which means the baby's mess is in my car. We also purchased a car seat for Nanny Mimi's car, so she can take the Dictator places.

Yesterday, the Dictator insisted on taking one of those individual pouches of oatmeal into my car. I should have said no, but we were in a rush and I didn't have the time or energy to convince her that it wasn't the best idea. Now, along with stale crackers and baby cookies, there is dry oatmeal everywhere.

We drive home mostly in silence. The Fiancé has a puss on his face.

"You should get your car cleaned," he says as we're pulling up into our driveway.

"I know, I know."

"And you shouldn't let her eat in here," he tells me.

"It's because of my whole 'pick your battles' way of parenting," I explain. "I just think it's not the worst thing in the world for her to eat in the car. So I let her. It's not that big a deal."

"And how's that whole 'pick your battles' way of parenting working out for you?" he asks, pointing at an empty juice box on the floor.

"Just fine, thanks for asking," I say, getting out of the car.

Because he complained, made fun of me, and criticized my car, I'm not going to tell him there's half a baby YumYum cookie stuck to the back of his coat, which obviously was on the passenger seat when he got in.

February 18
6:30 P.M.

Nanny Mimi took the baby to her arts-and-crafts class today. Since I was so lax about baby classes during her first year, I've decided to go all out and sign her up for swimming, arts and crafts, and gymnastics "classes." (I use quotes because they're not so much classes as something for parents to do to keep busy with their children. Not that this is a bad thing, I'm just saying.)

Nanny Mimi shows me the piece of artwork the baby made at class today. It's a piece of light-blue construction paper, with lines of orange marker scribbled all over, a piece of white string glued to it, two eyeball stickers, and one red pompom. I think it's the most precious piece of art I've ever seen. I think it's priceless. "I love it! I love it!" I say, hugging the Dictator and telling her how talented she is. I can't wait to show the Fiancé the first piece of art that the baby has made and brought home for us. I really want to hang it on our fridge, but unfortunately we don't have any magnets. I'm thinking of taping it or using a piece of chewed-up bubble gum to stick it on the fridge, when the Fiancé walks in.

Before he even takes his coat off, I run to him and proudly show him the baby's work of art.

"That's nice," he says, looking at what the Dictator made for a nanosecond before taking off his coat and turning his attention back to his BlackBerry. This annoys me. But how can I get mad? What could I say? "How could you not love this piece of art? Your *daughter* made this. Don't you think this is the best piece of art you've ever seen?"

I know it's a silly thing to get angry at. I also know that one could say the "art" that my one-year-old made is hideous and looks exactly like a one-year-old made it, but I still think it's brilliant.

Maybe men just don't get how important a baby's piece of art is, like mothers do. Though I know it's a one-year-old who made this piece of construction-paper art, I can't help but think the baby's a genius and may be the next Picasso. But that's just me. I'm her mother. No one expects me to be objective about these matters, do they?

February 20
5:30 P.M.
Like me, Tammy finds the hours after work, before bedtime, with her baby challenging, to say the least. Thankfully, there are a number of indoor play areas for kids that also serve coffee for adults. Thank God I have Tammy, who also has to kill time.

We meet at one of these indoor playrooms.

Tammy's child takes off crawling across the colorful floor. My child, however, is super-clingy. Every time I try to let go of her hand, she tugs it back. If I even step out of her sight for more than two seconds, she starts crying. I have to follow her wherever she goes. She didn't used to be this way. This clinging-to-Mommy thing is a new development, and not one that I'm exactly excited about.

"How long have we been here?" I ask Tammy.

"Seven minutes," she says, looking at her watch.

"Oh. That's it?"

"Yup. That's it."

5:40 P.M.
"How long have we been here?" I ask Tammy again.

"Um," Tammy says, laughing. "Twelve minutes."

"Oh. It seems longer, doesn't it?"

"Yes," answers Tammy. Thank God I'm not the only one who thinks paint dries faster than it takes time to pass at an indoor play area.

5:45 P.M.
"So, how old is your son?" a woman asks me. "He looks about the same age as mine."

"She's a girl," I say, not adding, "She's dressed in all pink, for goodness' sake!!!!!!!!"

How long will this last? When will my baby girl grow some hair?

5:48 P.M.

"What time is it now?" I ask, helping the baby down a plastic slide.

"5:48," says Tammy. Her child has crawled off and is playing with some toy trains.

"You want to go for dinner now?" I ask, praying—dear God— she wants to leave this place as much as I do. The place depresses me. I can tell that all the mothers here are just killing time, like we are.

"Yes! Let's go," Tammy says.

I'm sure that prisoners being released from behind locked bars experience the same feeling I do when they feel the air on their faces for the very first time.

February 28

Just as you start getting used to the term "playdate," which you'd never thought you'd say and which you hate, you start to understand why couples with children have "date nights."

I always laughed at Ronnie because Thursday evenings were her night to go out with her husband. I always believed that planning and scheduling a "date night" wasn't spontaneous enough (or at all) and that "date nights" were for some other type of couple, not the type of couple the Fiancé and I were.

But I get it now. After you have a baby, you kind of have to force yourself out with your partner, or you become the type of couple who stays in every night watching *Supernanny* and *Amer-*

ican Idol (both of which I love) or hanging out with other couples with children.

In fact, not only is it becoming clearer that the Fiancé and I might need to have a scheduled date night each week, it has gotten to the point where the Fiancé and I are making appointments to have sex.

"I'm too tired tonight," I'll say, then add, "But I'd like to have sex tomorrow night. Okay?"

I can't help notice that the Fiancé and I aren't having sex nearly enough. I can't believe I'm going to say this, but I'm always "too tired." It's no longer just an excuse to not have sex, it's actually the truth. And I can't believe I'm going to admit this, but so is the Fiancé. He too, on occasion, has said he's too tired.

It's not just that we both spend our days at offices and then have another full-time job when we get home now (the Dictator). It's because the Dictator, and I also hate to admit this, is again not sleeping through the night. One of us has to go into the Dictator's room, sometimes three times throughout the night, to give her a bottle of milk. We're both exhausted all the time. I know we're supposed to train her, by not giving her a bottle when she screams in the middle of the night. It just really is easier to go get one and hand it to her than it is to listen to her scream.

I've talked to my friend Vivian about this. Her baby, who is a couple of months older than mine, is also not a very good sleeper. She too has many sleepless nights. But Sara's baby is a good sleeper, as is Tammy's.

"We put Zack to bed at eight, and he sleeps right through to seven A.M.," she told me the other day when I moaned about another bad night. Why couldn't I have had a baby like hers or Sara's, who sleeps twelve hours a night? Too bad you couldn't custom-make your baby like you can custom-make a suit.

March 1

11 P.M.

Oh God. Did I really promise—rather, make an appointment with—the Fiancé yesterday to have sex with him tonight? I'm so tired. I'm just so tired. But a date is a date.

11:30 P.M.

We did it. I feel closer to the Fiancé. I must remember this feeling the next time I think I'm too tired.

Ten Mommy Moments People "Forget" to Mention

1. You will want another baby.
2. Your friends who don't have children will piss you off.
3. You will have to go on vacation without your child.
4. You will forget important milestones of your baby's life.
5. You will shop more for the baby than for yourself.
6. You will learn new mommy vocabulary.
7. When you leave your baby for longer than a couple of days, you will miss her more than you ever thought possible.
8. When you see your baby for the first time after a long time, you will never be happier.
9. Babies change at an alarming pace.
10. You will miss the days when your baby didn't move or talk.

The Tenth Trimester (18 to 21 Months)

Do I Really Want Another One of These? Do I?

March 15

I never wanted to have a baby. Ever. Well, I really didn't want to until I turned twenty-eight. It was like I had been slapped in the face—except not with a hand but a craving. I simply woke up one morning and had the somewhat desperate thought that I wanted a baby, even needed to have a baby, like a late-night craving for french fries after drinking too many gin and tonics. Even though, for most of my life, I had professed I never wanted that kind of responsibility and had never really imagined having a baby or being someone's mother.

I kept my baby craving under wraps, until I accidentally got knocked up, at my engagement party. The Fiancé and I, after all, hadn't even talked about having children. I had no idea if he was even interested in having children.

Well, it turns out, virtually the same thing happens when your first child is about eighteen months old. Though you hated the nine long months being pregnant, and though taking care of only one child, even with a nanny, exhausts you, and your sex life isn't hot anymore, and you would cut off your right arm for a solid eight hours of sleep, and you virtually have no social life, and you suffer from postpartum depression, suddenly you begin to think about getting knocked up again. Not only that, but getting knocked up again seems like a brilliant idea.

Why does this happen? Do all women feel this craving for another child when their first child is eighteen months old? Some scientist out there, I believe, should look into this.

A couple of days ago, I just started to think, "God, I kind of miss having a tiny little baby to hold." And "It really wasn't that bad being pregnant and having to stay up all night with a newborn," even though, yes, it was that bad.

And everywhere I look these days there are cute newborns in car seats at restaurants, being pushed in strollers and carted around in Baby Björns, just like when I was pregnant and noticed how many other pregnant women were walking the streets. I miss that time when the Dictator was so small and so cute and didn't require me to follow her around all the time because she may run into a wall or eat dishwashing detergent. I miss the time when the Dictator didn't refuse to get her shitty diaper changed. I miss the time I ruled the Dictator, the time before she really started ruling me. I now completely understand why people have more than one baby. The mind is an interesting thing. It represses the bad, and you only remember the good, like the first time your baby grabbed your finger and the first time your baby smiled. I now also completely understand why women never tell you the bad things about being pregnant, like how hard it is to walk around with that extra weight, how uncomfortable it is to sleep, and how difficult it is to deal with the sudden life changes. It's because time really does heal all wounds, including pregnancy.

Even I, who really did hate being pregnant, now find myself

thinking, "Was it really that bad, or was I just being a big baby?" And "Surely now that I know what to expect, being pregnant will be easier the second time around." I even think that maybe planning to have a baby, instead of unexpectedly expecting, might be easier and more romantic and, hey, wouldn't it be nice to actually plan on getting pregnant? I have to force myself to remember the bad. Because right now I'm only remembering the good, like how people smiled at me when I was pregnant, and how I could eat anything I wanted, and the joy of seeing the Dictator for the very first time.

"I think I want another baby," I say to the Fiancé.

I know the Fiancé very well, and I know there is no good way of bringing this topic up. So, instead of hinting about it, I just throw it out there. (It's amazing, really. Sometimes I hint for two hours about a new purse I'd like him to buy me, but when it comes to something as major as having another baby, I just blurt it out.)

"What did you just say?" he asks. I see the color literally draining from his face. And he's quite pale to begin with. I know he heard what I said just fine by the change of his color.

"I don't know. I've just been thinking about having a second child," I say.

"Why?" he asks.

"I don't know. I just want another," I say.

"No way," he says. "I'm too old. I still want a life. I don't want another baby."

"Well, can you at least think about it? That's all I'm asking. I just want you to think about it," I tell him.

"No. Beck, we already need so much help with one. How will we deal with two?"

"Can you just think about it? Please? Just think about it," I beg.

"No. I do not want another baby."

"Well, I do," I say.

"I don't," he says.

"It's not fair! I just want you to think about it! You can't just say you don't want another without even thinking about it," I argue, already on the verge of tears.

"Have you thought about why you want another?" he asks.

"Yes!"

"No you haven't!"

"Can you please just think about it?"

"Fine. I will think about it, but I don't want another child. How about a dog?" he asks.

Hmmm. Would it be so bad to get a dog as a consolation prize of sorts? I have been begging him for a dog for a while now. "So, you'll think about it then?" I say.

"I said I would. But, Beck—"

"What?"

"I don't want another baby."

After a few more rounds of "Well, just think about it" from me, and a few more "I said I will but I don't want another baby" from him, we go back to watching television. It may take some time to convince him about this second-baby idea, I realize. But at least he threw out the dog offer. And he has no idea who he's dealing with. When I want something, I'll do almost anything to get it.

Reasons to Have a Second Child

1. I have really great baby names. And they really shouldn't go to waste.

March 16

2 A.M.

Is that all I can come up with? That I have really great baby names that I don't want to go to waste? I lie awake and can't really think of another reason. I thought it would be a great idea to come up with a list of reasons to have another child, like the Fiancé suggested. It's just so hard to explain to the Fiancé, a male, that it's just a gut feeling I have. I can't explain a craving. You just have it. I can't really explain my postpartum depression. It just is.

March 17

2 P.M.

"So, how are you?" Vivian asks. I'm at my office, halfheartedly working. My editor won't call me back, though I've left three messages. This has nothing to do with the fact that I had a baby, I tell my still-paranoid self, and everything to do with the fact that all editors are overworked and can't possibly return all the messages they have on their voice mail immediately. That's what I tell myself.

"I'm good, good," I tell her.

"So, what's new?" she asks.

"Oh, not much. Nothing at all really. Just living my boring life as a boring mother. A lot of television. No, nothing new at all." Then I blurt out, "I think I want another baby!"

"What? Did I just hear what I think you said?"

"I know! Who would have ever thought it, but it's true. I want another baby!"

"That's great. I think you should have another one. You should!" she says.

Of course Vivian thinks I should have another baby. Most women who have more than one child always want other mothers to hop on their multiple-child bandwagon. Being a mother, I've learned there's definitely a mommy club and then another mommy club for those who have more than one child. Mommies with more than one child always wonder why parents with one child stopped at one, just like people with one child always wonder why childless people don't have any.

Then Vivian asks me the question I dread but I know I will be asked anyway: What does the Fiancé thinks about this?

"Well, he's going to take some working on to change his mind," I admit.

"Well, you can always get him drunk," she suggests.

"Um, yeah. I think accidentally getting pregnant while drunk only works once," I say, and we laugh. "No, he's way too careful about that now," I tell her. It's true. The Fiancé and I do not get drunk and do it anymore. We know all too well what can happen. "Unless I get him really, really, really drunk!" I joke to Vivian.

The other problem is that I don't think either of us have gotten as drunk as we did at our engagement-party celebration—the conception party, as it's now called, since the Dictator was conceived that night. Who has the energy to get drunk and then deal with the hangover when you also have to deal with a baby?

"Oh, he'll probably change his mind," Vivian says.

"I don't think so," I say, because I really don't think so.

"No, he probably will," she says. "How could he not?" Vivian's an optimist. What can I say? She married a toxic bachelor who actually begged her to have a second child. In fact, Vivian's husband probably wants her to have a third.

"No, I really, really don't think so. I'm going to have to be really smart about this. I'm going to have to not say anything about wanting another baby for another three months. The more I press him, the angrier he'll get and fight the idea. So that's what I'm going to do. I'm not going to say anything. I'm going to be the best mother for three more months and be so nice to him. And then he'll be so happy with me that the next time I bring up the whole second-child idea, he'll be more will-ing and ready to listen," I tell Vivian. I sound so convincing that I almost convince myself that this plan can work. And I don't feel bad about tricking the Fiancé into wanting another child by being super-nice to him because there are women out there who simply stop taking their birth control pills without telling their partners and trick them into getting them pregnant. I'm not judging these women. I'm just saying that tricking your partner by being nice is way better than tricking him by throwing out your birth control pills.

March 17
8 P.M.

I, of course, don't last three months not bringing up the subject of a second baby with the Fiancé. I think, however, I may have lasted more than three hours, which is pretty admirable. I mean, I am a girl. Much like wanting to get engaged, and screaming at boyfriends, "When are you going to propose already?" most women just don't know when to drop subjects of such impor-tance. Rather, we know but we just can't. It's out of our control. Like most women, I get something in my mind—this time, it's having another baby—and I can't stop thinking about it. Trying not to think about it only makes me think about it all the time. It's kind of like seeing the most perfect pair of jeans that you know cost way too much money, so you don't buy them, because they are way too much money and what is wrong with the world that a company can charge $450 for one pair of jeans? But then you can't stop thinking about the jeans. You even have dreams about the jeans. Next thing you know, you're back at the store, buying the jeans, because who were you kidding? You can either shell out the money and be happy with your jeans or make perhaps the greatest mistake of your life (not getting the best pair of jeans) and be miserable thinking about how you should have just bought them.

"How come you won't even think about it?" I ask the Fiancé, only hours after telling Vivian I wouldn't bring the baby idea up for three months.

"Beck. I don't want to talk about this now," he says. "We're having a nice quiet night and I don't want to get into it right now."

"Why not?"

"Because I don't," he says.

"Fine," I say.

"Don't fine me," he says.

"Fine."

(Silence.)

"Great. Now you've put me in a bad mood."

"And you've put me in a bad mood," I tell him.

(Silence.)

"Don't you love her?" I ask, about the Dictator. When all else fails, I figure, try guilt.

"Of course I do. But I also love our lives," he says.

I'm not going to give up, I tell myself. But I can't press this matter. I'm going to have to be smart about it, I remind myself again, and give him time to come around to the idea. Hey, I'm only thirty-one. I have a lot of time to get pregnant again. I have years, in fact, to have another baby. Didn't some woman in her sixties get pregnant? Technically, with the advance of technology, I could have thirty more years to have a baby. Though I don't think I want to be one of those women. Like finding that perfect pair of jeans, I want it now. I want to get pregnant now. I'm all about instant gratification.

March 18
10 A.M.

"I love you. You love me. We're best friends as friends should be!" I sing to myself in the shower. What is that song? Where do I know that song?

Gaa! It's Barney!

I'm not sure how that happened. Actually I do. I've watched all the Barney DVDs about seven hundred times each. Of course, I now know all the words to all the Barney songs. I also know all the words to the songs on *Dora the Explorer*. ("We did it! We did it!") Maybe I do let the Dictator watch too much television. I know all the songs and I wasn't even trying to learn them. In fact, I tried very hard not to learn them. But now they are stuck in my head. But, thanks to *Dora the Explorer*, I can also count to ten in Spanish now, which actually makes lifting weights a lot more fun.

March 19
4 P.M.

The stupid Fiancé wants to go to stupid Paris for a stupid romantic getaway. I know, I know. I should be thrilled. I've never been to Paris. I've always wanted to go to Paris. The Fiancé's cousin is getting married in Paris, and the Fiancé wants to know if I want to go. He suggested that we hang out in Paris, go to the wedding, and get some romance back into our relationship.

I do want to go.

I also don't want to go.

"I don't know," I tell him, honestly.

"What do you mean, you don't know? It's Paris! You've never been. You've always said you wanted to go to Paris. It's Paris!"

"Well, are we bringing the baby?" I ask. I know, even as I ask, that this is a stupid question.

"No. That will not be a fun trip to take the baby to Paris. It will be way too much with the time difference and walking around and staying in a hotel."

"Right. Well, how long would we be gone for?" I ask.

"Beck! I'm asking if you want to go to Paris. If you don't want to go, fine. But it's Paris! It's not a punishment."

I do want to go. I just don't want to leave my baby for so long. And let's face it: if you're going to Paris, you need to go for more than two days.

"Okay, I want to go!" I tell him.

"Do you?"

"Yes! Yes! I really want to go! It will be amazing. I've never been!"

"I'll look into the tickets then," he says.

"Great! This will be great!"

God, I don't want to go to stupid Paris. How am I going to live without my baby? Sure, I've left her with my parents for a couple of nights in a row. But I've always been in the same city! I was only a phone call away.

Think happy thoughts, Beck. You're going to Paris. How many women can say they get to go to Paris?

4:15 P.M.

God, I so don't want to go. How can I leave my baby? Yes, she sometimes drives me bonkers, but I always forgive her. How can I get out of going to Paris without hurting the Fiancé's feelings?

4:16 P.M.

Who am I kidding? I so want to go. It's Paris!

4:17 P.M.

I feel sick to my stomach for leaving her for more than forty-eight hours. What kind of mother would I be if I left her for longer than that?

4:18 P.M.

Of course, maybe it would be good for the Dictator to learn to be a little more independent. Right? I mean, I'm not always going to be with her. Right? And the Fiancé is right. It wouldn't be much of a vacation with her. Okay, I'm going.

5 P.M.

God, I so don't want to go. Or maybe I do. I don't know.

Midnight

WAAAA!

The Fiancé and I hear the screams. We've both been in bed for more than an hour. I pray he's going to get out of bed and get her a bottle. He's not moving though. Why isn't he getting up and getting her a bottle? Why do I have to do it?

"Fuck, she's crying," he says. Duh.

"I'll do it," I say, and feel my way in the dark out of the bedroom.

2 A.M.

WAAAA!

Who am I? Where am I? Right. The Dictator is screaming. Again. Again, I pray that the Fiancé is going to get out of bed and get her a bottle. I did it the last time. It's his turn. Why isn't he getting out of bed?

"Fuck, she's crying again," he says. Duh. "I'll get her," he says, literally stomping out of the room.

I fall back asleep.

4:30 A.M.

WAAAA!

No, seriously. This cannot be happening.

"I'll get her," I say. The Fiancé did go the last time.

6:30 A.M.

WAAAA!

Man, I can't wait to go to Paris! How soon can we leave?

"I'll get her," the Fiancé says. "I might as well just get up now and go to work. I'm obviously not going to get any more sleep."

"Okay. Don't forget to call the travel agent," I say sleepily. "We are so going to Paris."

Is this how it's going to be? I literally have to leave town to get a solid night's sleep?

March 20

6 P.M.

Mommyitis.

Today was the first time I heard this word. Like the words "sippy cup" and "onesie" and "playdate," there is certain terminology that you would never have in your vocabulary unless you've had a baby.

I was at the grocery store, buying a couple of cartons of soy milk. The Dictator refused to let me put her down. At the cash register, another woman in line saw me struggling with the milk while holding the Dictator.

"Oh, does she have mommyitis?" she asked. "I have an eight-month-old who refuses to let me out of his sight for even one second. He has mommyitis real bad."

"Yes, I suppose she does," I say. Luckily, it doesn't take a genius to figure out the meaning of mommy words. I'm not sure whether or not I actually like this one. On the one hand, it's a little too cutesy. Also, it sounds like a disease. On the other hand, it is a heck of a lot better than saying, "She won't let me put her down for a friggin' minute!"

March 21
11 A.M.

My mind, along with being full of children's songs and mommy words, is still also consumed with thoughts of babies. Babies, babies, and more babies. In fact, I don't think I have conversations anymore that don't include talk of babies—what they do, what they don't do, finding out people are having them or asking people when they are having one, or hearing about other people's babies, or talking about mine. My friend Heather, who I've talked to less and less frequently, is now going on and on to me on the phone about how she's not ready for a baby. She tells me she isn't even sure she wants one anymore, and how she loves being childless. I let her go on about her life without child and how she can't imagine how a child would fit into her fabulous, childless life.

I think she's lying. Of course, I don't tell her this.

It's funny to think that I once thought that way too. And maybe Heather isn't lying about not really wanting a baby. Maybe she honestly means it. She's a couple of years younger than me, so she definitely has time to change her mind. And most women do change their minds. Well, most women who profess they don't ever want children while in their teens or twenties change their minds one day, don't they?

Sometimes I read articles about older women, past the child-bearing age, who have never had children, who say that they were too busy working and enjoying life to even think about having children. I can't help but think they're lying too. Maybe they were busy working and enjoying life. But can't you be busy working and enjoying life *and* also have thoughts about having a baby? Can't you be busy working and enjoying life and get pregnant?

I can't imagine not having a baby. Though I was once the type who thought I'd never get married and never have kids (I also once thought wearing safety pins in your jeans and getting perms was a cool look), now I even want a second child. Oh, man, what has become of me? When did I stop wanting to take over the world? Why is my main worry now not how to get a promotion and a raise but how to trick the Fiancé into wanting to have a second child with me?

Noon
You know, it really bugs me when people say they "really don't want children" to women who have children. I mean, I don't tell people who have just cut their hair into bangs that "I can't imagine life with bangs." Do I tell my friends who have great, fun jobs interviewing celebrities, "I'm so glad I don't have to meet Jennifer Aniston?"

1 P.M.
Okay, it really, really bugs me that Heather said to me that she really doesn't want to have children and she can't imagine having a child. What is wrong with people?

3 P.M.
I'm convinced that women who say their lives are so much better without children are really jealous of those of us who have

children. Those of us who have children don't have to worry about meeting a good man to have a child with. We already have one, thank you very much. Young women who say they're not sure they really want to have children and that their lives are so much better without children to people who they know have children are just saying it in case one day it turns out that they don't have children. This way, they can say all along that they always professed they never wanted a baby.

5 P.M.

Why am I so obsessed, and upset, that Heather said that to me? One is because I know now, for sure, that our friendship is no longer the same. How can it be the same when my life is so different from hers, and hers is so different from mine? The slow death of any friendship is cause for concern and obsession. Second, it also really bothers me because I still can't shake the nagging feeling that she might be partly right about not having kids. I hate myself for sometimes still wondering what all the friends I used to hang out with are doing on the nights I'm at home watching reruns of *Friends* because I can't go out because I have a baby. It bothers me that I do sometimes wonder how much more fun my life might be if I was single, childless, and thought of myself as still fabulous. It really has hit me that I am not that person anymore. So, along with mourning the death of old friendships, maybe I'm mourning the death of the old me.

March 22

8 P.M.

I put my new plan—"Being the Best Partner Possible to Trick the Fiancé into Wanting a Second Child"—into action.

First, I put the Dictator to bed and tell the Fiancé to go relax. I change her diaper on my own. I put her into her pajamas on my own. I read her a story on my own. And then I go downstairs to join the Fiancé.

I hold his hand while we watch television.

I tell him that I'll get the baby if she cries. Of course she does, and I do, as promised.

When I come back, I tell him that I love him and that he's my best friend. Which may be going overboard. I think he's on to me. Argh. He's looking at me like he doesn't know me. Is it really that odd to him that I can be accommodating, sweet, and nice? Can't a woman tell a guy that she loves him?

10 P.M.

"I love you," I say. "You're my best friend."

"I love you too," the Fiancé responds.

I grab his hand to hold it again.

10:15 P.M.

"I love you," I say. "You're my best friend."

"I love you too," he responds again.

10:30 P.M.

"I love you," I say. I think I'm now actually cooing the words.

"I love you too, Beck," he says.

How can he not want to have another baby with me? I'm so nice! I'm the best woman he'll ever find. He's lucky to have someone so sweet like me in his life. I wonder how many days I can go on being so sugary sweet. I wonder how many days we can go on without arguing about something. I also wonder how many days I'll last without his help at all with the Dictator.

March 25

5 P.M.

I get my answer. I turn not so nice. I get sick. Viciously sick. My throat is so sore it feels like I'm swallowing knives. I have a fever. I'm freezing cold but burning up.

Nanny Mimi has gone home. I can barely move and the Fiancé has an important meeting and can't come home early. I get mad at him for not seeming to care enough to come home and help me out. For the first time—I can't believe it—the in-laws have plans and can't babysit. How can everyone do this to me when I'm so deathly ill and can barely manage to lift my head off the pillow?

The Dictator is grumpy. God, I miss the days when she would just lie beside me on the bed while I watched television.

What do women do when they are mothers and get so sick? I can barely form a sentence. I can't swallow. The Dictator needs to be entertained, fed, and bathed. Bedtime for her is still hours away. I'm going to die. I'm not going to make it.

April 2

I don't remember the last few days. It all seems like a dream. I know that I have been in bed for many, many days. Thank God for the in-laws, who took care of the baby after Nanny Mimi went home. I must stop complaining about them to the Fiancé. They are nice people. Even the Fiancé, after he saw how sick I was, helped out. He would put the Dictator to bed, and bring me soup, and let me sleep alone while he slept on the uncomfortable pullout couch in the spare room.

"So, where've you been?" Vivian asks. It's the first time in days that I've been to my office and answered my cell phone.

"I've been in bed. I've been so sick," I tell her.

"That sucks."

"I know. I literally haven't been out of bed in days. The good news is that I think I lost five pounds," I tell her. "My jeans feel great."

"Ah, the advantages of being sick," she says.

"I know! Sure, I was so sick I couldn't shower, but, hey, it's easier than going to the gym."

"So, how's the Baby Plan coming?"

"Oh, it's not."

"What do you mean?" Vivian asks.

"I mean that I realized that I'm not sure if I want another baby. I could barely take care of one when I was sick. I think I may have changed my mind."

"Well, you're going to change it back," she says.

"I don't know. I really don't think so. Maybe one is enough for me," I say. I really believe this.

"Well, you still have time."

It's true. I have at least a few years, I figure, to decide whether I want another child. For now, I'm completely happy with one.

April 3

My friend Cara has given birth to a boy. I buy her a blue Juicy Couture diaper bag. It cost a small fortune. I find myself way more generous to friends who give birth, now that I know what having a baby, living with a baby, and raising a baby entails. She might as well have a really nice diaper bag, because her life is not going to be so nice anymore.

April 15

1 P.M.

Cara calls me to ask me questions, thank me for the baby gift, and tell me about the first few days with her new baby boy.

2 P.M.

My friend Cara has made me feel like a bad mother.

Here's the thing. She wanted to know everything she could expect with her newborn.

"So, how many times did she go to the bathroom a day?" she asked.

"Um, I don't remember. A lot?" I answered.

"Do you remember when she first held her head up?" she asked.

"Um, not really," I told her.

"How about when she could sit up on her own?" Cara asked.

"Um, maybe around three months? Or four? Or two?"

Oh my God. How long does mommy brain last for? Have I lost all ability to remember? When did the Dictator first hold her head up? When did she begin to sit up on her own? When did I lose my short-term memory?

April 22

I am totally starting to understand why women scrapbook. Not that I'm even sure what scrapbooking really is. All I know is that ever since I had the Dictator, I hear mothers talking about scrapbooking and have read about stores now totally dedicated to the art of scrapbooking. As a journalist, I've received invitations from many, many people to learn how to scrapbook; I've even been offered scrapbooking supplies. I had turned down all offers.

I'm not the type who could scrapbook, I had thought. Scrapbooking takes organization. I'm the least organized person on the planet. All the baby's photos are stuffed in old shoe boxes, in drawers around the house, on tables everywhere. Looking for her photographs is kind of like being on an Easter-egg hunt. You never know where you'll come across them. I could be scouring around for a DVD I want to watch and I will find a pile of photos from when she was two months old. Or I could be looking for a new roll of toilet paper and find a stack of photos from her first birthday party under the washroom sink.

But suddenly I have realized that, like the photos scattered all over the house, my memories are also scattered. I really can't remember any of the milestones of my baby's life. I know she went from having a floppy head to not having a floppy head, from being able to roll over to being able to sit up on her own, from being able to sit up to being able to crawl, from being able to crawl to being able to walk. I just for the life of me can't remember the age she started doing it all. I know she once had no teeth and now she has a mouth full of them.

Does this make me a bad mother? I should probably have joined the cult of scrapbookers. At least then I'd know when she got her first tooth.

April 24

6:30 P.M.

I'm still worried about the fact that I can't remember every detail of the Dictator's life. Baby milestones happen at an alarming pace. And I'm not talking about the big important milestones, like when she took her first step. The Dictator changes from day to day now. In fact, she can go to sleep one night and wake up the next morning knowing three more words. Even her taste in foods has changed. But not for the better. It's changed for the butter. Literally.

"What is she doing?" the Fiancé asks.

"She's eating butter," I tell him.

"What?"

"She likes butter."

"What?"

"She likes butter," I say, overly pronouncing each word.

"But she's just eating it in a chunk. She's not even eating it with a piece of bread. She's just eating plain butter."

"I know. She likes butter," I say. The Dictator had kept saying, "Butter, butter, butter." I had tried to put the butter on a piece of bread, on some mashed potatoes, on some green beans. But, nope, she will only eat it in chunks, plain.

"That is one of the most disgusting things I've ever seen," the Fiancé says.

"I know. It is disgusting. But it makes her happy. What can I say? She likes butter."

"When did that happen?" he asks.

"Let me check my scrapbook," I say.

"What?"

"I'm joking. I don't know when it started. A couple weeks ago?"

"Why didn't you tell me?"

"Why would I tell you that your daughter is eating butter?"

"I don't know. Do you think she's going to have cholesterol problems?"

"Can babies get cholesterol problems?" I ask.

"I don't know. If she's eating a pound of butter maybe."

This gives me pause. Maybe the Fiancé has a point. Maybe I'm slowly killing the Dictator by allowing her to eat chunks of butter.

"Hey, we should be happy she's introduced a new food into her Survivor diet," I tell him.

"Butter is not a food."

"What is it, then?" I ask.

"It's butter."

10 P.M.

Along with Cara making me feel bad, and me obsessing that I really should remember the milestones in the Dictator's life, I can't stop obsessing about scrapbooking.

"Maybe I should pay someone to do a scrapbook for us," I say to the Fiancé.

"Do they have people to do that?"

"When it comes to babies, they have people to do everything. I just don't want to do it."

"Then don't," he says.

"But I kind of want a scrapbook."

"So find someone who'll do it."

I've come to think that scrapbooking is a lot like doing your taxes. I'd rather just hand over all my papers and receipts to an accountant and not have to take care of it myself.

May 2
8 P.M.

"Okay," I say. "Which one of you farted?"

We're having a nice family moment. Sort of. Well, we're all lying on the bed watching television. The Dictator is sleepily sucking on a bottle.

"Beck, why are you always so gross?" the Fiancé asks. "It's like I'm living with two children."

"I don't know. So was it you?" I ask him.

Crap. Baby gas leads nowhere good. It always ends the same way, in fact. It ends with a dirty diaper. Babies are like old men. They fart whenever, and wherever, they feel like it.

May 3
7:30 P.M.

I sometimes get the feeling that the Dictator knows more than she's letting on. When she does something wrong, or thinks it may be wrong—like touching my laptop—she looks at me with an evil grin. It's almost as if she's testing me. I pretend I don't care. Like when she falls, if I don't make a big deal and I even laugh, she won't cry. It's the times that I'm like, "OH MY GOD! ARE YOU ALL RIGHT? MY POOR BABY! ARE YOU OK???" that she starts bawling. So when she does anything bad, I pretend that I'm not bothered, figuring if she's trying to test me by throwing her sippy cup on the ground and I don't show that it bothers me, she'll stop doing it. I'm one step ahead of her. Bahaha. Except, the problem is, I do care. And sometimes I just can't pretend I don't. For example, right now, I'm sitting on the edge of the bathtub and the Dictator is acting like the bathtub is a swimming pool. And it's pissing me off.

"Don't splash me!" I tell her, when she takes a plastic toy cup, fills it up with water, and pours it onto my lap.

Splash!

Evil grin.

I hate myself because I am so bad at disciplining her. She's just so damn cute when she flashes that evil grin. No, I shouldn't laugh. But she's too cute. I laugh. God, this child is smart. All she has to do is flash me that evil grin, and I turn into mush.

May 4

7:30 P.M.

I'm really not too smart.

"How do you open this thing?" I ask the Fiancé.

"Beck, come on!"

"No, seriously. I can't do it. How do you open this thing?"

When the oh-so-hot male babyproofer came to babyproof our house, he did something to the cupboard doors under the sink in the kitchen. For the life of me, I can't figure out how to unlock it.

The Fiancé reaches down and, in a split second, opens the door.

"How did you do that?" I ask. I feel like I'm in some bad sitcom, playing a dumb woman who is clueless. Except I really didn't know how to open it.

"Shouldn't the question be," asks the Fiancé, "how you have gone months without opening this cupboard? That means you have not once turned on the dishwasher or gotten a garbage bag, because all the supplies are in here."

I should have never mentioned it. Stupid me.

May 5

8 P.M.

I get together with April, one of my old university friends. We're each sipping a glass of wine at a bar. I've learned, though I'm not sure it's necessary, to not talk a lot about the Dictator when I'm out like this. It's like some unwritten rule that as a mother, you just know not to talk a lot about your child.

It's not that they've explicitly told you, "You're talking too much about your child! I do not find it interesting that you have to bite her fingernails off when she has hangnails!" It's just something you believe to be true, even if it's not.

You learn, too, that when you hit around age thirty, it's no longer surprising when someone you know gets knocked up (it's only surprising that it's someone you thought would never settle down, not that they're too young to have a baby). It also becomes not so surprising that you learn you have a friend who actually desperately wants to have a baby, who is trying to have a baby but, for some reason, can't get pregnant, or, just as bad, can get pregnant but can't keep the pregnancy.

I knew April was trying to conceive. I had heard through mutual friends. And now she is telling me that she and her husband have been trying for a long time and getting bad news over and over again. I don't know what to say at first, and it makes me uncomfortable to be me, a mother. I, of course, give her suggestions, like names of acupuncturists I have heard good things about when it comes to treating infertility. I ask if she's considered adoption.

"We have," she says. "But I'm just not ready to give up yet." I can't imagine how awful this must be—feeling like you're failing at something you want so much, and you just can't understand why your body isn't doing it. When you already have a child—especially when you practically conceived by immaculate conception—it's distressing, at best, to discuss pregnancy with a friend who has miscarried or is trying to conceive and not succeeding. You wonder if your friend hates the fact that you have a baby, and you are overly sensitive about what you say. You feel awful that you had a baby and it's not working out for her, and you're not sure how much you should talk about your own child, how much or how little she wants to hear.

Unfortunately, there's not much else going on in your life but your child. So there isn't much else to talk about. Luckily, April is very open and doesn't mind discussing her fertility issues. She does ask about the Dictator, but I keep my responses minimal, like, "Oh, she's fine," and "She's hard work."

Why is it that some people get pregnant basically just looking at someone, and others, who really, really want it, have trouble? Mother Nature is a big question mark. All I know is that I desperately want my friend to get pregnant. I don't get why life is so unfair.

May 6

Sara, my mother friend who has a baby with a lot of hair, calls.

"So, does she have any hair yet?" she asks. It's become sort of a game now.

"Nope. No hair," I answer, and it's the truth.

"You can't even put it into a ponytail yet?"

"Not even close."

"Well, it will grow one day."

"Whatever."

I'm not holding my breath. I've almost come to terms with the fact that my baby girl will forever look like a little boy. Everywhere I look I see babies, way younger than the Dictator, with hair, hair, and more hair.

But talking to April has made me grateful for what I do have.

May 9

My birthday is in two days.

Of course, I've warned the Fiancé that I'll be expecting a big gift, like a Louis Vuitton purse, from him and the baby, or two smaller gifts, one from him and one from the baby.

"I also want something that the Dictator makes me," I tell

him. Cards made by the Dictator have become really important to me. I know, from experience, that the Fiancé doesn't give a rat's ass about the artwork the Dictator makes, so I know I have to warn him that I expect a scribble on a piece of paper by her.

The Fiancé picks up his cell phone. "Who is he calling?" I wonder. It's so odd for him to just pick up the phone and dial a number while we're in midconversation.

"Hi, Mimi," he says into the receiver. I look at him, stunned. He's never called Nanny Mimi before, though I know her number is on his speed-dial list. And why didn't he tell me why he's calling Nanny Mimi?

"It's Rebecca's birthday in two days. Can you please make something for her from the baby tomorrow?" he says to Nanny Mimi.

Okay, this isn't what I had planned. I should have mentioned that I also wanted the artwork from the Dictator to be somewhat of a surprise. But beggars can't be choosers.

May 11

It's my birthday. I get a designer purse from the Fiancé and the matching wallet from the baby. I also get a scribble on a piece of paper from the Dictator. See? It's good to speak out about exactly what you want for your birthday. That way you won't be disappointed. "You know, in three days it's Mother's Day," I tell the Fiancé, after I unwrap my gifts. He gives me a look. What can I do? It's not my fault that Mother's Day always falls the same week as my birthday. And every mother knows that Mother's Day is more important than birthdays.

"Your present for Mother's Day is a trip to Paris," he says.

Fuck. Right. The Paris trip.

I don't want to go anymore. How can I leave my baby? We're flying through my hometown to drop off the baby with my parents, who are watching her while we are on our stupid romantic vacation, before we catch another plane to Paris. Why did I ever agree to this trip?

May 17

We're at the airport. Heading to Paris. I'm so completely nervous. I've barely talked about going to Paris with any of my friends. It's just that to talk about it would have made it real. I'm not sure I'm going to be able to last away from the Dictator. Everything, so far, has gone according to plan. We've dropped the baby off with my parents. I should feel fine. I mean, my parents have raised four kids, so she should be fine. Right? She should be just fine. My parents are really looking forward to having the Dictator stay with them.

But what if the plane crashes? What if I never see my baby again?

May 19

We're in Paris and the stupid time difference means it's 4 A.M. back home and I can't call and check in on the Dictator. I feel so far away from her. I miss her so much. I can't stop talking about her. I keep asking the Fiancé if he thinks she's okay, what he thinks she's doing right now, and if he thinks she misses me.

Stupid Paris. Of course, this hotel room is quite beautiful. And the dinner we had tonight was fantastic. Maybe I'll be just fine without her, once I get through the withdrawal symptoms.

May 20

Okay, I definitely love Paris. I could live in Paris. The only problem with Paris is that there are babies everywhere. Everywhere I look there are babies that are not mine. No, mine is an eight-hour plane ride away. I miss the baby so much I can barely stand—oooh, cute clothing store. I must go in.

Sometime Paris time, midafternoon

I want to speak to my baby.

"We had a great day today," my mother is saying. "We went to the pet store and she loved it."

Okay, I'm in Paris. I shouldn't wish I were in some stinky pet store in some stinky mall back at home. But I do. I should be the one taking my baby to some stinky pet store in some stinky mall. I feel like the worst mother in the world. I tell my mother to put the phone to her ear.

"Hi, baby! Mommy loves you so so so so so much. I love you, baby, I love you!" I hear a bit of rattling around before my mother's voice comes on again.

"She's busy watching a DVD right now with your father."

I won't lie. I'm hurt. But how can I expect my eighteen-month-old to understand how much I need to hear her voice right now?

I also have to pretend I'm having the best time ever with the Fiancé. It is a fantastically beautiful city. But why do there have to be so many babies everywhere reminding me that I'm not with mine?

May 23

Only five more days until I get to see my baby. I do not remember ever wanting to see anyone so badly in my life. Though we had a great time at his cousin's wedding and the sights are spectacular, I hate the questions that keep popping into my head. Rather, I hate the one big question that keeps popping into my head. What if she doesn't remember me?

May 24

My plan today is to shop until I drop. Not for me, but for the baby. If I can't be with her, at least I can shop for her. It's amazing what they have for babies in Paris. All the baby clothes are so beautifully crafted, with so much detail. We're not in Gap land anymore.

"Look at this jean skirt," I tell the Fiancé, who, by now, is well aware that I will not pass any children's clothing store without going in.

"That's cute," he says.

"Look at the detailing. Isn't it amazing?" I ask, fingering the skirt.

"Yeah, it's cute."

"Should I get it?"

"Sure. It's cute," he says.

We walk up to the counter to pay for our one item. The clerk tells us how much the jean skirt is, and I plop down the credit card. The Fiancé is looking at me funny. Maybe he's shopped-out? I have bought a lot for the Dictator. Maybe he thinks it's time to stop?

We walk outside. "Do you know how much that was?" he asks.

I've given up doing the whole conversion thing. I can barely convert Canadian money into American money, and vice versa. I completely will not get euros. "It was 150 euros," I say, looking at the receipt.

"Do you know how much 150 euros works out to be?" he asks.

"No. How much?"

"Like, four hundred Canadian."

What? What the fuck? I did *not* just spend four hundred dollars on a skirt for my child, did I? "What? Are you telling me I just bought our baby a four-hundred-dollar jean skirt?!" I yell.

"Yes. We did."

"That's too much."

"You think?"

"Okay, no more shopping for her!"

"Thank God," he says.

If anyone should be getting a four-hundred-dollar skirt, it's me. I know better than to say this aloud.

May 25
Midnight

"You know, it's kind of nice being able to sleep and not having to worry that we're going to be woken up five times a night by a screaming baby," I say to the Fiancé as we're getting ready for bed.

"I know," he answers.

"In fact, I haven't slept this well in a long time," I tell him.

"Me neither."

It's true what they say. Once you have a baby, you always sleep with one eye open. You just never know. She could wake up. She could not. Either way, at home, I feel like I'm always ready to bolt out of bed to go to her. Even here, for the first couple of nights, I kept expecting to be woken up by screams for "BA BA!" Translation: bottle.

May 27

I miss Paris already. I love Paris. What had I been thinking about not really wanting to come here? The Fiancé and I had a fantastic time. The food, the shopping, the art, the museums. Sigh. We're on the plane back now.

An hour later
Four more hours until we land.

Only four more hours until I get to see my baby.

An hour later
Three more hours until we land.

An hour later
This plane better not crash. Oh my God. What if the plane crashes?

I can't wait to see my baby. What if she's forgotten about me? What if she doesn't know who I am? This plane better not crash.

An hour later
We've landed. My legs are literally shaking, like I'm an addict coming off heroin. That's how excited I am to see the Dictator. Why is it taking so long to get to the gate?

Twenty minutes later
Why are these people taking forever to get off the plane? Don't they know I haven't seen my baby in forever? I can't wait any longer. I might have to be one of those rude, impatient passengers who push their way through the aisles.

Finally, we get off the plane. The Fiancé has to jog after me, I walk so quickly to get through customs and then to the baggage claim, where my parents and the Dictator will be waiting for us. And then I see them.

"Mommee!!!!" The baby screams as I race up to her, and she laughs and laughs and laughs. I've never seen her smile so big in her life. I hug her and tackle her and roll around on the floor by the luggage carousel. I kiss her face a thousand times and smell her hair. God, I've never missed anyone so much in my entire life. And I've never had a better homecoming either. No one has ever been so happy to see me.

Maybe I should go away more often.

We get our luggage and I can't stop staring at my baby. She looks different. More mature. And, dare I say it? She may have grown a little bit more hair while I was gone. She is actually starting to look like a little GIRL!

Five Mommy Moments People "Forget" to Mention

1. You finally accept, and get used to the fact, that you're a mother.
2. You finally accept, and get used to the fact, that you have a baby.
3. You finally accept, and get used to the fact, that your life is different.
4. You finally accept, and get used to the fact, that your life will never be the same as before you had a baby.
5. You finally accept, and get used to the fact, that you like your life this way.

The Eleventh Trimester (21 to 24 Months)

No, Really, You've Been in Our Lives for Two Years?

June 14

It's Father's Day. While Mother's Day meant the world to me, Father's Day doesn't mean shit for the Fiancé. He just doesn't care about these things. Still, I had taken Baby Rowan's hand and scribbled, "Happy Father's Day. I love you, Daddy. Love, Rowan" on a piece of paper. I traced her hand too.

"That's nice," the Fiancé says, looking at the handmade card for three seconds.

I'm a bit hurt. I know the Dictator and I spent about twelve seconds making that card, but still. . . . It's from our child! And it is pretty cute. What's wrong with him?

June 17

I'm sweating, I'm so mortified.

We're at the counter of McDonald's, and the Dictator is having a major hissy fit.

"BALLOON! I WANT BALLOON!" she screams.

We had first walked to a toy store, where they also sold, unfortunately for me, helium balloons. I had thought I was being kind by buying the Dictator one. She loves helium balloons. And, somehow, my child now knows that the big M outside all McDonald's stands for french fries. As we were walking home, she saw the big M and started chanting, "French fries, french fries, french fries."

I had no idea she knew that. (As a fan of McDonald's french fries, I don't really mind.)

However, the Dictator, I also find out, doesn't really understand the concept of helium balloons. I should have explained to her that if she let go of the helium balloon, it would go up, and it would go bye-bye. I really should have. Because now here we are, with the balloon having sailed up to the roof of the very high ceiling in McDonald's. (It's a two-story McDonald's, if you catch my drift.)

She screams like I've just hurt her. Tears are streaming down her face like a waterfall. I look around to see how many people are staring at us. More than a few. How could they not stare? My child is acting like the worst child in the history of children, much worse than any child on any episode of *Supernanny*.

"It's just a balloon, baby," I try to explain. "I'll get you another one tomorrow. Okay?"

"BALLOON! BALLOON!"

"I'll get you another one tomorrow, I promise," I try to soothe her.

"BALLOON! BALLOON!"

Fuck. Fuck. Fuck.

The only way to get the balloon back would be to ask a McDonald's employee to get out a ladder, climb up, and try to reach it.

"Hi, I'm sorry. Do you happen to have a ladder to go reach my child's balloon?" I ask the seventeen-year-old who took our order. I can't believe I'm asking the poor employee to climb up a ladder, all because of one stupid helium balloon.

I'm grateful that the employee comes back to say he does have a ladder in the back. He brings it out and climbs it and gets the stupid balloon back.

"Thank you so much," I gush to him, thinking, "I think I'll send a nice thank-you card to this McDonald's location."

I take the balloon and say tersely to the baby, "Here's your balloon."

She stops crying and I tie the balloon to her stroller with a triple knot. There is no way I will let this balloon fly off.

When I'm out with the Dictator, I'm always a bit nervous. I worry that if she acts up, strangers will look at me and immediately assume I'm a horrible mother. I always feel like I'm being watched, and judged, when I'm out with the Dictator.

Can you understand why?

June 20

We're at Tammy's house for the evening.

We've just plopped our kids down at a mini-table with crayons and construction paper. The Dictator has a blue piece of paper in front of her, and she picks up a blue crayon.

"You know, children get more out of coloring if they use a different-color crayon than the paper they're drawing on," Tammy's husband tells me.

Once you become a mother, you can easily tell the difference between those parents who have read parenting books and those who haven't. I roll my eyes inwardly. I may have become a different person, but at least I have not become the type of parent who cares what color crayon her child draws with.

June 21

My friend Marci has just told me that someone we both know—someone we never thought would be a mother—is pregnant. I'm not as stunned as Marci is.

"Yes, supposedly she really wanted to have a child," Marci says. "So she just stopped using birth control and got pregnant. Can you believe that?"

"Yes, I can. She is almost forty, right? She had to do it soon," I say. April always wonders if she is having fertility issues because she didn't get pregnant when she was younger.

"Yes. I just can't believe she'd do it on her own," Marci says.

"I actually think it's great that she figured out she wants to do it on her own. And she went out and did it."

"It would be hard to do on your own," Marci says.

"Yes, it will be very hard. But a lot of women do it."

"I just can't imagine her being a mother. She seems like such a free spirit," says Marci.

"Well, that will change. I guess she just really wanted to have a baby. I'm happy for her." Marci, I can tell, is less happy for her. Part of this has to do with the fact that Free Spirit is not exactly what you'd consider mother material. But I know how Marci feels. When everyone around you is getting pregnant, even the ones who you'd think would be more comfortable with a martini glass than a sippy cup, it makes you think of your own fertility and whether it will happen for you.

I'm not worried about Marci. In fact, out of all my friends,

Marci is the one who, if push came to shove and she wanted to get pregnant but didn't have a partner, I could see raising a child on her own.

"My friend saw her at a restaurant the other night and said she was showing and everything," Marci says.

"You know, I think we should be happy for her."

"I'm trying."

"Try harder. It's a good thing. She wanted to be pregnant. Now she is."

"You're right. You're right," agrees Marci.

"You know it's going to happen for you, right?" I ask her.

"I know, I know."

But you never really do know anything for sure, do you?

June 28

I've lost my shit. I'm yelling at the Fiancé because I don't know who to yell at.

"Seriously! Who do they think they are?" I scream.

"Beck, they're only trying to help."

"I know! But honestly, I think they think they are her parents."

"They do not," says the Fiancé.

"They do too! Every time they come over they tell me what she should be doing, that she shouldn't be drinking out of a bottle, and then your mother tries to feed her, like she knows better than me!"

"That's just the way they are. They think they're helping."

"Your mother already raised you! She had her chance! She's my baby and I'll raise her the way I want."

"You're being ridiculous," the Fiancé says. "Your parents are the same way."

Even while I scream at the Fiancé, I know I sound ridiculous. It's just in-laws. Argh! The more they try to "help," the more they make me feel like a failure as a mother. No matter what I do, the Fiancé's parents think they can do it better. I say things like "She's not hungry." And the mother-in-law will be like, "She's hungry." I can't take it anymore.

"I can't take it anymore!" I scream again.

At this point, I'm screaming and crying. In fact, one could say I'm having an adult tantrum.

"Did you hear her tell me that she's taking her on the Disney cruise?" I ask the Fiancé.

"My mother is not taking her on any Disney cruise. She's not even two!" he says.

"That's what she said. She said, 'I'm going to take her on the Disney cruise.' She didn't ask me if it was okay to take *my* daughter on the Disney cruise. She just said she was taking her. She always does this. Is it too much to ask me—*her mother*—if it's okay to take her on the Disney cruise? Or if it's okay with me that Nanny Mimi take her to her office to visit? All I want is to be asked. *Not told*. I am her *mother*. She is not!"

"Beck, she just talks. Have you taken your antidepressant today?"

"NO!" I scream at him.

"Maybe you should."

"Maybe you should tell your mother to stop acting like she's the mother of our child. I'm her mother! I'm her mother! I'm her mother!" I say, stomping my feet. (Okay, at this point, even I think that maybe I should take my antidepressant.)

"Everyone knows you're her mother," says the Fiancé.

"Well, then, why don't they act like it?" I ask him.

"They just love her," he says.

July 1

I'm heading back to my hometown for a visit tomorrow. I'd like to see some friends. And this way, I can keep the Dictator to myself. I wonder if I'm being overly sensitive, but I don't think so. Why can't the in-laws see that the more they bug me, the more I want to leave town?

I ask the Fiancé if he wants to go out for dinner, just the two of us.

"Sure, that would be nice," he says.

"Okay. Great."

"Well, who's going to babysit the Dictator? Mimi?" asks the Fiancé.

"Well, I already asked and she can't because she has to do something with her father."

"So who, then?"

"Um, your parents?" I say quietly.

"Ah!!" He laughs.

"What?"

"So you do like them when you want them to babysit?" he asks.

"Listen, do you or do you not want to go out to dinner with me and have your parents babysit?"

"Yes, I do."

"Fine."

The in-laws do seem to drive me less crazy when I want them to babysit.

July 3

I'm back in my hometown and attending a book-launch cocktail party. The Dictator is staying over at my parents' house for the night.

"You look great!" says an old acquaintance, kissing me on both cheeks.

"Hey, thanks!"

"And you're a mother now!" she adds.

Argh! Once you become a mother, there's a whole new version of the backhanded compliment. Except you can't really get mad because most of the people who don't know they're actually giving you a backhanded compliment don't have children so they don't understand why saying something like "You look great . . . and you're a mother!" is irritating. It's almost like people believe it has to be one or the other. Either you look great, or you're a mother. You couldn't possibly look great *and* be a mother at the same time! Oh no.

But I'm used to these comments, so I just smile and say, "Thanks!" It is better than hearing, "You look so tired," which, of course, I mostly do. I'm a mother!

I've been thinking about compliments a lot lately. When I see a new mother I know, and I want to say something nice, I say, "You look amazing!" But I try not to say it like I'm shocked that they look amazing. Mothers, especially new ones, are sensitive to compliments, or backhanded compliments, or compliments that aren't really compliments, or basically anything you say to them.

I have to admit, I still love hearing "Wow. You look so skinny!" I know people are saying this wanting to add on, "And you had a baby!" Except now my response is "Yes, but I had my baby almost two years ago." It seems less like a great accomplishment to be skinny nearly two years after giving birth than it did, let's say, five months after giving birth.

While time does fly when you're a mother and see all the developments, for other people, who don't, it stands still.

"So, your baby must be almost two months old now," acquaintances will say to me.

And then I'll say, "Um, actually, she's almost two."

It's weird though. Even though I see how the Dictator has grown, there's no way I look older, is there?

July 4

What had I been thinking? Who had I been kidding? This was the worst idea I've ever had. Actually, it wasn't even my idea. It was the Fiancé's stupid idea. This was the worst idea he ever had.

He wanted professional photos of the Dictator. He heard about a well-known photographer in my hometown. Stupidly, he wanted this well-known photographer to take the photos of the Dictator.

Of course, the Fiancé wasn't with us as I attempted to get these professional portraits done. I took the Dictator to this very well-known photographer—who has taken photos of many well-known authors and politicians. The difference between the authors and politicians and the Dictator is that the authors and politicians probably didn't have temper tantrums and bawl their eyes out in front of this well-known photographer. (They probably had their tantrums in the privacy of their own homes.) The entire photo session took about an hour. There were about five minutes in that time frame during which the Dictator wasn't crying or screaming. She's such a diva!

But it was so interesting to watch a professional take a photo. Usually the one taking pictures of the Dictator is my father-in-law, or my father, two people who should not own digital cameras. "I can't watch. It's too painful," I usually end up saying when either one of them attempts to take a picture. Why? Because it takes them forever to figure out how to do it. And they still don't seem to understand that babies don't understand that they can't move while they're waiting for you to figure out how to use the camera.

This time, however, I was just embarrassed. Well-Known Photographer didn't seem to mind all the screaming. He was nice. But I minded all the screaming.

By the time we got out of there, I had a splitting headache and thought this man would really have to be a genius to have gotten even one good shot.

"How was it?" the Fiancé asks, calling me at home.

"It was awful," I tell him.

"What happened?"

"Well, we were there for about an hour and she screamed, oh, I don't know, for about fifty-five minutes."

"Oh no."

"Oh, yes. And now we're going to have to buy the photos from him no matter what."

"Why?"

"Because she was so bad that I'm embarrassed for us."

Like with tipping, every time this child is bad, it ends up costing us.

July 5

"You know, this baby is making me fat," I say to my friend Lena.

"What do you mean?"

"Do I look a bit fatter to you?"

"Not really."

"Look at this," I say, grabbing a handful of flab in the area right over my hip.

"That's skin! Everyone has that!" she says.

Lena has always been the type of girlfriend who will let me moan about weight gain. Even though she is super-skinny, she also complains about gaining five pounds.

"No, this baby is making me fat!" I tell her again.

"How?"

"Well, I always order her fries. I mean, I'm eating fries sometimes twice a day."

"But you're ordering them for her, right?"

"Yes, but she eats maybe two, and then they're sitting there on the table, so I eat them."

"You need willpower."

"Okay, if I had willpower, I wouldn't have gotten pregnant, and then we wouldn't even be having this talk about this baby making me fat because I have no willpower to stop eating her fries."

I finally understand why the Fiancé used to tell me, when we were dating, that I was making him fat. I usually finished half my plate. And he'd finish his meal and then the rest of mine. Just like I'm now eating most of the Dictator's.

It doesn't seem fair. First, you worry while pregnant that you're getting fat. Then you have the baby and try to lose the weight as fast as you can. Then, you finally lose the weight when your child starts crawling and walking because you're always chasing after her, and then she starts to eat human food, but not a lot of human food, so just when you're really sure you've lost the weight, you start packing it back on, because you're always ordering fries for your child, who only eats maybe three of them.

The worst thing is, I just never seem to get tired of french fries! Ever!

July 8
5 P.M.

"Fuck!" I scream, as I give myself a vicious paper cut while trying to open a piece of mail. It stings. I fight back tears. I've just arrived back home with the Dictator. The Fiancé is still at work.

"Fuck," the Dictator says.

"What did you just say?"

"Fuck."

"Don't say that," I tell her.

"Fuck."

Argh.

5:05 P.M.

"Fuck!" the Dictator says again.

"Oh, no. Don't say that! You can't say that," I plead with her.

"Fuck!"

"Oh, God. No. Um, luck! Mommy said 'luck.' "

"Fuck!"

Fuck! Fuck! Fuck!

5:06 P.M.

"Fuck!"

"No! Luck! That's right. Luck!"

"Fuck!"

"No, no. Daddy's going to be home any minute. You can't say that! Say 'luck.' "

"Fuck."

Fuck!

5:45 P.M.

"So . . . welcome back! Anything exciting happen today?" the Fiancé asks, giving me a kiss on the cheek and a bear hug.

"No, nothing," I answer.

"Why do you look like that?"

"Like what?"

"You just have a funny look on your face," he says.

"No I don't."

"Yes, yes you do. What did she do now?" he asks.

"Nothing!"

"Did she spill milk on the couch again?"

"No. She's been an angel."

"Fuck," says the Dictator.

"Excuse me? What did she just say?"

"Fuck," says the Dictator again.

I can't help it. I burst out laughing. I'm sorry, but it is kind of funny.

July 10

Marci calls. She tells me that she's heard our single friend had a miscarriage. I feel awful. Much like I find reading newspapers and stories about child abductions so painful, I feel terrible when I find out that people, even people I don't really know, have miscarriages. Especially if their pregnancy has been widely known. Ever since becoming a mother, I've become super-sensitive to these stories. She must feel so much worse than I feel for her. Even free spirits must feel the pain.

July 15
9 P.M.

The Fiancé and I are fighting.

"She said her ear hurts," I say to the Fiancé. "Does your ear hurt?" I ask, looking directly at the Dictator.

"Ear hurts," she says.

"Why didn't you take her to the doctor today? It's Friday night. The twenty-four-hour walk-in clinic is going to be crazy!" the Fiancé growls.

I know it's not the ideal time to be going to the twenty-four-hour walk-in clinic, which is also in a shady part of town, but what else can we do? My baby says her ear hurts. She could need medication.

"Why didn't you take her today?" the Fiancé asks again.

"Well, she didn't say her ear hurt earlier. She just started saying it now, and she's tugging her ear. That means she probably has an infection."

I'm pissed that the Fiancé doesn't seem to care that his child has an earache. I know he's thinking, "Can't we just wait until Monday?"

No, we can't. He grouchily drives us to the walk-in clinic so a doctor can check out the Dictator's ear.

11:30 P.M.

We're back from the walk-in clinic.

There was absolutely nothing wrong with the Dictator's ear.

"God, my head hurts," I say about my headache that just came on.

"Head hurts," says the Dictator. "My head hurts."

I would laugh. But the Fiancé is too pissed that we wasted our night in a waiting room at a walk-in clinic.

July 20

Somewhere along the way, I've realized that I say "What's the magic word?" about 293 times a day.

"What's the magic word?" I'll say when the Dictator says, "Bottle!"

In fact, almost every time words come out of her mouth, I'm demanding that she say "Please" and "Thank you." "Pleaseandthankyou," she'll always say, as if "Please" and "Thank you" are all one word.

"Blocks!" she'll say.

"What's the magic word?"

"Pleaseandthankyou," she'll answer.

"Water!" she'll demand.

"What's the magic word?"

"Move!" she'll say, pushing my legs out of her way.

"What's the magic word?"

It's so odd that she can learn so many things, do so many new things, speak so many new words, but for the life of her, she can't remember to say "Please" and "Thank you." It makes me wonder, what's the point of even reminding her? She never says it on her own anyway.

Midnight

"Can you turn the light off?" I ask the Fiancé.

"What are the magic words?"

" 'Fuck' and 'off,' " I answer.

He leaves the room, heading to the washroom, without turning them off.

"Pleaseandthankyou! Pleaseandthankyou! Pleaseandthankyou!" I scream out after him.

July 22

Along with me having to ask "What are the magic words?" a billion times a day, I have also made the grave mistake of buying a children's CD for the car. I now have to listen to "Bingo" over and over and over again while we drive. I really might have to check myself in to an institution.

August 1

"Okay, baby. Put this on," I say to the Dictator.

We're in the driveway, just having returned from the mall. She made me listen to "Bingo" twenty-six times in a row on the ride back. I bought the Dictator a fake-fur vest at the mall. It's pink. It's adorable. It cost seventy-five dollars.

"No!" she says.

"Please? It's so cute! Put it on for Daddy!"

"No!" she says again.

Argh! I just spent seventy-five dollars on this thing, and now she refuses to wear it?

"Come on! Just for a second. Feel it, soft! Like a cat. You want to wear the cat?"

"Okay," she finally agrees. "Cat."

We walk in. "Daddy," I call out. "Look what we bought!"

The Fiancé takes one look at the Dictator and bursts out laughing.

"That's hilarious."

"Isn't it?"

"Off! Off! Off!" the Dictator screams.

"Okay, I guess she doesn't want to wear it now," I say, taking it off of her.

"How much was that?" the Fiancé asks.

"I don't remember."

"Beck."

"Like, seventy-five dollars."

"Great. So she's going to be like you. Have a million things in her closet that she'll never wear."

"Oh, come on! It's cute!"

"She'll never wear it."

"I know. But it's cute, isn't it?"

Like mother, like daughter, right?

August 3

I've realized that if I say to the Fiancé that the Dictator needs new clothes, he's always okay with it. How can you argue if your child, let's say, needs new pajamas from Baby Gap? The best thing about always having to buy things for your child, who is constantly growing, is that I realized I can buy clothes for me too, without telling the Fiancé.

Now, I'll go shopping for the Dictator, but I'll also buy clothes for myself. I just put mine at the bottom of the shopping bags full of clothes for the Dictator.

Evil? Maybe. But hiding clothes I buy for myself under clothes I've bought for the Dictator that she actually needs (and sometimes doesn't) is easier than saying, "No, I will wear this. I promise!"

Just as men don't understand artwork done by their toddlers, they also don't really care about the clothes you buy for their toddlers. If I come home with a bag of clothes for the Dictator, he'll ask, "What did you buy?"

I'll answer, "Oh, she needed some new pants. And I got her some socks."

The Fiancé never asks to see what I bought. He's just not that into children's clothing, what can I say? When I take the bag upstairs, I run to my closet first, dump in what I bought for myself, and the Fiancé is none the wiser. Hey, I have friends who have secret credit cards they hide from their husbands. This is so much better than that, isn't it?

September 1

We go to Tammy's house, which has become our regular destination on Monday nights. Tammy, who owns an art gallery, has very interesting art on her walls. On one wall there is a huge painting of a naked woman, lying on a bed, holding a video camera. She has dark pubic hair.

"Mommy naked!" the Dictator says, pointing at the painting. "Mommy naked!"

Tammy and her husband start laughing. I'm mortified! Now Tammy and her husband think they know what I look like naked!

"Mommy naked! Mommy naked!" the Dictator keeps repeating.

Crap. Is this what her talking is going to be like?

September 3

"Can we take your car?" I ask the Fiancé.

"Why? Because yours is disgusting?"

"Do you think rats can get into cars?"

"Beck!"

"I know. But it's beyond cleaning up. I think we need to get me a new car."

"No!"

"I know. But there's a smell coming from somewhere in there and I can't figure out from where," I tell the Fiancé.

"It's probably a half-empty bottle of milk that rolled under your seat four months ago."

"That's what I think too. Can you look? I'm scared something's going to bite me if I put my hand under the seat."

"It's like I have *two* children," the Fiancé mutters, storming off.

Sentences I've Heard Way Too Many Times Coming Out of the Fiancé's Mouth Since Having a Baby

1. I can't believe she's up again.
2. It's like I have *two* children.
3. Have you taken your antidepressant?

September 6

I decide that the Dictator and I are going to go on an adventure.

I'm going to take her out for ice cream, because I'm a good mother. I'm also a very stupid mother.

I push her in her stroller to get her a chocolate ice cream cone—because I like chocolate—at an ice cream parlor just down the road. She doesn't actually want to eat the ice cream; she just wants to hold the cone. But the Dictator will not let me take it away. She just wants to hold the dripping disaster.

Outside the house, I run into an acquaintance and her husband who are on a walk. My child is covered in chocolate ice cream. I'm mortified. I know they're thinking, "How could she let her child leave the house looking so dirty?"

It's the same when I take her to the park. She could be perfectly clean when we leave the house at 6 P.M., but by 6:30 she looks like I sent her camping in the woods for a week . . . and then told her to roll around in a pigpen.

I had no idea children could get so dirty in a matter of minutes. No more ice cream.

September 8

"I wuv you, Mommy," the Dictator says out of nowhere.

I swear, I think my heart cracked a little, in a good way, like when the guy you've had a huge crush on for years admits to you that he's been interested in you for years.

It's the first time she has ever said those three words to me. They are the best and sweetest three words I have ever heard.

I give her a huge hug. "I love you too," I say.

September 9

"Where is Thumbkin? Where is Thumbkin? Here I am. Here I am. How are you today, sir? Very fine, I thank you. Run away. Run away," I sing to the Dictator, holding her thumb.

"What song are you singing?" the Fiancé asks, walking into the kitchen where we're hanging out. I know he's super-impressed that I know a children's song that's not Barney or Dora. I feel great about this, even though Nanny Mimi just taught me the words to it yesterday, after I heard her singing it to the Dictator.

"It's the Thumbkin song," I say, like he's so out of it for not knowing the song.

September 13

I love my daughter, I do. But sometimes she's embarrassing. It's bad enough when she cries in public, but now that she talks in public as well . . .

This evening we went to a Chinese restaurant with the in-laws. It was one of those nights that the Dictator was actually in a great mood, ate a bowl of rice, and behaved. On the way out, she yelled at the top of her lungs, "Good-bye, everybody! Good-bye, everybody!"

I'm not exaggerating when I say the entire restaurant turned and looked at us.

Is it wrong to be embarrassed by your own child?

September 16
5 P.M.

"Do not hit me!" I yell at the Dictator.

"Again?" she says. She thinks hitting me, her mother, is a game.

"No!" I say.

"Again?" she asks, smiling. And I feel a slap on my face, and see stars.

"Do NOT hit me," I say, tears welling up. For a second, I feel like hitting her back, and I feel awful about this. "Do not hit me again. You be *nice* to Mommy," I tell her.

"Again?" she asks.

Argh! Is this what people mean by the terrible twos? Have they started already?

"Do you want to go to bed?" I threaten.

"No yet," she says.

"Then you do not hit Mommy. Bad hitting."

"Again?" she asks, raising her hand.

"Do you want to go to bed?" I threaten again.

"No yet," she says, and takes her hand down.

Argh. I've created, well, a human. She's the Devil Child.

6 P.M.

"I wuv my mommy," the Dictator says.

My eyes well up. "I love you, Rowan."

"I love you, Mommy."

"I love you, Rowan."

"I love you, Mommy."

"I love you, Rowan."

My child is an angel.

September 29

"We've got to plan the Dictator's birthday party," I tell the Fiancé.

"Do we really have to? Again? Didn't we just have one last year?"

"Yes, of course we have to! Um, that's the thing about birthdays. They happen once a year, dear."

"Fine."

"I'll do it. I'll do the entire thing," I promise.

"Sure you will."

"I will!"

October 1

It's nearly Nanny Mimi's anniversary with us. I head to Holt Renfrew to buy her a present, with the baby in tow. We're at the Louis Vuitton counter. I know Nanny Mimi loves Louis Vuitton, and I thought I'd get her a nice traveling cosmetic bag.

As we're waiting to be served, the Dictator sees a beautiful model-like woman walk by. "Dirty woman, Mommy. Dirty!"

"No!" I say as harshly as I can, while whispering. "Shh! She's not dirty. She's beautiful."

"Dirty," the Dictator says again.

"Beautiful," I say.

The beautiful model-like woman is African American. I feel embarrassed and awful, and I check around to see if anyone overheard our little conversation. Luckily, I don't think so. And, luckily, the Dictator stops talking after a price tag on a scarf distracts her.

I'm so weirded out. I mean, it's not like the Dictator hasn't seen dark-skinned people before. Nanny Mimi, for example, is Filipino. Nanny Mimi's boyfriend, who the Dictator has met a hundred times already, is East Indian.

For some reason, I remember quite vividly asking my mother what she was buying at the grocery store when I was about six years old. It was a box of maxi pads, and I remember my mother saying when I had asked what it was, "I'll tell you at home."

God, I would much rather the baby ask me about tampons than have to explain why people have different-color skin, that's for sure. God, I miss the days when she didn't speak. Babies can be so embarrassing, even when they're your own. Especially when they're your own.

October 3

We're on portable DVD player number three. Don't even ask. Let's just say that you can't have a baby pour a cup of soy milk all over it and expect it to still work. The Fiancé is not a happy camper. "That's it. This is the last one," he tells the Dictator, when he arrives home armed with our third DVD player (or is it our fourth? I can't remember).

I'm positive the Dictator looked at him with an evil glint in her eye.

October 8

We're going to a concert! Tickets cost, like, $150 a pop. I hope it's worth it. The group is super-popular.

Yes, the Fiancé, the Dictator, and I are heading to see the Wiggles next month. We had to buy tickets now because we heard they sell out fast.

I know, I know. Pathetic.

The Wiggles are a group from Australia that I only know of because they are at the end of the Barney videos. The mother-in-law cut out an article from the paper about the group. They make like a gazillion dollars a year, doing kid shows. It makes me sick. Not that my life is now about going to concerts for kids. (The Fiancé and I have discussed the Wiggles when we see clips of their performances: Are they gay? Are they not gay? Does it really matter? No.) We're paying more than four hundred dollars for three seats to a concert we're not even sure the Dictator will be awake for, and even if she is, will she really enjoy herself?

It makes me sick that I didn't decide to become a children's performer. I'm serious. Why did I decide to become a writer, when I could maybe make more in one children's show than I do in an entire year?

I contemplate whether it's too late to make a career change.

October 9

The Dictator can count to ten. Well, sort of.

"One, two, three, four, five, six, seven, eight, ten," she'll say, over and over.

For some reason, she never says the number nine, no matter how many times I remind her about the number nine. Poor number nine.

She can also now sing the alphabet, except for the letters F, I, and V.

October 10
7 A.M.

"Beck," the Fiancé says, waking me up. I had an awful night's sleep. The Dictator, I think, was having baby nightmares. (What do babies have nightmares about anyway?) I had decided to sleep in her bed with her. Which would have been fine, if she had nice high-thread-count sheets like I'm used to sleeping on. Oh, no. The baby has Dora the Explorer sheets—a gift from Nanny Mimi—which are so rough, they feel like a cheap brand of paper towel when my face rubs up against them. But she loves her Dora the Explorer sheets and doesn't seem to mind at all that she's practically sleeping on sandpaper.

"Beck," he says again. I know the Fiancé well enough now to know when he's in lecture mode. I think to myself, "Did I leave the lights on downstairs? Did I leave a dirty plate in the living room? Did I shave my legs with his razor and not warn him?"

"What?" I say crankily.

"I woke up and went downstairs and Rowan was in the kitchen already," he says.

I jump awake. "What?"

"I thought I heard the pitter-patter of little feet, and so I went downstairs, and Rowan was in the kitchen playing with the light switches, turning them off and on."

"Really?"

"Yes. And I asked her where Mommy was, and she said, 'Sleeping.' "

"Wow."

"Beck?"

"Yes."

"This is why you have to remember to lock the baby gates. This is why we have baby gates."

Right.

October 11

I can't believe I'm a counter now. That's right. A counter.

"Rowan, if you don't pick that up . . . I'm going to count to three," I say.

The weird thing is, I've never used the counting threat before. How does a child know that counting to three is a bad thing? She could have just thought, "Okay, count to three. Then what?"

It's good though that the counting-to-three thing actually works. I'm glad, because if I got to three and she didn't pick up the deck of animal flash cards, I wouldn't know what to do anyway. What do you do after you count to three?

October 12

How have I forgotten to get married?

Vivian asks me today if I'm ever going to get married.

"I don't know. You know, we really haven't talked about it," I answer.

Raising a baby has taken over so much of our time; I'm not sure how I'd fit in planning a wedding.

"Maybe I should wait until Rowan is old enough to understand what's going on?" I say to Vivian. How many children can say they were at their biological parents' wedding, after all?

You know, maybe I do want to get married.

October 15
6 P.M.

It's the Dictator's second birthday. I can't believe she's now two years old. I also can't believe that makes me two years older as well. The party, which was from 2 to 5 P.M., is now over. I actually had a great time. Once again, we invited everyone we knew who had children to come over to our house. I had hired a clown to make balloon animals, another clown to paint faces, and a caricaturist for the older kids. I had helium balloons all over the house. I had also called a catering company to come and serve appetizers and a bar service for the grown-ups. I had ordered a cake shaped like Elmo.

"I'm just so impressed with what you did," the Fiancé says. "I can't believe you organized all that all by yourself. It was great, Beck. Just great."

"I did good, didn't I?" I ask him.

"You did great! I'm amazed you did all that. It was amazing."

Okay, it wasn't that hard. One company provided the clowns, the helium balloons, and the caricaturist.

Total cost of my two-year-old's birthday party?

Fifteen hundred dollars.

I'll tell the Fiancé that later. Right now, he's too happy with me.

October 15
8 P.M.

Because the Dictator doesn't really understand the concept of presents, I open them all for her. The reason to have a birthday party for babies is for the presents. It's not about making your child happy, I realize. I won't have to shop for games or clothes for another year. I'm so going to have a big birthday party for her next year.

Ten Things I've Learned Since Becoming a Mother

1. I couldn't live without the in-laws. But I sometimes would like to.
2. The Fiancé and I have to work at our sex life now.
3. Though I complain, I am so thankful I have had my child.
4. I have lost some of my old single, fabulous friends.
5. I have made some new, good mother friends.
6. I will always miss a part of my old life.
7. I look forward to the rest of my new life.
8. I still miss my old ass. I might always miss my old ass.
9. I could never love anyone as much as I love the Dictator. Though she can be really, really, really bad, as soon as she says "I love you," all is forgiven.
10. There will always be better mothers than me out there. There will always be worse mothers than me out there.

October 16

7 P.M.

"You have to come home right now," I tell the Fiancé, calling him on his cell.

"I was just leaving," he says.

"And you have to buy diapers," I tell him.

"What? I just bought a jumbo box last week," he says. "We couldn't possibly have used them all up. There were, like, 120 of them in that box."

"I know. But we used up all the ones with the picture of Elmo on the front," I say.

"So?"

"So? So? Well, she'll only wear the ones with Elmo on them. Just stop at the drugstore and buy some, will you?"

"What do you mean, she just wants the Elmo ones?"

"Just get Elmo ones, trust me . . . Hello? Hello?"

I think the Fiancé hung up on me.

Arguing with a two-year-old is like arguing with a two-year-old. The conversation, if you could call it that, went something like this.

Me: "What about the Cookie Monster ones?"

Dictator: "Elmo!"

Me: "How about this one with the blue bear? He's cute. So cute!"

Dictator: "Elmo!!"

Me: "What about Big Bird! How could you not like Big Bird??"

Dictator: "ELMO!!! ELMO!!! WAAAA!!"

7:15 P.M.

I speed-dial the Fiancé back.

"What now? Does the Dictator want special wipes? Does the Dictator want a private jet? Does the Dictator want a canary diamond?"

"No, I was just wondering if you remembered to buy a new DVD player. Remember? She threw it on the floor? Hello? Hello?"

8:00 P.M.

"Thank God, you're home!" I say, when the Fiancé walks in, holding up a jumbo box of diapers like a prize he had just won.

"You know, Beck, she's starting to get out of control," he says.

"I know! She really had a tantrum over not having an Elmo diaper."

"Great, the terrible twos are starting," he says.

"Just think. Pretty soon she'll be toilet trained and we won't have to worry about diapers anymore."

"Finally we can get rid of that thing," the Fiancé says, as we put the diaper on the Dictator.

"What thing?" I ask.

"That white thing in her room. You know what I'm talking about. What's it called again?"

"What thing?" I ask again.

"That thing! The thing we never used. The thing we never figured out how it works."

"Ohhh, you mean the Diaper Genie?"

"Yes!"

8:15 P.M.

"OW! Fuck! Fuck! Fuck!" I scream out.

"What happened?" the Fiancé asks, giving me a look because I'm using swearwords.

"She just butted me in the head! I think she broke my nose!"

I was trying to put the Dictator into bed, and we were fooling around, having fun. That is, we were having fun until she head-butted me. It was an accident, but my God, it hurts like a bitch.

"Fuck! I think my nose is broken! I think she broke my nose!"

Later that night . . .
who really cares what time . . .

• •

I'm lying in bed with a pack of frozen peas on my face. At least now I know how and why there are frozen peas in my fridge, unlike two years ago when I was so tired I walked into the wall and needed to ice my nose, after also thinking I had broken it. I feel somewhat proud of myself now, thinking how much I've grown up in the past two years. I may not even care this time that I might wake up with two black eyes. I can be myself around Nanny Mimi tomorrow. I look forward to seeing the head-butting Dictator tomorrow (or will that be in an hour?).

It took me two years to finally get, and come to terms with, my new life as a mother. At least I'm here now, I think. It took two years.

In fact, I now think I actually may be good at this mothering thing. I can't stop thinking that maybe the Fiancé and I, who somehow made it through the past two years without either one of us asking for a separation, should try for a second, now that we know what we can expect and everything. But maybe I should concentrate on that thing called "balance" between a happy home life and a solid career first. I haven't cracked that secret to a happy balance just yet. And maybe now is not the right time to bring up another child with the Fiancé, not that there may ever be a right time.

But I do know we still have to get through the terrible twos with the child we have now, the Dictator.

But, really, how bad can the terrible twos be? Surely, they must be easier than the first two years of being a mother, right? I'm not that naïve, am I?

For now, I'll sleep. Another day done. I'm wiped.

Acknowledgments

• •

Thanks to Denise Bukowski and the team at the Bukowski Agency, including David and Emily.

Huge thanks to Jill Schwartzman, Allison Dickens, Beth Pearson, Jordan Fenn, Linda Pruessen, and Kendra Michael.

Thanks to the mommies: Victoria, Dana, Tamar, Kama, Jodi, Tessa, Jasmine, Liza, and Rebecca, the best mommy friend a gal could hope for.

Special shout-outs to Louisa McCormack, Ken Whyte, Sherilee Olson, Dianne Defenoyl, Domini Clark, Ceri Marsh, Marcella Munro, Danielle, Joanna, Dara, Sheri, Carolynn, Valerie, and Nanny Mimi.

Thanks to the readers of ninepounddictator.blogspot.com.

The biggest thanks to the man who puts up with the most, S.J.C. I love you.

About the Author

REBECCA ECKLER is one of Canada's best-known journalists. Her work has appeared in *The New York Times*, *Elle*, *Fashion*, and the *Los Angeles Times*, and she is a frequent contributor to Canada's weekly newsmagazine *Maclean's*. She was a feature writer and the relationship advice columnist ("Advice to the Lovelorn") for the *National Post*. She now writes a weekly modern-parenting column for *The Globe and Mail*, Canada's national newspaper. Her first book, *Knocked Up*, has been published in nine countries. She lives with her fiancé, her toddler, Rowan (A GIRL!), and her King Charles spaniel, Ruby. She has no set plans to get married, have another child, or get another dog. Ever. Well, at least not yet, anyway. You can check out her website at www.rebeccaeckler.com.